T0356518

Horace

CAELUM NON ANIMUM MUTANT QUI TRANS MARE CURRUNT

THOSE WHO RUSH ACROSS THE SEA CHANGE THEIR SKY NOT THEIR MIND

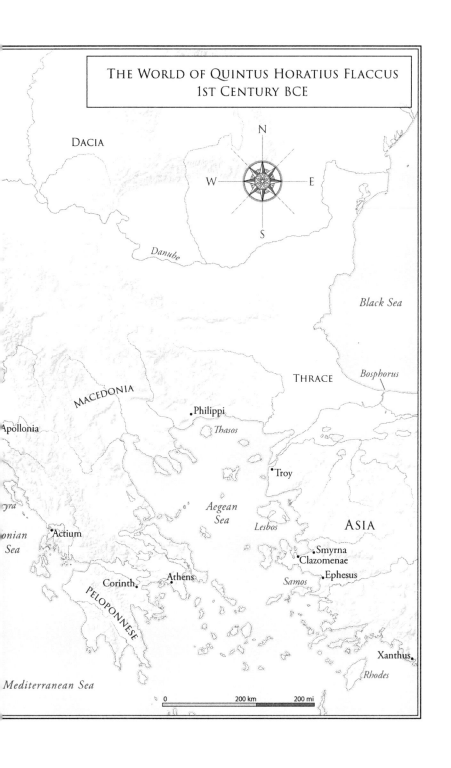

THE WORLD OF QUINTUS HORATIUS FLACCUS
1ST CENTURY BCE

N

W   E

S

DACIA

Danube

Black Sea

THRACE   *Bosphorus*

MACEDONIA

Apollonia

•Philippi

Thasos

•Troy

*Aegean
Sea*

Lesbos

ASIA

yra

•Actium

onian
Sea

Corinth•

•Athens

•Smyrna
•Clazomenae

PELOPONNESE

Samos

•Ephesus

Xanthus•

Rhodes

Mediterranean Sea

0   200 km   200 mi

Horace

Poet on a Volcano

Peter Stothard

· ANCIENT LIVES ·

Yale
UNIVERSITY PRESS
NEW HAVEN & LONDON

Published with assistance from the foundation established in memory of
James Wesley Cooper of the Class of 1865, Yale College.

Yale University Press books may be purchased in quantity for
educational, business, or promotional use. For information, please e-mail
sales.press@yale.edu (U.S. office) or sales@yaleup.co.uk (U.K. office).

Frontispiece: Beehive Mapping.

Set in the Yale typeface designed by Matthew Carter, and Louize,
designed by Matthieu Cortat, by Integrated Publishing Solutions.
Printed in the United States of America.

Library of Congress Control Number: 2024946036
ISBN 978-0-300-25658-1 (hardcover : alk. paper)

A catalogue record for this book is available from the British Library.

This paper meets the requirements of ANSI/NISO Z39.48-1992
(Permanence of Paper).

10 9 8 7 6 5 4 3 2 1

· ANCIENT LIVES ·

Ancient Lives unfolds the stories of thinkers, writers, kings, queens, conquerors, and politicians from all parts of the ancient world. Readers will come to know these figures in fully human dimensions, complete with foibles and flaws, and will see that the issues they faced—political conflicts, constraints based in gender or race, tensions between the private and public self—have changed very little over the course of millennia.

James Romm
Series Editor

To Max, Maya, Isabel, and Iona

And if a mad poet roams around with his nose in the air and falls into a pit, nobody will bother to pull him out. Like Empedocles, who leapt into the fires of Mount Etna, he may have jumped on purpose, yearning to be immortal.

— Horace, *Letter to the Pisos,* ca. 19 BCE

This mosaic of words, where every piece, as sound, as place, as concept, radiates its power right and left and through the whole, this minimum in the size and number of signs, this maximum in the energy of the signs achieved.

— Friedrich Nietzsche on Horace's *Odes,* in *Twilight of the Idols,* 1888

Contents

Contents

Horace

Introduction

In the autumn after Julius Caesar's assassination on the Ides of March, there was a meeting in Athens between two men who might never have met if they had stayed at home in Rome. Horace was a student, twenty-one years old, short and plump, somewhat nervous, the son of a former slave. Brutus was a politician and general, forty-one years old, tall, and severe in public and in private, the confident senior son of one of Rome's most aristocratic clans.

In 44 BCE Brutus was as famous in Rome as its hills. His family history was wound into the historical landscape of Rome (or so he claimed), and he himself was the living symbol of its liberty from tyrants, a claim that no one would deny since he was now Caesar's leading assassin. Horace was wholly unknown except to the teachers whom his father was paying to prepare him for a better life than he had had himself — and to keep him out of trouble.

On a campaign to finish what the assassination of Caesar had begun, Brutus was in Greece raising money, troops, and idealistic young officers. Horace, giving up his studies of Greek poets and philosophers, joined a band of student adventurers, most of them from families more like Brutus's than his own, and took up the cause of what he saw as virtue and freedom.

Their enemies were the young man whom Caesar had adopted as his heir, his sister's teenage grandson Octavian, and Caesar's glamorous fellow general Mark Antony. Octavian, the new, nineteen-year-old Caesar, was raising his own army, composed of his new father's veterans and avengers. Octavian knew much about Brutus. He knew nothing about Horace.

From Athens, Brutus led his followers east across the Aegean Sea, a danger in any autumn, and began the long march north with a growing band of soldiers whom he had persuaded or paid or both. Horace saw the popularity of his new cause and learned the pleasures of camaraderie along the way. He talked and drank, drank and talked. He did both with vigor. Away from Rome the distinctions of a socially stratified society more easily slipped away.

Horace stood by his new friends as they stripped the treasures of the ancient Greek cities of Asia, besieging, bribing, and murdering in the cause of freedom for Rome. He watched Brutus play judge and jury in his traveling court. He learned the postponement of ideals and the principles of war before peace.

This was not yet a civil war. Few Romans were fighting against other Romans. The massive Roman armies led by Caesar's avengers, Octavian and Mark Antony, were not ready. They had not even left Italy. The victims were impoverished peoples like the ones among whom Horace had been born, Asians and eastern Greeks whom he knew only from the epic poems of Homer, many of whom were murdered, the others raped and enslaved as they had been in so many previous wars.

Civil war was not to be postponed for long. The army led by Caesar's assassins stopped at Philippi in northern Greece, a narrow plain between mountains and sea, a strong position where Octavian and Antony, allies but rivals to be Caesar's political heir, were soon approaching to contest the future government of Rome – and much more besides.

Horace had time to watch and see what he had never seen: the preparations for a battle whose scale was set to exceed anything of which his father's friends had ever spoken. Romans had for half a century fought each other in the cause of haves versus have-nots. His childhood, his father's enslavement and ambitions stemmed from those wars. But the Battle of Philippi was on a different scale, tens of thousands of men readying to use their swords to rip away their fellow citizens' lives.

He was not himself on the front line – not till the end. His fellow officers knew that he was a writer, not a fighter. He did not have the distraction of leading a charge. For most of the time behind the lines he was a witness to what would never leave him: men stabbed and stamped upon, the ditches of blood that collected the remains, obliterators and the obliterated, the best of their ardor fueled on one side by passion for an ideal and on the other by the power of a single name, Caesar.

Horace was forever after, in ever different ways, a war poet. He absorbed what he saw and held it for release in fragments over the rest of his revolutionary creative life. He saw Brutus fail as a general, too impatient and impetuous, too fatalist for his cause and glorious in his suicide. When Caesar's chief assassin lay among some fifty thousand dead, the massed unknown alongside his fellow wielders of the daggers of the Ides of March, Horace was one of the nobodies. He had been an honorary member of the political class only since his success as a student in Athens and on the doomed march for liberty. He threw away his weapons. He escaped from the field among many others retreating into anonymity—a miracle as he came later to see it but at the time a commonplace for common soldiers, if they were lucky, once the battle was done.

Back in Rome he began the journey—political, intellectual, sexual, and poetic—that would lead him to become one of the greatest writers of a great literary age. He was a damaged man, at first almost a maddened man, an indulger of himself as soon as he could be, soon deft in the meters of his art and the tactics of survival. Eventually he became a laureate poet in an autocratic empire—appreciated by fewer than he felt he deserved, criticized and envied, but a poetic genius for all time.

Horace would write some of the West's most read poetry, sprung from a marriage of languages and cultures, from youthful ideals and a philosophical accommodation with reality, from peace and pleasure and a wry understanding of frailty at all ages. He left a life story within his words that remained unmatched for four hundred years, perhaps fourteen hundred. Some of his most self-revealing poetry has too rarely been read. Readers quickly came to rate his poems of wine and wistful pleasure more highly than those of troubled politics and explosive rage.

About thirty-five years after Philippi he wrote a letter to one of Rome's most powerful families which ended with a portrait of a mad poet on a volcano, a misunderstood perfectionist whose final act of control over his life was to end it by falling into fire and ash. He made his point lightly. He liked his every poetic point to be as light as it could be. He conjured an image of an unworldly artist with his nose in the air, liable to disappear without anyone knowing whether he was intending his fall or not. He summoned the story of the last Greek philosopher-poet, Empedocles, who threw himself into the crater of Mount Etna, possibly as a mad act of delusion about his own immortality, perhaps as a deception of his followers, maybe in mere confusion.

Horace was a wild poet as well as a wise and mellow one. He left behind a unique legacy of dark insecurity, bright pleasure, love, anger, and gratitude for life. He left a monument, as he put it, but even more a voice. He boasted that his poems would last into perpetuity and, unusually for the subjects of such boasts, they did last – and have lasted to our own day in the United States, Europe, and beyond, two thousand years later.

The art that made him proudest was his use of Greek poetry to power the poetry of Rome. He was not a translator but a transformer, and he was sensitive about the difference. He was a modernist in his ancient world. He was not the only – or even the first – to transform the future of literature by taking a fine knife to its past. But he was one of the most inspiring, quoted, and loved.

Among his own translators in modern times stand presidents, prime ministers, poets, and generations of students in school. John Quincy Adams, Ezra Pound, and Robert Frost stand beside William Gladstone, Jonathan Swift, William Wordsworth, and Rudyard Kipling.

Lord Byron was one of many, in his own day and since, for whom Horace's virtues were snuffed out in the classroom. Horace feared that form of fame himself – his future as fodder for those learning their ABCs. He has suffered from his fame. He lived an extraordinarily creative life but, more than any other ancient life, one that was adopted for the purposes of its adopters.

Friedrich Nietzsche, in the months before his own madness took hold, put Horace at the center of his case for the rugged virtues of Rome over Greece. His *Twilight of the Idols* in 1888 was a declaration of war on Horace's critics who thought the poet a mere copier of what had come before. Other admirers made their own claims.

Throughout his life Horace was both measured and maddened, controlling and controlled, but often liable to see worlds beyond any control. As Nietzsche showed, his lines were works of extraordinary literary engineering in which distant parts held up a perfect whole. The ordering of his words in Latin was in many ways alien to Latin speakers, but the poems found a peculiar familiarity when rendered into other languages.

Sometimes that familiarity was too easy. In a country which he saw as barbarian in his own life, Horace not only gained an English name but became a British imperialist, a genial English gentleman, a scholar of metrical technicalities, a poet whose sexuality was decorous and shrouded. His best-remembered phrases were plundered for meanings far from what he intended. Much of his life story was removed because it did not fit the requirements of his adopters. Horrors were buried under sweetness. Fake familiarity masked the truth of how alien was his work in so many ways.

For Horace the patterns of sound, the rules of long and short syllables, progression and pause within lines were not dry technicalities. Meter, the measurements inside a poem, brought power to his purpose. But they were undoubtedly alien to many. All meters were alien in their different ways, sound patterns all varyingly different in different cultures, their effects there to be felt but hard to explain, particularly in the work of Horace, to whom they meant so much.

Horace wrote in different forms, which gained their own technical names. These could easily be confusing. There were epodes (originally called *iambi*), satires (which he called *sermones*), odes (his *carmina*), and epistles, letters in verse, which were not letters in any regular sense.

Within this wide range of poetry Horace told readers more about his own life, both its attractive features and those we may find loathsome, than would any other writer before Augustine at the fourth-century rebirth of Christianity and Petrarch in the Renaissance a thousand years later. He told truths as well as approximations to the truth. He laid traps to deceive the unwary. What he told in his poems is a challenge to a biographer, a chance to make choices from what he tells us, to accept and reject, to make judgments, and to tell his story. He still lies behind his lines.

CHAPTER ONE

Son of a Sometime Slave

Quintus Horatius Flaccus was born on December 8, 65 BCE, a date of rare precision in the history of an ancient life. "Quintus" means "fifth" but did not necessarily mean that Horace was a fifth child. "Horatius" was the name of a mythical hero who had saved the early Roman Republic from the return of an invading king: there were many boys called Horatius. "Flaccus" means "limp," in a sexual sense, or "feeble" more generally – not an ideal name for a sensitive child but useful when Horace wanted to make himself the butt of his own jokes. None of these names was any more than a name. In an age when the names of ancestors, real or fabricated, were important for success, Horace had no ancestry that mattered beyond his father, who had once been a slave.

In Rome the aristocrat Lucius Manlius Torquatus was one of the two ruling consuls, the first of his family in a hundred years to revive its glorious political past, a history which mattered only to the Manlii family, but mattered very much to them. Torquatus was undistinguished himself, but his colleague as Rome's chief executive was Lucius Aurelius Cotta, from the heart of the city's ruling clique, whose sister was married to the young Julius Caesar. Although these consuls' success had come from prosecuting their opponents for bribery rather than any more glamorous campaigns, that was of little account. Even in the small town of Venusia, 150 miles southeast of Rome, where Horace began his life, the year of his birth would always be known as the year of these consuls.

Venusia was Roman: it was the town of Venus, Rome's goddess of love. It had strong walls astride the Appian Way, Rome's first highway south and the route for goods and soldiers going east to Greece. Venusia had also been a recent enemy of Rome. It was Oscan, a people whom Romans had not easily taken into their empire of Latin. Venusia recognized its own mythical founder, Daunus. Everywhere in southern Italy identities were mixed and obscured. Latin could be written in Greek letters, Oscan in the Etruscan alphabet of Rome's sometime kings. There were Venusians whose first language was Greek and who traced their history to the Homeric hero Diomedes, said to have passed by after the Trojan War. Horace's home was a contested town, militarily five years before his birth, culturally always.

Above Venusia stood Mount Voltur, a low, glowering peak whose slopes shifted from gray to blue with the passing hours and whose farmers moved with the seasons, keeping their goats high up during the summer and down in the valleys in winter. It was a landscape of thick woods: poplar, cypress, ash, and pine. Close and to the north was the clattering river Aufidus, a torrent of noise in December, when Horace was born, meaner in the months when the flocks needed it most. A little to the east beside the Appian Way was the Bandusian Spring, a well-known site for watering the thirsty. High in the farther distance, out into the sea, was Mount Garganus, its oak trees ever moaning in the Adriatic gales, battleground in the struggle against the slave army of Spartacus only eight years earlier.

That conflict with an enemy within was a shameful subject, safest not spoken of in Rome, not forgotten in Venusia.

Horace's father had been a slave. Italy depended on slavery, but, unlike in Greece and other places to the east, the status of the enslaved could shift. The line between free and unfree was clear, essential to life, but it could regularly be moved by war, ransom, reward, or an owner's favor. The stain of slavery never left, but it could fade. Horace's father may not have been a slave for long, possibly only in the aftermath of Venusia's failed rebellion from the Roman fold, possibly after another civil war battle. He was forever after a former slave.

The farmlands around the river and mountains were not the main source of family prosperity. Much better was the business that could be moved when trouble came. Horace's father sold salted fish and meat. He was an auctioneer, a seller of the property of victims of war. These were good times for a man who bought and sold and acted as a country banker. When Roman allies were demanding votes in Rome, when Roman armies were fighting to monopolize as many rights as they could, when Roman generals took different sides in desperate disputes, there was much war-torn property to be sold, for credit or cash, to those lucky enough to be living in peace. Horace's father invested part of the proceeds in his son's education. Learning, like a banker's skills, was easily moved from place to place.

The most novel weapon used to release land and livestock to the marketplace was proscription, a plain word that had become a term of terror. What originally meant nothing more harmful than a noticeboard bearing offers for sale had become a policy that brought profit to property dealers and poison almost everywhere else it fell. A proscription sale was once the result only of bankruptcy or natural death, a seller's desire to move house or city or to better his prospects abroad. In the years before Horace's birth *proscription* had become a single word for multiple horrors, the legal decapitation of those deemed enemies of the state; the legal right for the killers to swap severed heads for cash; confiscation of property; the paying of legal bribes for friends and family members to betray one another.

Proscription became part of Rome's political vocabulary under the city's first civil war victor, the theater-loving general and protector of the wealthy, Lucius Cornelius Sulla. It was a tactic of mass intimidation, and its message spread far: the deaths of some five hundred of Sulla's opponents discouraged many others. Those arguing for expansion of political rights and more equal ownership of land were the principal victims.

For Horace's father and thousands around Venusia, Sulla's proscription was still fresh and real. They had been lucky to lose only their land when generals needed to reward their troops. Forced sales paid for armies, but the fate of the newly landless resulted in insecurity and distrust that endured much longer. *Proscription* was a word pronounced in explosive P's, with a very particular sense of fear.

When Horace was learning his first letters at the local school, many of Sulla's former soldiers, their leader long dead, were still his neighbors. Some had learned the art of farming the parched soil, but many had not and treated the town as an occupier's barracks. Although Philippi, twenty-three years later, was Horace's first battle, his first taste of the military came from the boots and abuse of soldiers' sons in the classrooms of his southern Italian home. Horace was *libertino patre natum*, the son of a man freed from slavery, and he was not allowed to forget it.

War defined his start in life. When he was five years old, a new generation of generals was aiming for the primacy in the state that

Sulla had enjoyed as his own domain. Rome was ruled by what critics called a Three-Headed Monster, an alliance of political rivals. There was Marcus Licinius Crassus, vastly wealthy from the property of the proscribed; Gnaeus Pompeius, conqueror of the East, known as *Magnus,* "the Great"; and the rising Gaius Julius Caesar, whom Crassus was financing as a counterweight to Pompey and to keep the alliance alive.

These machinations were far away from Venusia, but as Horace grew up, the year 60 BCE, the year of the Monster, the beginning of Horace's education, became the start in his mind of the worst times, the realization that the instability of his father's youth was not going to stop in his own. To his father and neighbors, reading their calendar in the normal Roman way, the year was merely defined by the name of Metellus, the senior of its two consuls, Quintus Caecilius Metellus, whose wife, Clodia, was perhaps more famous in Venusia: her sexual affairs brought her even closer to the center of politics than Metellus stood himself, and sex was the kind of news that fastest spread.

This was a time of class warfare fought among the upper class. Sulla had his less extreme successors. The people had champions, but they did not produce leaders. Caesar was the populist on the rise. Clodia's brother Clodius was a client of Crassus's and supporter of Caesar who had changed the spelling of Claudius, the aristocratic family name, to make himself seem more plebeian. Clodius had a wealthy plebeian wife, Fulvia, whose open presence in politics was a radical act in itself. There was fighting in the streets and, barely more decorously, in the courts of law.

Clodia herself was notorious as the lover of the poet Gaius Valerius Catullus, and, according to the orator Marcus Tullius Cicero, sexually available to anyone willing to pay the price of entry to the baths. When Horace was nine years old the scandalous Clodii, their exploits dramatized by Cicero in a notorious trial, were celebrities known far down the Appian Way and beyond.

The name of Brutus meant much less at this time. In Venusia it would have evoked his distant ancestor, who expelled Rome's Etruscan kings. Legends were more durable than news, more pervasive and more liable to be believed than whatever gossip came from the Forum, a new speech by Cicero, or the latest jostlings between the three heads of Rome's ruling alliance.

In the year when Metellus was consul the young Brutus, aged around twenty-five, was still enjoying student life, learning rhetoric from the great performers of his day, building on the grammar he had studied at school. Brutus studied politics from boyhood too. His teacher had been the fashionable former Greek slave Staberius Eros, whose classroom was a place where the battles for Rome were fought in miniature. Eros became rich enough to give free lessons to any boy whose family had lost its fortune in Sulla's proscriptions. Sulla's own son used to throw his weight around in class as though he were his father. Others fought back against the little dictator like enemies in a real civil war. Brutus had early lessons in the language of liberty and tyranny, in the competing visions for the future of Rome, but this was not the next phase of learning that Horace's father had in mind for his own son.

Horace, like Brutus, was going to be educated in Rome, but he was going to have a very different teacher. Rome was essential if the son were going to fulfill his father's hopes. The temptations of Rome could be shunned. To that end Horace's father was prepared to be his son's chaperone, even to pretend to be a slave again, his own son's slave.

In around 55 BCE the two set off up the Appian Way, the road used by all classes at all times, by senators and wine salesmen, soldiers and seekers after work, the stronger barging aside the weak, mile after traveling mile of square-cut stones. Venusia was three hundred miles from Rome, not so very far away along this wonder of their world.

The road was a lesson in itself, straight where it could be, sinuous only where it had to be. To the left was Mount Voltur, the haunt of bears and wolves, where Horace had roamed before the classroom called. The road ran over the river at Pons Aufidi, the gateway to the countryside he knew less well, the battlefields of the Italian wars which the Appian Way was built to banish into history. Then came Beneventum, the former Oscan town of Maleventum, renamed from "bad" to "good" in the spirit of Roman superstition or maybe optimism: at Beneventum two centuries before, the Greek king Pyrrhus, famed for his costly victories, had suffered his decisive defeat, the last time Roman power over Italy was threatened from across the Adriatic.

After Beneventum came Capua, the town whose luxuries had softened up Hannibal for defeat, the site of the gladiator school from which Spartacus began his revolt, the start of the long line of crucifixions, all the way to Rome, by which Crassus had executed the survivors of the slave army. Then came Suessa Arunca, birthplace of Gaius Lucilius, a poet of the previous century who had been both a friend of the grand and a pioneer satirist of Roman life. From Tarracina on the coast the road ran through marshes, straight as a spear, to Rome's southernmost gate.

Bovillae was the last stop, a town loyal to the family of Julius Caesar. Violent riots regularly spilled from the capital into its suburbs, because Rome was in a state of civil war even when war was not fought by armies in its streets. Its citizens had been due for a week of parties to mark the city's next age, its *saeculum,* according to the priests who measured the years, but the due date was denied by the consuls. Horace's father aimed to shield his son from the city mobs and from any allure that such as Clodius and his sister might have for the impressionable.

Keeping a distance from Clodia and her friends was perhaps not so hard a task. Horace would never have met the ironically nick-named Nola, the "sexually unwilling," and the "Medea of the Palatine", Cicero's taunts when he accused her of poisoning her husband, Metellus. Clodia was already seen as Lesbia in the love poems of Catullus, but for Horace, still young and not yet a poet, she could have existence only in his dreams.

What Horace's father wanted to avoid for his son was the more general moral and political contamination of the capital, a threat even when the priests had postponed the nighttime parties of the *Ludi Saeculares,* the Centenary Games. He did not want to take him from the sons of the centurions and leave him among the idle rich and suppurating poor. Medea was a fictional witch queen from Greek tragedy: on Rome's Esquiline Hill were women who claimed a real power of witchcraft, perverting and poisoning both bodies and minds. He had the fears of a man for whom so much harm, through the strife of civil war, had come from Rome.

Horace's schoolteacher was to be a strict scholar, Lucius Orbilius Pupillus, originally from Beneventum. Orbilius was not prospering in Rome, as Brutus's tutor had. He was a literary conservative in his taste, drumming into his pupils the harsh sounds of Greek classics in Latin. He insisted on a close study of the *Odyssey* through a pioneering translation by a Greek actor and sometime slave, Livius Andronicus. All writers in Latin struggled with the techniques of sound and meter that were so natural in Greek, literature's accepted senior language. To read Andronicus's Homer in its rhythmic meter from the Italian countryside was to handle delicate glass through a soldier's glove. This did not detract from the moral lessons of epic poetry. Horace wrote on wax tablets what his teacher wanted to see. Orbilius was a wielder of the classroom whip to prove the superiority of his views.

Orbilius's pupils went on to study Homer in Greek, just as the boys did in the grander schools. But there was a nervousness about Greek, even among the many who knew it well. Romans had conquered southern Italy, which was deeply Greek, and then Greece itself, but that did not end their sense of cultural inferiority; indeed it heightened it and sometimes created defensiveness. Pioneering Latin poets, rough in language but also in criticism of their peers, were still models for a good Roman to be proud of.

There was Gnaeus Naevius, a wild critic of Carthage, chronicler of Rome's war with Hannibal, and Lucilius himself, the great satirist, citizen of Suessa Arunca, who had known many military heroes of the previous century but kept an artist's distance from them. Lucilius had chosen literature over politics. He wrote about himself and his friends, about bad manners and meandering journeys. To Horace there was the seductive sense that Lucilius's whole life lay open to his readers like a picture on a temple wall: it was a sense that he would turn into self-exposure of his own.

The old man from Suessa would have found many new targets for his satire had he still been alive. No amount of lessons and chaperoning could protect Horace from the radical ambitions and massed madness of Rome, the Monster politicians, the magicians, the criminals, and the starving, the squalor of thousands packed close beside Rome's walls, the peculiar differences between country living and that of the city.

Lucilius had been a pioneering artist. He had stared at human faces and seen beneath the skin, seen fears as well as features, *mors, icterus morbus, venenum,* "death, yellowing eyes, poison." He had seen bodies with *gangraena herpestica,* the "crawling of gangrene," men so thin that they were *vivo monogrammo,* a "living outline," and so deformed that they could be characterized only in Greek. Latin was a junior language. It needed educating itself. A Roman writer had to be an inventor, a verbal engineer. Lucilius was a model to Horace from the start.

Around the time Horace was arriving in Rome, new opportunities were arising for the soldiers and their families in Venusia. Those who had never settled to country life could join a new army. Their older sons, if sneering at the locals was no longer sufficient satisfaction, could answer the call from Crassus to accompany his invasion of an unknown empire east of the Euphrates. This was a personal project by Rome's wealthiest man from which everyone who joined him was promised precious metal: real wealth, not a few acres of mountain.

There were already Roman armies in Gaul and Spain and lesser opportunities along the Rhine and the Danube. Conquest was the business of Rome. Loyal legionaries were in high demand. Crassus could not be too fussy about where he recruited. The Three-Headed Monster ruled on the basis that no single head should mess with the ambitions of another. Caesar and Pompey may both have had doubts about whether Crassus was wise, or even well enough equipped, to attempt the conquest of Parthia, a sprawling borderless country that stretched out from the far reaches of Pompey's conquests to the edges of China. But they did not intervene.

Any doubts were in the streets around the Forum. Senators wore black to protest their impotence to interfere. Soothsayers and priests showed their opposition to the Parthian War — or the opposition of those who were paying them — but only by noise and smoke. The younger generation was divided. Brutus stayed aloof. His brother-in-law Gaius Cassius, his fellow pupil in Eros's school, became Crassus's second-in-command.

The army departed in a cloud of expectations, gathering new recruits along its route to the Aegean Sea. Then came a long season of silence. In the school of Orbilius, as in every other part of Rome, Parthia became just another distant story until rumors returning along the Appian Way began to suggest the biggest military catastrophe in any Roman's lifetime.

By 53 BCE, only a year after his departure, Crassus was dead, his army destroyed, his head stuffed with molten gold as a message from his destroyers. Arrows and camels had killed Romans as Gauls and Germans never had. Survivors returned to their farms if they were fortunate, to the streets if they were not. The Three-Headed Monster had now only two heads, Caesar and Pompey, who, with no balancing power between them, were soon at each other's throats. Caesar, conqueror of Gaul, crossed the Rubicon into Italy in 49 and became an invader and an outlaw. The two fought a full civil war. Pompey's head and body were separated on an Egyptian beach, and Caesar became the single ruler of Rome, its dictator-for-life. Horace, directly involved in none of this but seeing and hearing it all, began quietly the next phase of his education.

CHAPTER TWO

Poets and Assassins

The university of the Roman world was Athens. Mere politics was no reason for Horace's father to pause the progress of his son, whose gifts were clear, if only to a few. Horace left Rome through the same southern gate as the soldiers of Crassus, and the same port, Brundisium, which took almost all Romans to Greece, the country where at this time they either studied or fought.

Greece meant both the battlefields on which Caesar had defeated Pompey and the marble-columned painted walkways in which a young man might learn the ways of philosophers and poets. Four hundred years before, Athens had had its own empire. The temples of the Acropolis, their massive sculptures of half-men, half-horses trampling and dying, were the product and surviving proof of that power. The Athenians whom Horace met were now no longer imperialists — or even free. They were ruled by a governor sent from Rome, and much of their greatest art was being transported to the homes of their conquerors.

Cicero and his fellow writers from Rome liked to take the tourist stroll through the remains of Plato's Academy. To visitors, especially the young, the stones still stood for liberty, free thought, and free speech. Even where the sculptures showed the harshest brutalities of war, the mythical Centaurs assaulting civilization on its knees, the Parthenon was a place of freedom. Athenian democracy had lasted barely a century in its purest original form, but its legacy lived on, in libraries and bookshops and the life of inquiring minds.

Horace himself was for the first time free. There was no Orbilius with a whip. There was no father dressed as a slave to keep him out of trouble. There were other young men whose parents were ambitious enough to afford further education. His father had left him with only stern advice. Athens was a city of free women and boys, freedom in every way. Leaving Rome was a way of getting a life. In Athens's competing schools of life and art he could choose a new curriculum.

Within the libraries of Athens lay works of which he hardly knew, some wholly new to a student fresh from the wax tablets of his cloistered school. It was not always easy to identify what was available to be read. Papyrus rolls, made from Egyptian reeds laid vertically and horizontally in strips, were only as clear a surface as the skills of the maker had made possible, sometimes centuries before. They were often anonymous until their box was carefully opened. Sometimes there was a tag bearing the name of a writer, in many instances not.

There was not just the work of Homer but the works of poets whose languages and interests were very different. Homer's heroes lived and died for glory: dead leaves beside the rivers of Troy stood for the decade lost to fighting for fame. Other poets from around the same time lived for sex and wine: dead leaves for them were a warning to enjoy life while one could.

Prose was mixed with poetry. Three-hundred-year-old speeches by the Athenian orator Demosthenes in defense of Greek freedom from the rule of the father of Alexander the Great sat alongside Hesiod's advice to farmers from three hundred years before that. A box of Homer's *Iliad,* whose story Horace had learned in the Latin of Livius Andronicus, would be indistinguishable from one with much shorter poems from the same age as Homer and Hesiod, epigrams by the pleasure-seeking Mimnermus and by Archilochus, utterly different in another way: personal, vicious, *iambic,* to use their technical Greek name.

Mimnermus's was a name that regularly appeared. He was a patriot, a pleasure seeker, and a reporter, who described a total eclipse of the sun. He was fearless. He dared to criticize Solon, one of the great sages of Athens, for preferring death in his prime to a painful old age. How to have a good death was a common subject in the papyri. Mimnermus suited some of Horace's ideals of what a poet might do.

But the mood and manner of Archilochus better fitted Horace's own. The poems under this unfamiliar name, unrolled and rerolled in the delicate scrolls, revealed a soldier who was no Homeric hero but more a mocker of heroics, a mercenary with the special cynicism and realism of that trade. Archilochus came from Paros, a Greek island that had become rich from quarrying marble. His father had founded a frontier town in Thasos, an island of gold mines and medicine farther north. Archilochus's mother had been a slave. He was illegitimate, no part of any assured social future, someone whom Horace could understand.

Archilochus had made his money by fighting others' wars. He had hoped to settle down with the daughter of a local landowner. The pair were engaged and the marriage date was imminent when the girl's father broke off the deal, sparking a stream of iambic abuse from the disappointed groom, setting out Archilochus's sexual enjoyment of both the daughter and her sister who hanged themselves out of shame, it seemed. Or maybe the first daughter became a prostitute, and Archilochus turned down her advances. There were various versions, even within Archilochus's own work.

Horace did not have to read much to discover that poetry was not just about kings, queens, and warriors; it was about a man's own passions and hatreds, misogyny and lust, his penis like that of a grain-fattened ass, the sexiness of a fat-ankled whore, wine, and his own troubled soul. Archilochus wrote enthusiastically about all the pleasures of sex, "falling upon a woman's flesh, thigh to thigh," the feel of a woman's mouth, "head-down, as she did her work like a Thracian drinking beer through a straw."

Archilochus experimented with different kinds of material and meter, with the sounds and rhythms that intensified sense. His most aggressive poems were prominent in the collections of his work, but he was more than an iambic aggressor. He observed the division between men who were like foxes and knew many things, and those who were like hedgehogs, who knew only one big thing. In a poetic world of Homeric bards looking up and writing about their betters he was a fighter himself, not always a very good one, throwing down his shield in one very popular poem, and running for safety in an unmanly way, reassuring himself that he could always get a new shield tomorrow. Life, by contrast, "could not be retrieved or repurchased after your last breath slips past your teeth."

Words of rage and self-exposure, playing himself and playing roles from ordinary life had served Archilochus well. His mother might have left him illegitimate and his marriage might have not gone according to plan, but hundreds of years after his death he had a shrine to himself on Paros. Inscriptions recorded his greatest lines. Visitors revered him alongside the Muses. In Greece even a brutal poet was a man to be respected. His monument was in the place where he had been born but also in the libraries of Athens and thus the world.

The libraries held many hundreds of different papyrus rolls, products of writers centuries apart in age, their identities hidden until the borrower began to untie them, unroll and read them. Names were not always clear, but many stood out as favorites. The reader had always to take care. Papyri that had been white and smooth in the dry air of Egypt could be creased and crumbling farther north.

Alongside Archilochus lay the much later Callimachus of Alexandria, a master of invective, pioneer of brevity, and believer that a big book was like a *mega kakon,* in one of his famous phrases, a big evil. Callimachus was renowned as a giant and a genius, a philosophical librarian whose pen took no prisoners. He was a literary grandee from the capital of culture.

There were also Alcaeus and Sappho from the humbler island of Lesbos, passionate and personal poets who wrote to be sung. Alcaeus might seem just another political buccaneer, a soldier singing of love and wine and the evil of tyranny. But in a different way from Archilochus, he struck a chord. The sound of Alcaeus wrapped itself around his sense. Sappho was a poet as original in her way as Homer. Hers was an extraordinary voice of sweet grace and sexual longing.

Alcaeus and Sappho had their own reasons to be writers, their own ambitions in art, their own methods of measuring sounds and stresses in their lines. They sang of their own lives, in the first person, with an *I* not a *they,* in the present tense, with a *now* not a *then.* They had fewer imitators than Archilochus, and the fashion for their songs did not seem to have lasted, but hundreds of years after their deaths, they too were still alive.

Horace was himself able to write in Greek. That was not unusual. He considered writing his own Greek poetry until the sense of carrying wood into an already crowded forest became too strong. Many Roman writers used Greek in contexts where there were not the right Latin words, in places where they wanted to show off their learning. Greek was the language not only of descendants of Greek settlers but also of the learned everywhere, and Athens was where it was learned in its finest forms.

While Horace read closely, absorbing the sound and spirit of what he found, not all his fellow students were so attentive. With him was the son of Marcus Tullius Cicero, whose name was famed even in Venusia: the teenage son had the same name as the father but not much else in common with him. In the Rome that Horace had left behind the elder Cicero was the foremost orator and power broker among the great, enemy of Clodius and Clodia – and an everyday writer in Greek as well as Latin. The younger Cicero did not seem likely to reach such heights. Athens for him was more a finishing school than a university.

At the start of his illustrious career the elder Cicero had needed to overcome the stigma of being an outsider, a *novus homo*, "new man," since no member of his family had been a senator before he was. He had bought a grand house from Crassus, grander than the one which Rome's richest man had for himself, attracting the suggestion that he was trying too hard for social success. The young Cicero had no such insecurities and a generous personal income from two apartment blocks which his father was dedicating to his education, one for the poor on the Aventine Hill, the other on the Argiletum, the main road from the slums of the Subura to the Forum. He could also call on his father's closest friend, Titus Pomponius Atticus, the wealthiest Roman in Greece, who was living in louche retirement from the perilous fray at home.

Cicero the father, in addition to writing essays and dialogues and speeches, thought of himself as a poet, even though this view was perhaps not widely shared. The young Cicero was no writer of any kind, bringing paternal delight with even the slightest stylistic improvement in a rare letter home. He was learning oratory in Greek under a florid teacher whom his father ordered him to leave. He saw his future in the family business of politics – though his first step, fighting for Pompey against Caesar, had required the arrangement of a pardon from the victor. Caesar usually liked to pardon well-connected Romans if he could.

Horace was starting life from a much lower base. His father was far below a novus homo, he was a former slave. However successful his business of auctions and banking, he would never be a senator. Horace had an income but not the proceeds of large rented properties. He had no friends in Athens apart from the ones, young Cicero included, he was rapidly making – in the bars around the Acropolis if not in the libraries.

To all these students in Athens, at the end of March 44, came the news of Caesar's murder. The simple act was a shock, the dictator stabbed in full view of the Senate by the daggers of some of his closest friends, well-known men, the sometime school friends, Marcus Brutus and Gaius Cassius, to the fore. Rome had already lost Crassus and Pompey, two of the heads of its Three-Headed Monster alliance. Suddenly the city was headless.

It was hard to comprehend how explosive and resounding a shock this assassination was. One of Horace's fellow students was the young Lucius Calpurnius Bibulus, who came from a family almost as hostile to Caesar as it was possible to be. Bibulus's father had failed to become one of the Monster's heads as he felt he should have been; he had endured an unusually public nervous collapse after the murder of his two eldest sons in Egypt; and he blamed Caesar for it all. The younger Bibulus was also Brutus's stepson. There would have been justified rejoicing in whatever Athenian bar he heard the news – but trepidation too for anyone with a sensitive turn of mind. After the shock, what?

The aftermath, as it seemed from early reports, was a curious calm, a desire to return to normal business as quickly as possible, almost to pretend that the years between the deaths of Crassus and Caesar were no more than a stage show that had run its course, its audience free to go home. Deals were being done. News passed quickly between Rome and Athens – down the Appian Way and across the Aegean. Old Cicero, excited by the killing and prime among the pretenders of normality, was in close contact with Atticus. Caesar's chief lieutenant, Mark Antony, was a man with whom they could do business. Young Cicero was well placed to brief his student colleagues.

Fresh details came with every ship. There had been further violence, though nothing of the magnitude of the killing itself. Caesar had supporters in the streets who were less enthusiastic than Cicero and Antony for compromise and pretense. The poet Gaius Helvius Cinna, known among the educated for his epic on mythological incest, had been killed in a very literary error of mistaken identity because one of the assassins had a similar name.

Nor did Caesar's former soldiers, fueled by the loyalty of their service together in Gaul and against Pompey, accept that the show was over and that they should return to their beds. Old Cicero changed his mind (he had a very flexible mind) and told Atticus that the assassination and its aftermath had been botched. The conspirators, he wrote, should have killed more of Caesar's supporters, particularly Antony, in order to ensure that the Monster did not grow replacement heads.

This perception was correct but too late. A new head was already growing. Three hundred miles away from Athens, in Apollonia, another part of the university of Greece, was the teenage grandson of Caesar's sister. His name was Octavian. He was slight and frail in health, but Caesar, who had no children of his own, had known the boy just well enough to adopt him in his will.

Octavian's mother thought this a dangerous inheritance and hoped that the legacy might be divided, the money coming to her son, the politics left to Antony and Caesar's other supporters in Rome. Octavian disagreed. Caesar's troops – and the mass of the Roman poor who had enjoyed his generosity – disagreed too. They wanted another Caesar. Octavian was ready to be that Caesar.

The port of Athens began to receive ships filled with Romans escaping the uncertainty, followed soon after by the assassins and their sympathizers fleeing the possibility of vengeance. The most glamorous of the arrivals, in the late summer of 44, was Brutus himself, bringing the blood of Caesar on his hands, his famous name, and a high-flown rhetoric about restoring ancient freedoms. The Roman students of Athens, steeped in Greek poetry and the city's short-lived democracy four centuries before, were a readier audience for him than were the men and women of the Roman streets.

The people of Athens welcomed Brutus too – to their hot streets, to their air that was always healthier than the swamp mists of Rome, healthier now in every way. Athenians were proud of their tyrant-fighting traditions. No visitor to the Agora, the ancient forum of the city, could avoid the bronze statues of the male lovers, Harmodius and Aristogeiton, who in 514 had assassinated the brother of the last tyrant of Athens, clearing the way for democracy to begin. Theirs was a murky story of hidden daggers, sexual jealousy, and heroic silence under torture, all of these distracting from the inconvenient truth that Athenian democracy had been born mainly through the military assistance of Sparta, the state that was already its rival and soon to be its enemy. But truth had not hampered the myth.

The immediate aftermath of the ancient tyrant's assassination had been four years of repression and terror. But as any visitor could see, there was no dead tyrant among the statues: the message was that tyranny was never dead, only absent. There was no bronze whip of the torturer, no whip of the lover, only the moment of killing, the old and bearded Aristogeiton with a cloak over his arm, the young Harmodius thrusting out his murder weapon.

Art could be deceptive. Art was partial. Art was part of politics. The Athenians welcomed Brutus and planned a similar bronze tribute to him and Cassius, the old friends, related too by marriage, who had become the assassins of Caesar. Dead leaves of autumn blew in piles around the pinks and blues of painted columns. The smoke of roasting meats announced parties to celebrate these new great days.

Brutus himself, in part to conceal his military options from his hosts, became a student and teacher alongside his admirers. He was well versed in the arguments for and against what he had done. Was tyranny to be opposed at all costs? Was civil war worse even than tyranny? Was tyranny so destructive of liberty that no good could be done while a tyrant was alive? Horace read and learned. The tyrant-fighting poet Alcaeus had sung and marched on the same path of freedom that Brutus had chosen. This was a dazzling time for a young man from the countryside of the Italian South.

Brutus was living two double lives in his year in Athens. Not only was he a general with a school satchel, he was caught between starkly different versions of what was legal and what was not. So were his supporters.

According to one version of what was law in Rome, Brutus was a legitimate provincial governor. Precisely which would be his province was disputed, but the principle was fixed. That was his prize in the compromise deal that Cicero had brokered with Mark Antony in the Senate after the assassination: there was to be no official thanks to the assassins but neither was there to be any loss to them. Brutus's trip to Athens was a station on his way to the status that he would have held if the killing had never taken place.

According to Octavian's rival law, eventually passed in August 43 in the assembly of the people, Brutus was a criminal. So was Gaius Cassius and the lesser assassin, the poet Cassius Parmensis, who was a captain in Brutus's fleet. Like all assassins and accomplices, they were proscribed, their lives and property forfeit. Proscription, the word synonymous with terror when Horace was a boy, had come back with a new vengeance.

Cicero, the young soldier bearing the famous name, was more use to Brutus than was Horace. Cicero's father, though ecstatic at the death of Caesar, had not been trusted enough to know about it in advance, still less to wield a dagger: he was too liable to see arguments against an act as well as those in its favor. His son was simpler in parading his hatred of tyranny, and Brutus sent him to meet Greeks who might join his fight, seemingly inevitable now, against Octavian and Mark Antony or support him with money and supplies. Brutus's plan was to join Gaius Cassius, his fellow leader of the assassins, in the Greek cities of Asia on the other side of the Aegean to find money and mercenaries as best they could and match, or ideally outmatch, the army of the new Caesars.

In the meantime Brutus studied philosophy and made friends. He was conservative in his tastes; he had already written treatises on Stoicism, on the superiority of ruling only oneself, on the supreme need *vivere honeste,* "to live an honorable life." A more fashionable school of thought was that of the Athenian Epicurus, whose garden, which he recommended everyone should copy, had been a haven for those avoiding the disturbance of politics: freedom from the fear of death and avoidance of pain were the key Epicurean virtues. Horace found attractions in Epicurus, whose garden ruins still survived and who, by Greek standards, was a modern philosopher, dead for little more than two hundred years. Brutus did not.

There were many forms of freedom, said the philosophers of Athens. Their biggest star that year was Cratippus, originally from Lesbos like Alcaeus and Sappho, who had been a friend of Cicero and comforter of Pompey after his defeat. Cratippus was a more traditional philosopher than Epicurus, trained in dissecting arguments more than promoting a doctrine. He spoke about dreams as a source of truth beyond the material world. Brutus attended his lectures. Life was not a simple choice between avoiding politics, as the most devoted Epicureans argued, or avoiding civil war, as Stoics had argued to him in opposing Caesar's murder. There was pragmatism, the reasoning of issues case by case. Brutus listened and learned and also taught Latin rhetoric.

In the autumn of 43 the numbers of aristocratic refugees from Rome rose sharply. Octavian and Mark Antony were in an uneasy alliance, but they had agreed on their tactic for raising money and purging Caesar's opponents. A new law, passed in November, extended the proscriptions beyond the assassins and their accomplices to anyone seen as sympathetic to them. Names of the suddenly guilty appeared on white boards around the city, at first just a few, then hundreds. Anyone wanting revenge or reward or both could exchange severed heads for cash in the Forum.

It was a new time of terror. Slaves gained freedom as well as fortunes for decapitating their owners. Neighbors solved long-festering land disputes. Wives betrayed husbands, the indebted their bankers. There was a seedy profession of hunting down the proscribed and a grateful mass of unemployed ex-soldiers to fill its ranks. Horror stories grew as they traveled, but the core truth was clear enough.

Those who could escape Rome had few choices. There was Sicily, which was controlled by Sextus Pompeius, the surviving son of Pompey, Caesar's last rival for absolute power; but Sextus's demands on new arrivals were unclear. There was the army of Cassius in Asia, approved by the Senate but unattractive for the many proscribed who lacked military skills. And then there was the more ambiguous, and maybe less demanding, Athenian milieu of Brutus and his students.

One prominent arrival in Athens was an intellectual aristocrat whom, like Brutus, Horace would have been unlikely to meet if society were as it so long had been. Marcus Valerius Messalla Corvinus, a distant relative of Octavian, was committed to the principles of the old republic. He brought a letter from Cicero packed with Greek philosophical justifications of what had gone well — and what not so well — since Caesar's death. Messalla was himself a writer, a historian of his own time, a flowery orator in what he hoped was Cicero's style, and a poet who wrote satires and erotica. He had an erratic half-brother, Lucius Gellius Poplicola, who was also soon expected on a boat from Rome.

Bibulus, the young man whose father had broken down and died in enmity with Caesar, was already waiting to greet Brutus, the husband of his mother, Porcia. Like Messalla he had ambitions to be a writer and was planning a history of his family's recent times, one which owed much to comparisons with the war at Troy. Bibulus likened his mother to Andromache, the wife of the Trojan hero Hector. They were a family in which history was almost all of the present.

Another young idealist was a wealthy wine maker's son, Lucius Sestius, whose childhood, though very different from that of Horace, had been no less torn by the politics of Rome. As a small boy he had stood in court as little more than a stage prop, theatrically frail, to help Cicero rouse the sympathy of a jury for his father in a corruption case. Cicero's successful defense, part of his long-running assault on Clodius, had owed more to his claimed benefits for political moderation (in general) than to any particular facts. The young Sestius retained many of the failed principles of those days.

Not all belonged to the highborn and high-minded. Brutus could not choose his supporters. He knew enough about war to see that violent opportunists were more necessary than gentle poets or retiring philosophers. Among these was Rupilius Rex, his fellow praetor for the year 43, the rank just below consul. This Rupilius, famed for vile words and venomous revenge, was proscribed along with Brutus and chose Athens too as his place of safety.

Horace himself heard the news from Rome with a horror that was more dispassionate than direct. He had no friends or relatives likely to be proscribed. The populist revolution was eating only the rich. Messalla and Gellius needed to be out of town, so too Rupilius, who was Rex in respect of his alleged descent from one of Rome's kings – and had the manner to match. The mere son of an auctioneer from Venusia did not need to be away from Rome, except for the reading of poetry.

The young Cicero very much needed to be away. His father, long naively hopeful about Octavian, had been conducting as aggressive a rhetorical campaign against Antony as had ever been heard in Rome against any man. His speeches were called Philippics after Demosthenes' vicious assaults three hundred years before against Philip of Macedon. The father of Alexander the Great had threatened the free constitution of Athens; so too was Antony threatening Rome, a "gangster" who expected gratitude from Cicero merely for not murdering him.

In December 43 Antony's tolerance for Cicero was exhausted. He exercised his right to add the entire family of Cicero to the proscription lists. He and Octavian had an agreement not to veto the other's choices. News soon reached Athens that a gang led by a soldier called Laenas had taken up the challenge.

The killers expected that the price on the head of such enemies would be high enough to make it worth all their whiles. The younger Cicero was with his new friends in Greece, but the older was caught after a failed attempt to join him by sea. The winter waves were too high. The great orator and philosopher was notorious for indecision. Most educated Romans, Horace included, had a fear of the sea.

Cicero showed his final fatalism on land. He headed toward one of his own villas, where he would be easily found. His carriage was intercepted. There was no struggle, but Laenas's men made an easy job hard, three strokes of execution and the last sinews severed by a saw. The hands that had written the Philippics, packed around the stubborn head, were carried back to Antony. Cicero's tongue was pierced by the dress pins of Antony's wife. His brother and nephew died too. The soldiers took away their cash in return. This was the most notorious story of the proscriptions – though not the cruelest or most brutal – and it shook the exiles of Athens.

Brutus began to find recruitment to his liberators' army much easier. The young Cicero, under mortal threat even in Athens, was living testament to the values that they claimed to be fighting for. Sestius, using the family wealth from vineyards and pottery factories, became the manager of his mint, maker of the coins that would promote the assassins' commitment to liberty. Brutus offered Horace the chance to be an officer. It must have seemed an unlikely proposal. Horace had come to admire men like Archilochus and Alcaeus, who were fighters as well as writers, but he had never trained for war himself. He had absorbed only the spirit of war and, as winter turned to spring in the birthplace of political freedom, as the scent of new leaves smothered the damp and dead, that was enough.

CHAPTER THREE

Behind the Lines

Halfway between the ruined site of Troy, on which so much imagined history hung, and the wealthy island of Rhodes, which the assassins hoped would finance their future, lay Clazomenae, a city known for wine and wheat, swans and olives, its name derived from the clacking of wings. Horace had many new things to see. He was with Brutus and his backers on the Asian side of the Aegean. They had passed by large towns like Smyrna, and tiny coastal villages like Lebedos, barely more than two hundred yards square. They had played the roles of tourists and bandits. Their main task was to raise troops and money, to suborn supporters of Mark Antony and Octavian by bribes and threats, and eventually to join Cassius's army for a joint attack on their enemies. Horace enjoyed travel as he had never known it before.

On their way to Clazomenae some of their methods sat uneasily with the reputation of liberators. When the citizens of Xanthus preferred their own freedom to that of Caesar's assassins, Brutus's army oversaw a mass suicide rather than a surrender. Swimmers attempting escape found themselves in fishnets carefully laid to catch them for the slave trade. The freedom fighters from Rome did not take their cue from the imagined world of Greek democracy but from the brutish realism of the scenes above the Parthenon columns: half-humans, driven wilder by drink, raping and smashing human heads.

Rhodes was left to the small mercy of Cassius, who took all its treasure, public and private; when desperate citizens hailed Cassius as their king, he said he was an enemy of kings, a boast which neither saved nor reassured them. Up and down the coast where Greek ideals had begun, the story was of sieges, the choice of surrender or destruction or both.

Clazomenae was a city with two centers, one on an island, a retreat when the threat was from Persians in the East, and the other on the mainland, ready for enemies from the West. Alexander the Great had ordered a causeway built between the two. The city minted particularly beautiful coins featuring Apollo and the swans which pulled his chariot through the sky. It was there that Horace sketched a wartime scene, one of his earliest, an episode not of the bloody sort that attracted his literary companions, but more commercial, an everyday story of life as an occupier.

Brutus was experienced enough to know that not every aim could be achieved by murder, torture, looting, and rape. He did use maximum intimidation to ensure that the cities of Asia would not vengefully attack his rear as soon as he had moved on. But his soldiers also had to be fed; they needed corn and wine and other commodities which, if pillaged, tended not to reappear in the markets, where they might be pillaged again.

If suspected gold were not found, the search could be resumed the following week. If food were not found, the army would be hungry—and liable quickly to lose its loyalty. Brutus's officers needed to trade as well as raid. They needed to buy as well as steal;

and inevitably contractual issues arose whenever one negotiating side had the monopoly on force and the other on food.

Horace was as watchful a student on the warpath as he had been when he was recruited. He was marching with an army for the first time in his life. He was away from his libraries, and his eyes saw more of the novelties going on about him than from the literary past. He was not yet a poet himself, but he noted scenes that might become poems, not the horrors of siege warfare, which might have suited some poets, but the daily disputes, which offered a different kind of drama. He took a glancing gaze at events around him. He embellished bits of dialogue. He saw short scenes and edited them to be shorter in his mind. He was ready to write in a manner closer to Archilochus than Homer, one that was "Horatian" for the very first time.

His central figure was Rupilius Rex, one of the less literary of Brutus's followers from Rome. Part of Rupilius's job, and of many like him, was to buy what kept the army fed. Rupilius's antagonist, in Horace's account, was Persius, a local supplier who felt that he had been insufficiently paid for his wines and wheat, or cheated in some other way.

Persius was a thug who had sauced himself heavily with the cheapest Italian wine. Both men appeared in a form of commercial court in which Brutus himself was the judge. Whatever Rupilius's disagreement with Persius, he too had proven his love for the vinegars of Italy. The result was something of a brawl. The courtroom audience was mostly Roman, and Persius was getting a hard time.

Cleverly, the stout trader launched into lavish praise of Brutus and all his officers, one by one, apart from Rupilius Rex. The drunken officer, outraged by his exclusion, hit back. The battle of words went on until Persius slurred out his opinion that Brutus should assassinate Rupilius. That was, after all the way that Brutus's family always dealt with would-be kings. The audience laughed. That was the reality of life on the long road to northern Greece, where Antony and Octavian were heading too, to a then little-known town, Philippi.

By the time Horace's companions set up their base for the coming battle against Octavian and Antony, they could reasonably be confident of victory. Some of their idealism might have faded, but they had more troops, more money, and a securer source of food than their enemies. The Greek cities behind them were either conquered or cowed. Their new soldiers seemed loyal to their newly wealthy employers – even if many spoke in languages that not even the most literary Romans understood. Everyone had heard Cassius give a rousing speech of liberal reasoning and lavish rewards.

Horace, Cicero, and Messalla had enjoyed weeks of tourism through countryside that they knew from literature. New friendships were made. There was a flamboyant character called Marcus Lollius, with high ambitions for the future – if any of them were to have a future. They had passed the plain of Troy – even if its ruins were invisible except to the very credulous or drunk. They had crossed the Bosphorus like Alexander the Great – in their dreams at least. Some were headed next to Thasos, the island close offshore where Archilochus had fought, written poetry, and found fame.

While the legionaries were under strictest discipline the staff officers were free to fraternize with each other and with party givers along the way. Wine, in poets' language, broke the resistance of many dragging days. The local Thracian tribes were violent drunks by reputation, and some of that repute was true. Drinking stories were told. Liber, the wine god, was surely the god of liberty too.

Empty flagons lay in piles by the side of the roads, the "dead soldiers" of a journey that in the marchers' high hopes would reach victory without too much death. Some of the pleasure seekers were even assassins themselves. A special place was held by Lucius Tillius Cimber, the man who had laid first hands on Caesar on the Ides of March, tugging down the dictator's toga so that the first dagger could strike. Cimber had his own boy to bear his brimming cups while they were full, and his terra-cotta bottles, which were not yet dead but would be soon.

Thasos, once one of the wealthiest islands of the Aegean, was to be the safe place for the treasury of the assassins' army. Its walls, for which democrats had fought would-be tyrants three hundred years before, were now ruined, but it still had a defensible harbor, necessary against both naval attack and the storm tides of autumn, the fast-reversing winds from north and south. It had its memories of Archilochus, its quarries of blue-gray marble, pebbles like the herons' eggs of Italy. It was the greenest Greek island, with forests like those on Mount Garganus. It had a salt lake. Food and wine were readily available to replenish stocks.

Thasos was no longer rich enough to attract invaders, though its marble was prized for victory monuments and memorials. The gold mines which had once lured its neighbors were even longer gone than the walls — and with them the pioneering doctors who had since taken their trade elsewhere. Archilochus's wars had been over new mines on the mainland, with exotic names like Dugout Forest, and these too were exhausted. Thasos had once had a small empire itself, a cause for which Archilochus had lost a fight and notoriously thrown away his shield, confident that he could always afford another one. His poems were the principal survivors of those days.

There was little on the ground to remind Horace and his friends that the final miles of their march were through an empire that, like the empire of Athens, had long gone. Archilochus had hated the greed of the men of Thasos. Its central mountain ridge was as ugly as "a donkey's back," and all the troubles of Greece had pulled it down as though the mythical "stone of Tantalus" hung in its sky.

Their final stop was on a narrow strip of land between the mountains, the sea marshes, and the sea. Philippi itself was not their destination, merely the nearest town, founded by Philip of Macedon, father of Alexander and enemy of all free cities, on the site of a colony that the Thasians, in their distant heyday, had called Crenides. The town was incidental to the battlefield. Horace's march ended in a well-protected camp on the mountainous side, where Brutus ordered his friends and soldiers to prepare for battle.

In front of them a stream, called locally the Gangites, ran slowly to the marshland. When they looked along the sluggish water they could see the camp of Cassius at the southern end of the battle line the two leaders had chosen. In legionary warfare it was essential not to be outflanked; the enemy had always to be prevented from slipping round and attacking from the rear. Cassius had the protection of the reed beds and stagnant pools, Brutus the greater safety of the mountains.

There they waited for the heirs of Julius Caesar to arrive, watching the rise of a long wooden wall with gates and towers, the fortifications for which Roman soldiers were as famed as for fighting. While the winds blew for the coming winter there was time, perhaps too much time, for all to talk about the future, about which side would win and what would happen after victory and defeat. Horace was loyal to Brutus, but then Horace was part of no one's military calculation or political hopes. Others of his friends were less certain.

News flowed ahead of the advancing armies of Octavian and

Antony: their soldiers were tired and hungry, northern Greece was not as rich or fertile as Asia, yet their morale was contrastingly and surprisingly high. The banner of Caesar, it seemed, was bright in the eyes of soldiers whom Caesar had always inspired and helped before his Senate friends had turned their daggers on him only eighteen months before.

Inducements to change sides – promises and threats – came with the news. Julius Caesar had made himself famous for clemency. Many of those who murdered him, former fighters for Pompey, had been previously pardoned by Caesar, not least Brutus himself. The continuing fate of the proscribed was proof that the new Caesars might be less understanding to their enemies. No one could be sure.

The arrival of the enemy forces intensified the dilemmas of the doubtful in the assassins' army. Octavian, whose soldiers Horace could most clearly see, was himself invisible. Antony, by contrast, camped close by, across from Cassius at the marshland end of the line, was everywhere rousing the morale of his own men and mocking the fears on the opposite bank of the stream.

There were plots to kill both Brutus and Cassius. Lucius Gellius, the wayward half-brother of Messalla, was implicated and then pardoned. He defected to Antony nonetheless. Cassius's friend Quintus Dellius was a waverer. Horace's first sight of a battle line was very different from his first meeting with Brutus, or the wine and parties along the way. The wind of politics was swirling with the wind from the sea. The army in which he served was filled with mercenaries paid from the forced contributions of Xanthus and Rhodes. Others were paid by local leaders, all keen to sniff the future.

Some tribes had members on both sides. News flowed between them in mysterious languages without the need for code. Archilochus had written that a mercenary could be trusted only if he had a spear at his back. For all those paid wages to fight, the prime aim was to be still alive for the next payday.

Why were they fighting for Rome so very far from Rome? It was not a new question. It was what a hired soldier was used to. Caesar had defeated Pompey in Greece. Caesar had chased Pompey, just as Caesar's army was now chasing his assassins. It was better politics to destroy foreign land than one's own. Greece was an easier place to land troops and to hire troops. Yet the more important answer was that while this ground was Greek it was Roman too. It was on a Roman road, the Egnatian Way. For Horace it was surrounded everywhere by reminders of what Greece had given Rome: its history, its mythology, and its art. To Roman soldiers it was Roman.

Life at Philippi was familiar, albeit with an alien familiarity in which Roman distinctions of class and tribe were collapsed, and local ambitions to be Roman were fragile, fired like glass, brittle, ready to break at a touch. Horace was benefiting from the chance to advance through Roman society but was putting his life in the hands of mercenaries whose only interest was money. It was all a long way from Venusia.

Who was the most accomplished general? Cassius and Antony had the best claims for that title, Brutus not so much, and Octavian not at all. Archilochus had jibed against tall commanders who stood with feet astride and took too much care of their hair: Antony would likely not have been his choice. The poet from Paros preferred the short and bandy-legged type, a man full of spirit: Cassius maybe.

Brutus would have to have been Horace's choice. There was due loyalty owed to the man who had brought a poor student from academe to high society. But Horace would have dodged the question if he could. He had more interest in the meter Archilochus used for his joke than in the question of military genius. The ancient poet had employed not his usual rising iambic, short syllable followed by long, but the falling trochaic, long syllable followed by short. How did that work? Why did it work? How much did the measure of a line need to match its matter? Horace's education since arriving in Greece had been in every way in which poetry was made.

Horace was an officer in a way he could never once have imagined, a very literary military tribune, an honor from Brutus given usually to the young and grand. The rank came with a permanent status in the hierarchy of Rome. He became an *eques*, a knight, a member of the class immediately below that of the senators, not an equal of those who had assassinated Caesar but higher than his father had achieved or would ever achieve. The gift came with a gold ring.

As the combatants faced each other for the fight, Horace and Octavian, unequal figures in almost every respect, had the same good fortune of being deep behind the front lines. Neither man was a fighter, neither very fit—Octavian frail, sick, and exhausted by the march, Horace, fuller figured, better rested, but new to the sounds and smell of war, no part of any one's military plans.

Even from the mountainside camp of Brutus it was impossible to see everything that was happening on the battlefield. The marshes were almost two miles away. But for any man of imagination, it was clear what would happen if neither side gave way. Some two hundred thousand men, all trained as part of Rome's usually triumphant killing machine, stood in two opposing armies, each in three lines, taunting each other, sallying and retreating, bubbling up and falling back like two pots about to boil.

One day collapsed into the next. The weather was foul. It was hard for the soldiers to find a dry level place to sleep at night, or to fall asleep if they did. Insects flew in as strict formations as the soldiers. Sleeplessness fueled every fantasy, but everywhere was a sight to strike awe. None had ever seen such a weight of Roman against Roman. Horace had been intended by his father to join a higher class, whose best young men would be ambitious in pursuit of Germans, Gauls, and their own pleasures of peace. Instead they were arrayed, yet again, against one another.

Like every other student of his time, Horace had heard only by gossip and boast how Caesar had defeated Pompey at Pharsalus, six years before and some hundred miles to the south. Now, all too clearly, was the time for the survivors, and a second generation, to fight a second round. Horace had willingly joined that fight. He had no need to be there, no social pressure from a family steeped in the history of politics and war, only the novelty of being wanted by one of Rome's most idealistic and grandest men. His watchful father was far away.

It was Brutus who had brought him to Philippi, promoted and rewarded him, armed him for the first time in his life. Messalla and Cicero had then welcomed him to his new world, protecting him from the charge that he was still *libertino patre natum,* an overpromoted son of a father who, even if briefly, had been a slave. He was with lesser-known men such as Lollius whose origins were somewhat higher than his own but whose ambitions were much higher. He was in a new world, on the brink of something new again. Behind thousands of less fortunate contemporaries whom Horace hardly knew, all of them armed with swords and spears that they were expected to use, he was beginning to see, as vividly as the dust allowed, what mass death might be like.

There would soon be a riverbank of blood unless these soldiers of Brutus and Cassius decided that the assassins' ideals were no more than ideals, that the lure of Caesar's name was too great and the financial offers to them too small. Some of their officers had made that choice, some of the local allies too, but the legionaries, trained most of all to be loyal to each other and their standards, were standing firm.

Now at the far end of the lines, Antony was strutting and shouting, a persuasive and inventive thug, probing into the marshes, it was said, secretly and then in full view, proving, or trying to prove, that Cassius could be caught from the rear. But in the camp of Brutus there was great faith in Cassius as a commander. He was much the more militarily experienced of the two assassins. He had had to surrender to Caesar after Pharsalus, but that was hardly a disgrace.

The timing of the coming battle was much discussed. There was a strong case for letting Antony strut, taunt, and probe a while longer, to make the new Caesar's men wait, to stoke their fears of hunger and cold as the autumn turned to winter. But in the outcome of such talk, as in so much battlefield talk, reason and intention played a lesser part than accident. The fighting began for no clear reason in the center of the line, and, as after the lighting of a long fuse, the explosions inexorably followed.

Horace was in reserve, able to see and hear more than those ahead of him, even if he was doing less. Dead bodies, stomachs slashed by swords, chests skewered by spears, fell in a ripple from the mountains toward the marshland, precise details fading with distance, the pattern not hard, however, to predict. The living stamped their nailed boots on those whose lives had ended. After the first roars from what seemed a machine of men the line grew quieter, a grinder of metal and flesh. Immediately ahead of him the battle seemed almost to be going well. It was hard to see much farther than immediately ahead.

The front line was pivoting on its center. The signs from nearby were much better than those from afar. Horace's friend Messalla was leading a massacre of some of Octavian's most newly arrived allies, men with the ancient military reputation of Sparta. In front of the mountains Brutus was clear leader of the winning troops, the river now in their rear, ahead of them Octavian's crumbling lines even though there was no sign of Octavian himself. Beside the marshland Antony's men were now across the river, charging up the gentle slope that should have held them back. Cassius seemed to be in retreat. Horace was still free to observe: Brutus had no need of his reserves on his own part of the front, but in order to help Cassius he had to slow his advance.

After more hours of slaughter, the news came that the battle story was still one of two parts but that the assassins had suffered much the greater loss. Behind Octavian's badly dented lines Messalla's men had killed two thousand Spartans. Cassius's lieutenants on the farther side had seen no such success, unable even to protect their camp.

The first Battle of Philippi was over. Cassius had overseen a catastrophe. He had not recognized the reinforcements sent to help him and had committed suicide rather than risk the "mercy" of Mark Antony. The winners on both sides returned to their camps, more like porters than soldiers, staggering under the weight of silver and gold stolen from yet another owner.

Horace moved with the camp of Brutus to the marshes that had been so much less protection than the mountains. The troops of Cassius had to be consoled, encouraged, and bribed with promises that their lost loot from Rhodes would be replaced. Cassius's wavering friend Quintus Dellius had already gone to Antony. Others had to be dissuaded from following. The body of their dead commander was to be taken to Thasos, where supplies could be replenished and there was marble for a splendid tomb in blue and gray.

———

There followed almost three weeks without further fighting, only fresh bouts of taunt and posture, long nights of pleasures and parties too, dead wine flasks piling again like soldiers but this time on top of the barely buried battle dead. Horace was stationed with Brutus above the marshes on the higher ground that had once been Cassius's camp. He drank with a new friend called Pompeius, possibly a distant relation to Caesar's friend and enemy, Pompey the Great, possibly not. Family ties were as much a matter of stories as of truth.

This was now an ill-omened place, where Brutus was more a fatalist philosopher than tactician. Time was still on his side. Octavian's camp was flooded and frozen. Octavian had long left it for safety in the rear, leaving Antony to lead their troops. But Brutus's little patience was exhausted. He offered Messalla the overall military command and was refused. He ordered the killing of those captured three weeks earlier. There was a second battle, timed again by chance more than by intention. The lines again clashed. Swords pressed. Stomachs spilled. Chins fell to the foul ground. The thin river flowed again with the blood of Romans, the richest and the poorest side by side.

Horace briefly found himself sharing charge of a legion. There were moments of extreme need when loyalty was more important than experience. There was bravery on both sides. Horace noted the courage of some of his traveling companions — and the absence of it. He saw that Octavian was hardly more a man of military action than he was himself. The fighting fell back to the last broken line of the liberators' army. From this point in the minds of the victors, and in all other minds, their name was dead along with their cause. They were merely the assassins' army and soon not an army at all.

At the end it was a horror to be alive. Antony's officers began touring their enemies' tents, spearing where they thought there was money or a man who might have killed Julius Caesar or been a killer's friend. This was a last opportunity of the proscriptions, soldiers seeking bounty on a Greek battlefield as wives, slaves, and debtors had done in Italy. Brutus followed Cassius into suicide. Brutus's lawyer and his closest friends followed their leader. Those with little chance of mercy from Octavian did not test that chance.

Horace was among the mass who did not know their fate. He had not killed Caesar. He was of the class that had not been invited to the killing party – and he never would have been, even if he had been in Rome at the time – too young, a nobody, useless for an act that required public proof that Caesar had lost the confidence of his peers. He was an acolyte of an assassin. That was all.

But he was in no way safe. He held an honorable, if somewhat honorary, rank in Brutus's army. His life was in the hands of the victor, and even less reliably in the hands of victorious soldiers. To be a prisoner of any war risked a future life as a slave. To be pardoned was for some a different kind of slavery; many of Caesar's assassins had been motivated by the shame of having to ask him for their lives. To lose a battle was a loss of status and sense of self, perhaps to be followed by a fresh sense of both, perhaps not.

Although Horace had not been one of Caesar's assassins, to a soldier scouring the battlefield for scalps he might look little different from his drinking companion Tillius Cimber, who had been a true assassin, or from the son of the Cicero, who had praised the assassins, or from others who were either among the sea of dead or in flight to fight again where they could. Lollius was somehow with the officers of Antony. Neither Cimber nor Cicero, Messalla nor Bibulus, was anywhere to be seen.

His arms and insignia betrayed his loyalties. Poetry provided only a small part of his lessons in survival. To throw away his shield was merely the first necessity. No part of his armor would ever help him stop a pair of thugs from mopping up a survivor.

When Archilochus had joked about jettisoning his shield it was not clear why he had originally put it down, perhaps to have a piss beneath a tree, or to eat or to take some other pleasure available to a soldier of the strong in the land of the weak. One of the glories of poetry was omission, what the poet did not need to say. All that was clear was that Archilochus intended to get another, to hope that the lucky Thracian tribesman, finding such a shield while fighting the gold diggers of Thasos, would have good joy of it. Archilochus would soon have a better one. Horace did not want another shield. He did not want any further official place in anyone's army. He wanted to go home. He wanted to disappear.

Flights of imagination are part of any human flight, the hope of the seemingly impossible, a journey to what might not still exist. On the fields of Homer's Troy, by the river Scamander, so much grander than the red stream before his eyes, a god might sometimes come in a cloud, pluck a hero from danger and deposit him in safety. Horace knew those stories. In the school of Orbilius in Rome, in the libraries of Athens, he had read how poets had imagined escape. He might now think of the same way, even if he could not confidently hope for it. Disillusioned, changed, and confused, he left for the coast.

CHAPTER FOUR

War Poet

*P*roscripti, "belonging to a man proscribed," a single word that meant both the proscribed man and that something belonged to him, the word divided in two, *proscript* and *-i,* the two thoughts brought together in the magic of Latin. This was the first word of what may be Horace's first poem, the raising of the voice to gain attention, the place where his art, as well as the verse, began.

Proscripti Regis Rupili pus atque venenum, "The pus and poison of the proscribed man, Rupilius Rex." That was all that belonged to this Rex, disgusting fluids alone. At its very start the poem, set in that commercial court on the march to Philippi where Horace had sat himself and heard quarrels over the price of wine, pointed to the fate of anyone deemed an enemy of the dead Caesar. It pointed to the still fresh horrors of Rome, those that Horace had not seen, and the nightmare of the battle through which he was living still.

The first word did not sound out only at the start. Its sense spread throughout the whole. Proscription made a man a refugee, hardly a man at all, a mere target for bounty hunters. This was a *satura,* a "satire" in its original modest sense, a title that meant literally a sausage skin into which anything might be stuffed. Eventually back home, Horace took a vivid memory of the road to Philippi and cut and squeezed it into thirty-five lines named after the intestines of a pig.

For *Regis,* the second word, the poet's voice was still raised: a king — no, a man called King — something belonging to him, the *-is* linking him for a Latin speaker to *proscripti,* both endings meaning the same. Then came *Rupili,* linked in the same way. The still unknown subject of the poem was something associated with Rupilius Rex, the Roman officer who had the wine-soaked courtroom fight with the witty trader Persius at Clazomenae, the town of swans, as Brutus's army marched north to its defeat.

Then at the end of the line came the subject, the *pus et venenum,* the "pus and poison," the running sore that represented the nastiness of Rupilius but the nastiness of more than Rupilius alone. This was a poem of its time. In Rome, Brutus had wanted to stop Julius Caesar becoming a king. In Asia he had behaved like a king himself. Brutus had left Rome as a refugee — with a long family lineage but a price on his head. In Clazomenae, Brutus had been judge and jury in his own court, lord of a small and poisonous domain that he hoped would not be small for long.

The poem pushed on. Everyone in every corner chemist and barber shop knew the story of how Persius ended his defense by challenging Brutus to execute Rupilius Rex: after all, was not that the thing for which Brutus and his distinguished ancestor and namesake were famed? This was the joke. They were king killers, back in the ancient times when the Tarquins were kings of Rome, and they were proud of it.

Or at least, Horace could suggest that: *opinor,* "I think," the last word of the second line. He could suggest that anyone in Rome seeking a shave or buying ointment knew the story, or that to all of Rome's *lippis,* its many men with "sore eyes," the tale was an old one. Rome was full of survivors telling war stories. Horace's subject was the suppuration of the body politic as well.

He added the detail of an eyewitness: Rupilius was like an angry grape farmer mocked by passersby for being late with his pruning, and how the mongrel glutton Persius, *hybrida,* the first word of the second line, "half pig, half wild boar," Greek, half Asian, with the worst qualities of all, hit back. Persius was smart. He knew how to hurt a man. He flattered Brutus as the sun of Asia and all Brutus's officers as health-bringing stars — except Rupilius Rex, who was left to splutter on his own.

Horace was using his poem to describe a duel. He had seen many such commercial conflicts of war. They were much more common than acts of actual fighting. He had literary models too that were Greek. He looked back into Homer's *Iliad,* as Orbilius would have approved, using epic meter but instead of epic grandeur introducing a fight between grubby merchants.

Proscripti Regis Rupili pus atque venenum
hybrida quo pacto sit Persius ultus, opinor
omnibus et lippis notum et tonsoribus esse.

The pus and poison of the proscribed man, Rupilius Rex,
and how the mongrel man, Persius, got his own back
is known, I think, in every chemist's shop and barber's.

This was what a poet could do and others could not, playing with tones of voice, concentrating so much into thirty-four lines, slurring the vowels in the last line, *operum . . . tuorum,* to show that Persius was a drunk.

> at Graecus, postquam est Italo perfusus aceto,
> Persius exclamat: "per magnos, Brute, deos te
> oro qui reges consueris tollere, reges, cur non
> hunc Regem iugulas? operum hoc, mihi crede, tuorum est."

> But Persius the Greek, once sozzled with Italian vinegar,
> shouts out, "By the great gods, Brutus, I beg you
> who used to topple kings, why don't you cut
> Rex's throat? That is your family business."

Lucilius and Archilochus had a kind of freedom which Horace, fortunate to be back home, could aim to extend — with care and without being dull. Any memory of Brutus, a man defeated, dead but still a beacon for some, was a sensitive subject in the new Rome. A glancing strike at him was better — and safer — than a sword through the stomach or a stab to the throat. A poet's boundaries were sound and meter, the long-short-short syllable rules of the hexameter line. His skill was that of the architect and mosaic maker. A poem was like a building — or an artful floor.

This short satire was a war poem in pieces, a jigsaw where key pieces were deliberately lost. It was a poem of Philippi, but the closest Horace came to showing the whole was in the sounds of the *P*'s: *Proscripti, Rupili pus, Persius, opinor, lippis,* consonants as a code. He entered the court story when the case itself had already begun, with no precise explanation of its cause; he left it with Persius's jibe about killing kings but no hint of Brutus's reply. Early in, early out, letting the silence talk, the arts of the best storyteller always: Horace's life as a poet had begun.

———

Horace had been lucky to reach Rome. Like so many Romans, he feared and hated sea journeys and at the end of his voyage home had barely escaped drowning off Cape Palinurus, near Naples. Palinurus was a mythical Trojan helmsman who died before he could find a new life in Italy. Horace had been close to the same fate.

On landing he found that his father, like Brutus his patron, was dead. The businessman who had hoped for a higher life for his son – and had sacrificed himself to its pursuit – never saw what his efforts had achieved. Horace now had grand friends. Young Cicero and Messalla were already back and making their peace with Octavian, the one forgiven for the words of a father, exploiting Octavian's guilt for the death of Rome's greatest orator, the other forgiven for the massacre of Spartans who never mattered much.

Lollius was back too. He had persuaded one of Antony's officers to let him dress as a slave, and together the two men, loser and winner, returned to Rome, one dressed as the slave of the other, the same disguise Horace's father had once used. Whether such friendships would survive in the fragile politics of Rome after Philippi was uncertain.

Young Cicero was now responsible for holding Greece for the heirs of Caesar. Messalla, it was said, had surrendered to Antony the army's money, supplies, and weapons on Thasos. Others of the defeated army had sailed away to keep up the liberators' fight. Many of Horace's Philippi friends were missing, their fates unknown. News was scarce, unreliable, and quickly manufactured to meet the needs of the new world.

In Venusia the boots of encroaching soldiers extended farther into the countryside around the town. Returning men again demanded the reward of land. More of those who had stayed at home lost their homes. Horace, at age twenty-four, no longer had either land or home. He took a job in Rome as a public clerk and had to pay from what little he had for the privilege.

Thanks to his father he could read papyri; he could copy; he could make counterparts of legal documents, transcribe, avoid errors of originality. He was confused, angry, liable to hit out in his own forms of rage, but he could survive, as he had on the battlefield. He could watch and note what was safe on the torrid city streets, and who was saying what about Octavian and Antony, the rival victors of his war.

Springtime in Rome was when its walkways welcomed back walkers, when the sodden pumice bricks looked like dry sponge again, when its oozing water disappeared into the air, and it was good again to be outside. Rome's tumbling tenements were still the lasting memorial to Caesar's banker Crassus, who had hoped for a different legacy as an eastern conqueror. Crassus had owned tens of thousands of tiny rooms where men and women ate, slept, drank, and had sex, where privacy, if there were any privacy, was a curtain, and windows looked out on other rooms that were the same. Someone else owned them now, but the high houses were unchanged.

Those with any room, or part of a room, were fortunate and knew it. A huddled mass of the homeless filled the shelter of the city walls, their numbers swollen by those who had depended on Caesar and had no one yet to replace him. There were sellers of magic, traders in drugs that promised sexual success or in simple sex itself if the love charms did not work. Laws on life or death did not extend far into a throng for whom the spring was a brief relief between icy rain and shade-shattering sun.

Higher on the hills were bigger houses whose pumice was faced in marble, many also first built by Crassus, copied by competitors, inhabited by Antony and other prospering survivors of the civil wars. There was still much more marble on Thasos. Rome was a rancid slum which even the rich found hard to avoid. Cassius was better housed in death than he had been in life. His surviving supporters, those who had marched with Brutus too, found the slowly warming weather one of the few certainties of spring in Rome in 41 BCE. It was a scene for only a certain kind of poet following the models of Greece, a brutal realist, not one writing of fresh grass, gamboling goats, or boys and girls on rose petal beds.

Rogare, "You ask me." This was another first word, another raising of the voice. *Rogare longo putidam te saeculo viris quid enervet meas,* "You ask me why your long decaying body keeps my cock limp." You ask me why I can't fuck you! O I'll give you an answer! Twenty lines of poetry beginning with a shout like that was a louder cry for attention than any report of a court case on the road to Philippi.

The tale from Clazomenae had been mere wry observation, the bedroom disaster a scream in the dark; the first was one of his *saturae,* the second one of his *iambi.* He was experimenting. In both poems the poet began the story of the event after the event had begun, the most dramatic way, as he had already come to know. At the start of his second new life in Rome, Horace was writing varieties of poems which showed not just his war stories but his postwar rage to anyone who might care to read.

The question to be asked, inspired by the bold brutality of Archilochus, was to a woman from a house high on the hills whose appearance, he wrote, was like a stinking whore from the hovels below. Why was Flaccus so flaccid? she dared ask him. Well, he could begin his answer with her blackened teeth, pass tactfully by her plowed-field face, and focus on her filthy arsehole, which was as open as a sick cow's. After that: well, there was her flabby stomach, thin thighs, and thick ankles. Her collapsing breasts were a bit of a come-on, although he had seen better on a horse.

His subject had a few points in her favor. There was her wealth, of course, her fat pearls, her family — so very unlike his own — whose triumphs had once filled the Roman streets. On the cushions of silk in her bedroom lay papyri of philosophical tracts. Horace knew nothing of silk: almost no one did in Rome, and the word itself, *sericos,* was a novelty in Latin. But he loved papyri. He was a big reader.

She should remember, however, that his cock could not read. If she wanted him to harden up, she had better "put her mouth to work." *Ore allaborandum est tibi.* The message was a shock: oral sex was much more of a taboo subject in Rome than in Greece. The effect was even clearer when the poem was read aloud. *O* for "orifice" was added now to the *P*'s of Philippi.

Poverty was fueling Horace's anger. He had not been rich when he first came to Rome but he had had his father's support. In Athens, and on the road to Philippi, he had lived the life of the rich with some very rich men. Now he was worse off than when he had first left Venusia. Deeply affected by what he had watched on the battlefield, confused by his escape, he wrote his first poetry. He did not expect to make money out of it. No one did that. His poems were an expression of himself, both his learning and his rage at having seen and lost so much.

While Horace was working at his clerical job he was copying routine documents for the Roman state. In his poems he was showing a unique contempt for his own state. His inspiration was what he had read in Athens, the literary jibes of Archilochus of Paros, the artful attacks by Callimachus against his long-winded colleagues at the courts of Alexandria. For five hundred years Greeks had attacked each other in verse; but there was no counterpart anywhere to what Horace was writing on his return from Rome's Greek civil war.

His officer friends were gone, helping Octavian fight battles at home. Cicero and Messalla and so many more were needed for work. The victors had to distribute land to their troops. They had to take that land from those who owned it, or thought they did. It was also Octavian's task to appease the grandees of the Senate who thought that they still stood in charge of the country. He needed brutality and diplomacy by turn. He needed every friend and favor he could find.

The latest news from the fields of Italy was in every local barbershop. It was harder to know what was happening to Antony farther away. At Philippi, Antony had been the leader. To many he was still the senior of Caesar's successors, and he had much the more glamorous new assignment. But Octavian was Caesar's son in Caesar's country.

Antony's whereabouts were not even fully known. He was still, it was said, in Greece, moving east to ensure the loyalty and yet deeper penury of the cities that had supported the assassins. After that his destination — or so it was less certainly rumored — would be Parthia, the graveyard of Crassus, where he would avenge the defeat of Caesar's banker and bring back the legionary eagle standards lost at Carrhae.

Little of Horace's work as a clerk was touched directly by the ambitions of either man. Octavian and Antony were nothing much to him. The contracts and tax bills of daily life continued. His clerk's job was to make the ordinary happen. The new uncertainties were a cloud over any future, but perhaps that cloud would pass. In the meantime he owed nothing to anyone. He did not know anyone to whom he might want to owe anything. He wrote about what was close and current.

Returning to the same sexual subject in a different poem he aimed to outdo Archilochus in an even more vicious piece. *Quid tibi vis, mulier?* "What do you want with me, woman?" The first words of the poem were the same cry for silence as *Proscripti,* the poet's loud-voiced call for attention. In the rest of the line he entered new realms: *nigris dignissima barris,* "black elephants would be more fitting" for you.

Quid tibi vis, mulier? Nigris dignissima barris. What did the woman want with Horace? Horace was ill-equipped to meet her unreasonable sexual demands. Black elephants? *Barris* was not even the standard Latin word: it was a name that stressed trumpeting and squeals. This would have been a brutal opening even for the boldest poets of Greece.

Horace had almost certainly never seen an elephant himself. There were all sorts of novelty beasts in Rome but not in Venusia or on the road from Athens to Philippi. He knew little more than that they were big beasts with big penises (if one were to risk getting close enough to look). Roman soldiers had sometimes fought against elephants — in the days when Hannibal brought them across the Alps and, before that, when King Pyrrhus brought them. Aristocrats in the cause of Pompey had used them vainly in Africa against Caesar's feared legion of Gauls, the Lark, which won the right after that campaign to emblazon elephants on their shields. There were no elephants at Philippi, but they were part of the language of the soldier, one who was angry and spurned. Horace was clothing his resentment in the rules of meter, but the bitterness was no less bitter for that.

"An octopus or stinking goat lies in your armpits," *polypus an gravis hirsutis cubet hircus in alis:* whatever else was slacking, his poem was not going to slacken. This woman who needed an elephantine cock smelled already like the most disgusting animals. Horace conceded that he himself was merely a youth, but did she think he had a stuffed-up, snotty nose? No, he could smell everything about her. Her own nose was a stinking sore. His sense was acute. He was like a dog with a pig when it came to smelling. He did not miss a single salt hint of cuttlefish or sick goat stench when she was protesting about his limp cock and wanting to reach a sexual climax anyway, writhing, rubbing lizard-shit rouge on the bedclothes.

And as well as gagging at her smell, he had to hear all her taunts against him, her fury that with other women he could perform three times a night but with her he was Flaccid Flaccus. He had to hear her boasts about her sometime favorite shepherd, the one whose cock needed no cultivation to be as stiff as a young tree on a mountain. She certainly did not forget all the presents she had sent Horace, the purple sheepskins that made him the envy of his friends. He couldn't give her what she wanted. He didn't want to give her what she wanted. And then she wailed that she did not deserve his neglect.

He began as he meant to go on.

Quid tibi vis, mulier nigris dignissima barris?
munera quid mihi quidve tabellas
mittis nec firmo iuveni nec naris obesae?
namque sagacius unus odoror,
polypus an gravis hirsutis cubet hircus in alis
quam canis acer ubi lateat sus.

What do you want, you woman fit for black elephants?
Why do you send presents and letters to one

who is only young but whose nose is all too clear?

I smell octopus and goat in your armpits,

like a keen hound who sniffs where a pig is hiding.

And he ended the poem hardly any gentler. This second effort on a theme of bedroom life, like the first, was about impotence and rage. It was a bit longer and also a bit more complex. The sexual failure was shared. It was about indifference as much as failure. It worked through dialogue. It was a story told from different points of view. There was attack and then surrender. It had some literary flourishes, such as the shepherd. Many great Greek poets of Alexandria liked fantasy shepherds. Archilochus had rejected old women and compared oral sex to Thracians sucking beer through a straw. Women and donkeys were a commonplace. Horace was hitting harder, but he had chosen his predecessors in poetry for a reason. He could go beyond them. This kind of episode was real enough. It was all too real.

CHAPTER FIVE

Connoisseur of the Concealed

There were houses on the Subura and there were hovels. There were unbuilt spaces packed with the homeless. The spaces between the houses held more tales of the Subura than did the homes. There were apples for sale and drugs for hiding inside the apples. There were women selling sex and women selling drugs to enhance sex. Wild dogs streaked through the crowds. High-flying birds circled the Esquiline and Viminal hills up above. If the Forum was the palm of Rome's hand, the Argiletum, the main street of the Subura, was the middle finger.

Julius Caesar, in his own poorer days, had lived in this drain, which ran down to the Forum from the city's northwest wall. As soon as he had bribed his way into the job of chief priest, with its own house in the Forum, he left. But he never stopped passing through it. The Subura people were his supporters. No one could live in Rome, especially not Horace in his still impoverished days, and avoid passing through it. The men and women of the Subura were the early people of Horace's poetry, snapping and screaming in full view of each other and of anyone else who cared to watch, or could bear to.

At o deorum quidqid! "But whichever of the gods" is controlling the world, why this torture? The sound here was as sharp as the sense. Horace began a poem with a line that his friends from Athens would have recognized from Archilochus, but the speaker of the line is a helpless Roman, not a Greek, a sight before Horace's passing eyes as well as the eye of his reader's mind. In the Subura words and visions merged.

At the center of the poem was a "prepubescent boy," miserable but not yet defeated, "stripped of his toga and identifying tags, a sight that would soften the godless hearts of Thracians": *insignibus raptis puer, inpube corpus, quale posset inpia mollire thracum pectora.* Then there were two snake-haired women with spades in their hands. This was a live burial, a living sacrifice, described in a hundred iambic lines in details not seen before in poetry, only in books for witches themselves.

There was food for the boy but placed just beyond his reach as the earth fell around his limbs. The agony had to be long for the spell to be strong. The women wanted his liver to dry slowly in the sun and his bone marrow bit by bit to become spongelike. All soon would be harvested and powdered so that men might buy the witches' drugs, might eat or drink them, and want sex that they otherwise would not.

This was how the Subura was for Horace—prostitutes and priestesses, clients and customers, infection for the healthy even where there were any healthy to be found. This was how Rome was when the safety of his schoolroom and his father's small estate defined the years before Philippi. He was now a poet of urban squalor, not a temporary tourist. He was mixing past art and present reality as though he were making a potion himself. He was becoming his own alchemist. He had to leave.

——

He had choices of how to go. None of them was easy. He could return landless to the country. Some men were happy being poorer than they once had been — even when they were working on land they had once owned. Perhaps he too would be happy in Venusia again. He would be far from the Subura and the burial pits of the pharmacists, far from the beds of women who taunted him and whom he taunted in return. As a worker of land he might enjoy quieter nights though tired days.

But he had never worked land before. Nor, very much, had his father. They had both escaped the fields that in Greece and Italy appealed most to city dwellers when there was never any prospect of their working them. And Venusia, much more than the streets of Rome, was like a war zone. Its fields were battlefields, their boundaries fought over more than were the wines and drugs of the Subura.

There were many poems in which city men imagined a countryside they could barely remember, urban purveyors of rural scenes, poets who had written in sophisticated Alexandria about shepherds in Sicily. Horace did not want to return to the hills of bears and eagles where he had been born, or to any other place of war. The smell of the streets was the smell of art. He would do his imagining in Rome.

He had heard the dreams of land told by soldiers on the road to Philippi. He did not share them. He was not even sure that any man had ever dreamt them. They were each other's dreams. He had seen the reality in Venusia. The country always looked better when seen from the town — or from a foreign road. The countryside poems of Alexandria were called idylls. Horace, still fresh from Philippi, did not have an idyll in him, although for sixty-six lines of a new poem it seemed as though he did.

Beatus ille, "Blessed is he." Horace was experimenting, learning to tease and trick, to be witty, to write words which would be wittiest perhaps when read aloud. *Beatus ille:* again, as he had learned, the first word focused the main point, how to have an idyllic life.

Blessed was that man, the poem went floridly on, who, like the great men of old, kept far from business and soldiering, from sailoring and politics, a man who was free to prune his vines and tend his cows, whose honey was sweet, whose wife and slaves were loyal, and whose pears bounced off his happy head.

And so on, and so on, exclaimed the unnamed speaker, through all the charms of olives and fat oysters, the delights of doves in their cotes, until four lines from the end he revealed himself as not a farmer at all but a city banker named Alfius, a man who liked the idea of country living but liked the profits from town life more. No sooner had Alfius liquidated his assets, all ready to invest in arcadia, than he took a deep breath, changed his mind, and put his money out to market again.

That was the poem, the trick and the tease. Horace was gently mocking those who dreamed, gently exposing the reality. Gentle mockery was maybe a better kind than the harsher sort. This Alfius got satisfaction from his country dreams. He took pleasure in thinking of his money invested in someone else's farm labor. There was nothing wrong with that.

Horace was not hostile to the character narrating this poem. If the poet had been himself that kind of investor, he too could have planned to live vicariously through money, imagining one life while living another. But he was not. He had a job which, while not arduous as farming was arduous, was repetitive, responsible, and dreary. He had to get away another way.

Maybe he could travel south, down the Appian Way, through the springtime marshes he had first passed with his father on their road to Rome, not veering eastward back home to Venusia but keeping straight to the western toe of the Italian boot, the narrow strait to the real Sicily, not the one imagined in the idylls of Alexandria. The war against Octavian and Antony was still being fought there under the smoking shadow of Mount Etna. He would not become a fighter himself. His few hours as the leader of a legion at Philippi had assured him of that. But he would be back among old friends.

The three coasts of the triangle island were controlled by a naval commander who was not one of Caesar's assassins or even consistently sympathetic to them but was absolutely not subject to Caesar's heirs. Sextus Pompeius was the flamboyant son of Pompey the Great, Caesar's last open rival for supremacy at Rome. Sextus had seen his father's head severed on an Egyptian beach by men who wanted to ingratiate themselves with Caesar. But he had not joined the campaign of Brutus and Cassius. Possibly he had anticipated their defeat. He was a power at sea whom Octavian and Antony still had to defeat if they were to claim what Caesar had held when he died.

Horace did not know Sextus. But it was likely that his first friend from Philippi, Pompeius, with whom he had shared so many parties on the road, might be in Sicily with the man who shared his name. Sextus had attracted his greatest support from Romans who distrusted Caesar but were not willing to kill him. Those later proscribed by Caesar's heirs had flocked to Sicily. Now too Sextus had Horace's fellow escapers from Philippi, including the assassins Gaius Cassius Parmensis and Decimus Turullius, who did not want to give up the fight or who felt they had no choice but to stay with their fighting friends.

Horace was most aware of Parmensis as a writer, the kind he least wanted to be, as bombastic as he was prolific, as rough as the satirist Lucilius whom he had read as a schoolboy. But he was not hostile to Parmensis, and he very much hoped that Pompeius was still alive. He just had no wish to join them.

He was seeing and writing very darkly. In a second short poem, the character of the speaker was not clear until the eleventh of eighteen lines, a war poem that both reminisced about war and predicted a death in future war. The grim weather, like the *Threicio Aquilone,* "the north wind from Thrace," was the reminder of Philippi: the poem might almost have been set there as they waited for battle.

Horrida tempestas, it began, a "foul storm": the weather had drawn down the sky to the earth and what could anyone do but hold a party to lighten the mood? *Levare,* "liberally" to "perfume the air," *perfundi nardo,* and drink fine wine from the year when Torquatus was consul, the year of Horace's own birth.

The speaker, it then became clear, was the centaur Chiron, tutor of the greatest Greek hero, Achilles. The opening mood before the party was darkness from an alien world, one which Horace knew as a reader and whose battlefield from Homer's *Iliad* he had passed by as a soldier. It was the dark world into which Horace had now returned, the alien madness he had found and felt. Chiron's prophecy, more certain than a mere prediction, was that by the icy rivers of Troy, Achilles would die. There was a possible lightening of only a certain kind, *vino cantuque levato,* the "lightening of wine and poetry," and nothing beyond that.

Even less attractive than a journey south was a journey north. There were battlefields there of a different kind. Both Antony and Octavian needed to reward their victorious troops with land, and Antony, who was still in the East, had to believe that his men were receiving an equal share of the spoils. Trust between the heirs of Caesar was fading. It was not always clear what were equal shares and what were not. Few of the recipients knew anything about the land — or about any land. Their farms were dreams. But men fought bitterly for dreams.

From west to east the towns of Italy were filled with men who knew best war and the reasons for war. Octavian was now a very visible leader—not the man who had hidden in the marshes at Philippi but a decisive commander of the *metatores,* the measurers managing the spoils. Antony was represented chiefly by his wife, Fulvia, now on her third marriage to a supporter of Julius Caesar, a ferocious woman who in the proscriptions had stabbed the dead tongue of Cicero with the pins of her jewelry. His younger brother Lucius, too, was a former consul. Fulvia and Lucius made a formidable pair, but one was female, the wrong sex for battle in Roman eyes, and neither was known to those who needed to trust them, their actions perhaps little known to Antony either. The conflict was ferocious nonetheless.

Horace wanted no more to do with soldiers. He was not even sure what side he would be on. The countryside was as crazed as the town. He dreamt of total escape—and he said so in a poem aimed directly at his fellow Romans, an act of bravado even bolder than his brutality to the old woman who failed him in bed.

The first word once more said it all, the raising of the speaker's voice, *Altera,* "Again." *Altera iam teritur,* "Again, now, the grinding down." This was the start of a poet's speech from an imaginary podium. What was happening here? For a second time his hearers were pulling their own country down on top of their heads. Roman was fighting Roman.

The stark message of the speaker was that this new catastrophe for Rome was Rome's own fault. No one else was bringing back the horrors of the years when Sulla was dictator. Italy's savage tribes around its stagnant lakes had not done as much as Romans were doing to themselves. Nor had Spartacus, nor Hannibal.

But the poet had a plan. *Arva beata,* out to "happy fields," that was where Romans should go, getting away to distant islands in the ocean where all was good, everything blessed. This was the public rage of Archilochus charged with Horace's own rage. It was a powerful conceit for a state clerk, a copier of documents, an overseer of copiers, to play the role of orator in a Roman assembly. He had not lost the status he had won at Philippi. He still had the gold ring of his new class. But he had advanced himself on the losing side and was still libertino patre natum, the son of a sometime slave. To call for mass exodus from Rome, even as a poetic fantasy, was a bolder step than he had taken before, a madder step, some might have said, the words of a madman who, no longer in the bedrooms and torture pits of the Subura, might this time be noticed.

Horace could best escape through poetry. Escapism was central to a poet's purpose. The fixing of words into metrical mosaics was an answer to the hideous disorder of war. Many great men of his time had written poetry to free themselves from the business of daily life. Cicero and Julius Caesar were both poets in their own minds if not so much in the minds of others. There were soldier poets, politician poets, playboy poets, and, most seductive to Horace, poets with patrons.

Horace's problem was not whether through poetry he could imagine himself somewhere else but whether by poetry he could escape the need to have any other business. He was not a soldier or a farmer or even a lawyer. He needed the time and space to be a poet in an age when poetry purchased neither.

No money had ever come directly to Archilochus or Lucilius from the papyri Horace had found in Athens and studied in Rome. In the Alexandria of the royal Ptolemies there were jobs for poets as scholars, librarians, editors of the classic poetry of Greece – and writers in their own right. Rome had no royal court and no such work.

There was talk of a man called Gaius Cilnius Maecenas, rich, flamboyant, a proud Etruscan, slightly foreign at Rome, not a senator and not intending to become one, not a holder of any office except proximity to Octavian's office and very content with that. The word on the streets of Rome was that Maecenas loved literature — also that he had plans to clean those streets of witches. This Maecenas, it was said, loved fine wine and had a fondness for roasted donkey. He was a somewhat bombastic writer himself, more enthusiastic than refined. Failure as a poet was his most direct link to the lives of Cicero and Julius Caesar, but he was already known for generosity to poets.

Horace wanted a patron but not a patron of the usual kind. The poetry he wanted to write was not the poetry that people were used to, the poetry that at some lowly level rich men might pay for. He had no ambition to write epics of military exploits, the kind that might flatter a general who saw himself as the Achilles of his time. He did not write lectures in verse, the explications of farming or philosophy that might appear to be of practical use. He could not write of great virtue at great length.

He was beginning to write about writing, rarely a topic with a wide appeal. He began criticizing other writers, some of them much loved and only recently dead, others still alive. Lucilius, he said, had written at the speed of a flooded river; from Cassius Parmensis, his colleague in the cause of Brutus, the river of verbiage was also turgid. Horace was beginning to attract criticism to himself for pointing these vices out.

He was mocking rather than stinging, making readers laugh at a victim rather than take him seriously. Mockery was not always preferred. An aggressive assault implied at least that the opponent was worth attacking. And who was this Horace, anyway, to be laughing at his betters?

He was a taker of risks. That was clear enough. Literary criticism was no safer than any other kind. Lucilius had the protection of the powerful Scipio family. Horace had nothing. When Horace was not writing about writing he still sniped at men who, if not directly named, knew exactly who they were. He subjected the sexual niceties of the Esquiline and Subura to his growing technical control of words and meter.

He put three words in a first line, two of them very strange words, *Ambubaiarum collegia, pharmacopolae,* "The flute-girls' societies, the fake doctors." This was the opening of a scandalous poem whose first word was not just a shout but a shout in the Aramaic language of the East, and whose second two were also like nothing usually seen. A hexameter of only three words, *dah di di, dah di di, dah di di, dah di di, dah di di, dah dah* with only two breaks between words? That did not happen very often, not in Greek. Horace showed that it could happen in Latin and now had.

Poets were free to innovate. Poets were different. Horace was a poet. Therefore he was a different kind of man. Take apart the words of Ennius, a rough pioneer in Latin epic, and there were still the *disiecti membra poetae,* the "limbs of a dismembered poet." This was a metaphor but one that might still have been fresh in his mind. Horace had seen enough dismembered men at Philippi and might easily have been a limbless poet himself. The key point was to *be* a poet.

He knew what that meant. The rules of meter were his boundaries: he liked to press them but not break them. That was part of his personal as well as his poetic character. Rules were a defense against ill-disciplined madness as well as bad taste. In Athens there were textbooks on long and short syllables, on whether a vowel was long by its nature or by its position before two consonants, or whether a vowel might disappear before another vowel. In Italy for two hundred years there had been looser rules. Horace was a disciplinarian but not, he hoped, a man of routine.

And the two words, *ambubaiarum collegia,* came before he began his real subject. All those Syrian flutists were a blind. Every one of them in flimsy eastern undress, all grouped now in respectable Roman institutes, was a distraction. So too were those dodgy quacks and mendicant priests, everyone who was upset at the death of Tigellius. Who? A playboy singer admired by Julius Caesar, by his Egyptian lover Cleopatra, and by Octavian as well, it was said.

None of this city riff-raff mattered. Almost immediately after Horace had shown off his three-word line, he changed his subject, now not the death of a crooner, introduced by a word as long as Homer had used once for a long spear used at sea, but a battery of good advice about sex. Were married women worth the danger? Sex with whores and slaves was surely the better option, second-best sex a useful diversion from the dangers of the better kinds, sex with free women who had once been slaves the best of all.

With whores dressed in transparent silks a man could see what he was getting. With matrons wearing thick robes to their ankles, in extreme cases with an extra flounce to the floor, he could not. Horace cited the fashionable poet, critic, and literary theorist Philodemus, prolific friend of the great, for his wisdom in preferring the woman who is available when *iussa venire,* "ordered to come over." The woman who says *post paulo,* "in a little while," or *si exierit vir,* "when my husband is out," was too much trouble.

Vividly Horace set out the perils of pursuing other men's wives, the horrors of the husband's unexpected return from the country, the smashing of doors, the howling of dogs, comic but not quite, the maid's fear of torture, the wife's of disgrace, the lover's dread of undressed flight if he was lucky or being buggered by the stable boys if he was not.

The lover's *muto,* his "cock," speaks crossly to him: Why am I demanding *magno prognatum deposco consule cunnum,* "cunt descended from a mighty consul," the word of greatest offense landing hard at the end of the line. Why aren't I satisfied with commoner conquests than those in the white that the consuls' wives wear? Of course, some men love the risk. There was that *mirator cunni Cupiennius albi,* "Cupiennius, connoisseur of the concealed."

This was a sequence of shocking language in Latin. It was intended to shock. The word for a cock, *mutonis,* was not commonly committed to papyrus. *Cunnum* and *cunni* were common in speech, a common obscenity for vagina, but still had subversive power when written. Horace's words for women's bodies, especially the sought-after parts *in medio,* "in the middle" of the body, were drawn from those of horses and other animals appreciated by traditional Roman men — and from siege warfare. Horace was not afraid to be a satirist of the old school, discursive, shamelessly sexist, dismissive, his pen dipped in the contemptuous ink of writers who had come before him.

At the same time Horace was also modern — and modern in his own way. His poem demanded knowledge of Roman historians and comics, of the philosophers of Athens and of Alexandria. He was calling for his readers to be alert and alive to something new. Those *ambubaiarum collegia,* the women who played for parties and stayed when the party was over, were just the artful start of his poem. More new tricks lay ahead. Various more men of Horace's Rome, identified or not hard to identify, were subjects before the poem was over.

Horace was anxiously assembling his iambi for a wider readership. These poems, linked by their variable debts to Archilochus, ranged from a kicking for cowardly dogs to the ill effects of garlic on his entrails, as bad, he wrote, as snake blood, as mysterious as the methods of witches. *Mala soluta navis,* "May the ship" leaving port with stinking Maevius on board "come to a sticky end." In this poem he was wishing death at sea for a malodorous man with a murky sexual reputation.

Horace's output was already impressive, but, in order to attract a patron it would help to have a completed set of poems. For Maecenas he was not finishing his poems fast enough. He needed to up his speed despite his open contempt for poets who put quantity over quality.

Horace could be pushed only so far. He was no obsequious courtier-in-waiting. The attack on garlic referred hardly subtly to a dinner with Maecenas himself and ended with a wish (gentle but clear) that for any future offence the great man's girl of the moment should escape to the far side of the bed.

Maecenas blamed Horace's slow pace of writing poetry on excess attention to sexual pleasure. Horace did not disguise that the great patron might be right. You ask, he says, why *mollis inertia cur tantam diffuderit imas,* "soft lethargy has so overcome me." The answer: *me libertina nec uno contenta Phryne macerat,* "the promiscuous Phryne chews me up." Whether or not Maecenas knew Phryne, whether she was a real woman or a representative of women, the excuse was clear.

CHAPTER SIX

Out of Here!

In the houses of the Esquiline in 38 BCE men and women were still adjusting slowly to the roll call of the dead at Philippi. Survivors filled the places left by the fallen. Some held land and offices far beyond their previous expectations. Others saw that the dice had been thrown, and yet again they were the losers. In a rigid hierarchy it might be worse to lose the second time than the first. Fate was a cruel master, but bad luck and poor judgment were crueler. The next throw might be catastrophic. It was a time to take the pleasures that one could.

Octavian ensured the distribution of all the old offices. There were elections to the offices of quaestor, praetor, priest, and consul as though nothing had changed at Philippi. Some men held provinces and privileges that Caesar himself had promised them. Yet those offices, as well as many of the candidates, had changed, subtly, significantly, and sometimes very sharply.

Victorious alongside Antony, the new Caesar was only half the dictator that the old one had been on the morning of the Ides of March. His advantage over his rival was that he held his half of their power in Rome, the center of the empire. His priorities were to watch Antony as closely as he could, to plan the defeat of Sextus Pompeius around the coast of Sicily on behalf of both of them, and to distribute land to their men. He had little time for the city itself. Horace was a small cog in an idling machine.

Octavian pardoned those of the assassins' supporters whom he hoped he could turn to and others like Horace whom he did not know. He relied on new men — he had no choice. He had to take risks. He had to rely too on old men, men like Gaius Asinius Pollio, who was fighting Dalmatian tribes across the Adriatic, writing about his exploits as though he were Julius Caesar in Gaul, and claiming his seniority as a reason for backing neither Octavian nor Antony, only Rome.

What was missing most in Rome was reliable information about Antony's progress or lack of it. There was the constant need to keep alive the waning trust between the two Caesars. No one was fully satisfied with the result at Philippi, not the highest or the lowest, not the politicians, not the poets, not even those who wanted to be both.

For anyone who wanted military promotion the best man to lobby was Octavian's student friend Marcus Vipsanius Agrippa. The two had met each other in Apollonia at the same time as Horace was meeting his own fellow students in Athens. Agrippa was not a Roman aristocrat; in fact, he was somewhat ashamed of his name. But much more useful than any ancient lineage was his marriage to the daughter of Cicero's Athenian friend Titus Pomponius Atticus, a man both fabulously rich and skilled at riding political tides.

Back in the spring of 44, Agrippa had been among the first to encourage Octavian to accept Julius Caesar's legacy — and he was with him still. In 38 his biggest responsibility was the navy: the requirement for hundreds of new warships, with the latest weapons, all to be secretly assembled at an inland lake needing new access to the sea. Sextus's spies were everywhere, sometimes, it seemed, in every house. Pompey's son made a special appeal to slaves: any who escaped to Sicily were promised freedom in exchange for service on his ships. And for thousands of wealthy conservative Italians in the South a victory for Sextus over Octavian was their best chance of continuing their old lives on their old lands.

For everything else on Italian earth Octavian's man in charge was Maecenas, the other loyal friend, whom ambitious Romans needed to know. In that same year, 38, a set of poems was circulating for the first time which Horace recognized as mixing models he had found in Athens with the real life of his time, idylls from Alexandria with the tragedies of the newly landless in Italy. The poems were called *Bucolica,* "pastorals." Their characters were Italians in the guise of Greek shepherds and Greeks in the guise of Italians. Their themes were both hope and desperation. Their author was Publius Vergilius Maro. Maecenas was their sponsor.

Vergil was an older man than Horace, quieter, more reserved. He had lost his lands in the north of Italy just as Horace had lost his in the south. Vergil had not been at Philippi, but Philippi had changed both their lives. Vergil was ahead of Horace in translating their loss into art.

There were echoes of the fourth of Vergil's *Bucolica* in Horace's bitter poem beginning "Altera iam teritur," its opening scream of *Altera,* "Again," its evocation of past glories, present horrors, and the distant dream, maybe no more than a dream, of something better. Vergil was drawing on his own Greek models, but his bitterness went beyond another's words. Horace was drawing on Vergil, and his feeling was yet more intense. He met Vergil, and through him met a poet of a different kind, Lucius Varius Rufus, who had ambitions in epic. Through Vergil and Varius, Horace gained a formal meeting with Maecenas.

The encounter was short. Horace was shy. Maecenas was the busy first minister of Rome, no part of the senatorial aristocracy but doing much of what that aristocracy had once done. Horace could not define himself by long Roman ancestry cither, but there their similarities ended. Horace described the only ancestor he knew, his father, not for want of a better man to claim but as the best man he could possibly imagine. Maecenas said little. For nine months Horace heard no more until the simple request came that he join the great man's *amici,* his "friends," the network of social debt and service, far beyond friendship, that held Rome together, whoever was in control.

Not long after that Horace was no longer a clerk, or, if he kept the job as a sinecure, was leaving the work to others. He was leaving Rome too, on a journey south which Vergil and Varius were set to join, with others swelling the party along the way, in an embassy that Maecenas was going to lead for Octavian to Antony. He already knew the way ahead, the marshes of frogs and heavy mosquitoes, the steep climbs, the fountains, the strange worlds of every different town. He was going close to his old home in Venusia, but he was not going there.

Egressum! "Gone!" "Out of here!" He had the first word of a future poem. He had found his way. He would escape.

Among a small band of walkers, riders, and slaves bearing litters, Horace left the Capena Gate on the south side of Rome. It was springtime. He was free. A first journey out as a friend of Maecenas would be very different from his first journey into Rome with his father acting as his slave.

Out of Here!

He was walking with the well-known scholar and teacher Apollodorus, whose responsibilities included improving Octavian's Greek. Maecenas liked to enliven his journeys with learned conversation — about the Greek and Latin language (Latin was thought to be a descendant of Greek), laughter and tragedy (which was the better and where?), the local country arts, and the wit of the city. Thanks to his father and the university of Athens, Horace could join in.

Apollodorus helped men to be writers. He was an authority on poetic meter. Maecenas, like many Romans aspiring to greatness, saw himself as a bit of a poet, happy to talk about long syllables and short, the light running foot of the iambic line, as their own feet trod the path. Horace adapted Apollodorus's name for the poem he was planning to write, using a synonym for the sun god, Heliodorus, to be witty but also to signal to a knowing reader that this satire would be about more than meter alone. Octavian had no known literary aspirations himself, but the presence of his rhetoric teacher was a sign, if only in a single name, of the man whose political future lay at the journey's heart.

Horace had an older Latin poem in mind as well. Lucilius had written his own satire on a southward journey from the Capena Gate to Sicily. Horace would have the same opportunity — and in the most newsworthy company of his time. He could be both reporter and poet, tactful about facts that mattered to others, truthful in what mattered to him most. His art was already to hint and to tease, to take the reader into cul-de-sacs as well as corridors. Apollodorus might be a major figure when he came to write his new poem — or he might be no more than a shadow for his mighty pupil.

The first section of the stone road was a lesson in a history that had so nearly come to an end. It ran like a spear through a sculpture gallery of monuments to the wealthy Roman dead, the closest site to the city where memorials were allowed by law. Horace had seen them all before. However much they were reminders of how Rome's past had produced perpetual civil war, they were still too familiar for a travel tale.

To begin making a poem from an event was to use first the art of selection. Horace's concern was with the new and the here and now. The tombs of Lucilius's patrons, the Scipios, would be of no more news to a Roman reader than those of the ambitious bakers and wine merchants whom his father might have joined had he lived. What was fresh was first of all how quickly they would have to walk, where they might stop for rest, whether some might move ahead more speedily than others, and who next would join the journey and when.

For his first night he slept gratefully in a little inn at Aricia only fifteen miles from Rome, enough of a journey for a man whose best marching days were five years behind him. Horace was in the slower of the parties when they divided to cross the Pomptine marshes. Those with longer legs, those keen to hitch up their tunics like sportsmen, those men could go on ahead if they liked. The break was a good choice, even if the drinking water was foul and his sickened stomach became an enemy to the rest of his body.

The two groups came back together again to take barges through the watery hinterland of Forum Appii, a frontier town where to move far from the road was to enter deepest rural Italy, the insects fierce, the frogs croaking noisily at night, and the drunken boatmen dangerous to the unwary traveler. Civilization, as Horace saw it with his new confidence as a city dweller and his new friends, returned only at the end of the marshlands: Tarracina, high on its bright white rock.

There they waited for the diplomats, Octavian's team led by Maecenas, for Antony, Caius Fonteius Capito, polished, smooth, cold, and as somewhat more a neutral, Lucius Cocceius Nerva.

Horace could not be confident of his reception from Capito and Nerva. Maecenas, libertine and intellectual, was amused by a tubby poet who had fought for Brutus, but there were far more Roman grandees who might not be. Horace had to spend too much time spreading ointment on his sore eyes.

At the next stop they met a country grandee at whom everyone could laugh. The aedile of Fundi, the local mayor, wore a broad purple stripe on his toga, a mark of rural distinction to which only senators, and therefore not Maecenas, were entitled in Rome. Tactless, or merely pompous, he had put on full regalia for his distinguished guests, parading his finest medals and a tray of hot charcoal in case anyone might want to propitiate the gods. This butt of jokes, like Horace himself, was a former clerk, but Horace was happy to join the mockery. A few years earlier, this mayor of nowhere might have merited a poem in the bitter style of Archilochus, dedicated solely to himself. Now Horace had moved on.

The party planned to use wayside inns no longer. They would stay with friends. At Formiae much of the land was owned by the family of Mamurra, Julius Caesar's extravagant military engineer and his male sexual partner, if one believed the taunting epigrams of Catullus from a time of greater freedom. But the group stayed at a house owned by Lucius Licinius Murena, a relation of Maecenas's wife. Capito's cooks produced the food. The local wine, the Caecuban, was renowned as one of Italy's best.

After the dinner party at Formiae, the poets' party began. At Sinuessa, some twenty miles on, Vergil and Varius arrived, along with their friend and admirer Plotius Tucca. Horace was thrilled. This was what he had come for, time with other poets in the presence of a man who supported poets to write poetry.

All three writers were ready to share their philosophical sympathies. Varius followed Epicurus, the Athenian thinker who, as Horace knew, preached the avoidance of pain, the pursuit of pleasure, and that the only way to peace was the elimination of the fear of death. So too had Caesar's assassin Gaius Cassius and others on the road to Philippi. Varius's best-known poem was *De morte*, "On death," which, more relevantly for the journey, contained some sharp criticism of Antony. Horace and Vergil's interests in Epicurus were more selective.

Maecenas was something of an Epicurean too in his appreciation of pleasure, his lack of interest in political structures, and particularly in his open mind about what poetry had to do. He did not expect poets to be teachers or flatterers, though he was not opposed to either of those roles. He stood for allowing poets to display artistry for its own sake and for the pleasure of those, like himself, who loved art.

Epicurus had urged upon his disciples a special care if they needed to be among the powerful. He preferred, as far as possible, to keep away from politics. For the embassy members in spring 37, as for Cassius in spring 44, it was impossible to stay very far away.

The party had to commandeer a government guesthouse for a night. Maecenas slept well enough to join in some competitive sport the following day, one of the games with feather-stuffed balls, feinting and passing, which the Romans had adapted from the Greeks. Horace and Vergil, claiming sore eyes and stomachache, preferred some daytime sleep, perhaps aware that playing with a patron could be dangerous to more than arms and back.

After that it was time for a night at Cocceius's villa. There was a literary cabaret of a sort, though not one in the style of Vergil, Varius, or Horace; it was more in the manner of local comedy in Oscan, the language still dominant in the deeper parts of the countryside. There were jokes in favor of Maecenas's generosity and — carefully — at his expense.

The talk became loftier in tone, leaning back into a literary past. It was wise for poets to earn their keep. Burned thrushes over a spit in Beneventum were like the victims of Vulcan on his Mount Etna volcano. These were poets who could give a patron what he wanted, not just what they wanted to give. If the thrushes themselves could be rescued from the blaze, so much the better.

The road was soon skirting the fields and hills of Horace's home. The only place to stay was a rough villa where the hearth was filled with damp logs and leaves. His eyes, sore in good air, streamed in the air that recalled his childhood. He hoped that a girl of the house might join him for the night, optimistically perhaps, as he was the most junior of the party and a local boy among the glamorous visitors from Rome. He waited till midnight, feeling more and more a fool, before sleeping, dreaming, and ejaculating in his bed.

Their destination was still some eighty miles away, but on most of the coast road the surface was fit for carriages. Water was sometimes scarce and bread coarse, but the journey was swift. Brundisium was the only port on Italy's eastern coast that could welcome Antony and his attendant fleet. The time for learned discourse was over. This was the place for diplomacy – also the only port for a hostile fleet if the rivalry between the two heirs of Caesar were to turn to war in Italy.

As a reporter of this poets' journey he made a simple start, *Egressum magna me accepit Aricia Roma hospitio modico,* "After I was out of mighty Rome, Aricia welcomed me in a modest inn." One hundred and four lines later he wrote a no less simple conclusion, *Brundisium longae finis chartaeque viaeque est,* "Brundisium is the end of a long journey and a long story." In between was a series of missed opportunities, stops, and diversions, an itinerary edited and elaborated by chance. Sexual disappointment came after distant sights of homeland hills, sketches of diplomats at play, and the croaking of frogs. Heliodorus never reappeared in his story, whatever the part of Octavian and his teacher in the trip itself.

Horace had last seen Antony at the Second Battle of Philippi. He was there as visible as Octavian had not been, easy to spot among the front lines of his men, tall, broad, bearded, brightly armed, looking as much as possible like Hercules, from whom he claimed descent. He had personally taken the surrender of thousands of Brutus's troops. While Octavian was despised by the losers, his fellow victor was respected — even as his officers were ransacking the camps for signs of assassins.

Since that time no one in Rome had seen Antony — who was preparing for new battles and seemed well placed to win them. His provinces included both Gaul and the East, the only two places from which in living memory Roman commanders, Sulla and Caesar, had launched a successful assault on Rome. He had the option of invading Parthia and winning the glory of avenging Crassus. Along the road through Clazomenae, where Horace had marched north with Brutus, were towns offering Antony devotion, almost the status of divinity. Capito, his agent on the journey to Brundisium, was ready to be his agent in his wooing of Egypt. Its queen, Cleopatra, once the lover of Julius Caesar, was already transferring herself and her country to the man who was the new Roman power in the East.

At home in Italy, Antony was no more than a name. Once a familiar in the Forum he was a presence now only through his wife, Fulvia, a veteran of politics whose attitude toward Cleopatra was perhaps predictable but in practice unimportant and unknown. It was Antony's absence that was problematic for him and helpful for his rival. Roman soldiers liked to see their commander. They did not take easily to command by a woman, however long her experience of Caesar's cause, and however determined she might be.

They were easy prey to the propaganda that both Fulvia and Cleopatra, whatever the jealousies between them, were together in acting outside their natural state.

There had already been fighting between Fulvia's and Octavian's forces around the town of Perugia. Again the issue was the confiscation and redistribution of land. A new farmer plowing his fields could find slingshots fired by soldiers on both sides who had recently been on the same side. There were some addressed to Antony's wife which bore a question scratched in the lead at the point of a dagger: Did Fulvia want to defeat Octavian or to fuck him? When Octavian was victorious, Antony was too far away to respond, torn between the acquisition of vast wealth (and Cleopatra) and what must have seemed tedious bureaucratic consolidations at home.

Both rivals needed watchful, wary diplomacy. Maecenas's embassy of poets was part of an intensifying process, one of many such exchanges. There was wavering in the strength of both sides and still the threat to both from Sextus in Sicily. Then Fulvia suddenly died, and new reports arrived from the East. The Parthians had not waited to be attacked and had made their own attack on Antony. These were events to celebrate.

Fulvia's was a very convenient death for Octavian, not considered suspicious but as significant as her life had been long ago as wife to Clodius, Caesar's rabble-rouser when Horace was first on his way to Rome. Once Antony was without a Roman wife Octavian could show a generous spirit and buy time. His way of keeping Antony close was to offer him marriage to his sister Octavia. His way of keeping his partner at a distance was to invite him for talks and not come himself. Neither a victory nor any other kind of clarity was close. At the end of the journey to Brundisium the weary travelers could expect many calls on the diplomatic skills of Maecenas, fewer on the skills of the poets.

—

The combatants were making ever more exaggerated claims on public support. Since the dead Julius Caesar had been promoted to divinity, Octavian was the son of a god; and since Caesar's family was already acknowledged as descended from the goddess Venus, Octavian could be doubly divine. Antony claimed descent from Hercules – and had a fighting costume of long sword and low-slung tunic to prove his point to his people. The third player in the military balance in 36 BCE, Sextus Pompeius, saw himself as the Neptune of the Sicilian seas, second among the Olympian deities only to Jupiter the sky god, whose temple dominated the Roman Capitol.

Horace's closest sympathy was with the Epicureans, for whom there were no gods. If by chance that confident claim turned out to be false, then any gods that existed would have nothing to do with men, and certainly not be investing them as proxies for wars on earth. This was a powerful argument but not, in the years after Philippi, a popular one.

Horace saw the prime virtue as avoiding supercharged superstition and mass death. By contrast, voters and soldiers wanted an outcome. In Horace's eyes Sextus was commander of the few who had escaped Philippi, very many of whom had earlier escaped the proscriptions, and thousands of freed slaves. Octavian was master of Rome and, most important, of Maecenas. Antony was the one he knew least but whose courage he had seen in battle. These were merely men, and it seemed far from obvious to him that they needed to be at war.

Horace was not a politician. He only watched while politics was going on. When fake gods jostled to exploit the craving for certainty, Horace was more frustrated than engaged, lashing out at what he saw closest at hand, the world turned upside down in Rome, and still nervous about his own place in it. A beneficiary of turbulence, a son of a former slave who now knew people in high places, he turned his iambi brutally on the pretensions of others who had risen from the same dirt as himself.

His subject was hatred, his own as much that of anyone grander. *Lupis et agnis,* hatred between "wolves and lambs": for a man born in the countryside there was no better example of natural hatred than that.

The reader or hearer of this poem would not know at first what or who was hating what or whom. It ended with a characteristic glancing blow at Sextus, but the hatred in it was not among men at the top. There was no natural hatred among Octavian, Antony, and Sextus, attenders of the same clubs and lectures, descendants of generations of Roman grandees, if not of the divinities they liked to claim. Horace's hatred, delivered with all the venom learned from Archilochus, was for someone nearer his own level.

Videsne, "Do you see him?" That one strutting down the Sacred Way, still with the whip scars on his back, now in a billowing toga, farming great estates down the Appian Way, sitting in the knights' seats at the theater. What a disgusting parvenu! Boldly he went on. Well may the people question the point of sending massive ships against that pirate Sextus, when we promote such a man as that in Rome!

Horace was picking up the rhetoric against Sextus that was all around him, fanned by Octavian's supporters in Rome. But he was also anxiously picking at his own place in a changing society. Brutus had given Horace a military post, a knight's gold ring, and the right to sit in the knights' seats. From Maecenas he was hoping for some reaffirmation of that status. Those southern estates of the upstart were a reminder of where he himself was born.

Hatred of the newly rich was his theme. This was not new. But after Philippi there were many more newly rich. When he was a schoolboy under the rod of Orbilius notices on the walls in Rome warned of a man whose only sexual opportunity, not so long before, had been sucking donkey cocks. But not now! Oh no! The man had just been made consul: the world was at his feet, or wherever else he wanted it to be.

Horace knew everything about the disdain of the city poor for the poor of the country. Everyone had to look down on someone; that could never be stopped. A poet who followed Archilochus and was merging his own experience with the models of the greatest Greeks would never want it to stop.

But war might be stopped. For Horace the Neptune of Sicily was part of the past, part of what he was escaping. A Caesar against a Pompey: that was also the story of his schooldays. Diplomacy could surely bring a deal. He had seen Maecenas at work. Antony could be negotiated to defeat, Sextus surely as well. There did not need to be war. He said so more clearly than at any time since he himself had witnessed the mind-wrenching horror of limbless corpses in faraway fields, so many thousands of the dead.

He took up again his poet's role as orator to the Roman people. It was conceit that he found a comfort. *Quo, quo scelesti ruitis?* "Where, where are you criminals heading?" After Philippi their swords had gone back in their sheaths. They should stay there. Had not enough Roman blood flowed? If anyone were to ask what right Horace thought he had to be hectoring his betters, he had the beginnings of answer. He was a poet—with a protector, if not yet a patron. Maecenas was a man high in the new world who knew what poetry allowed—and what was allowed to poets.

Philippi had decided nothing except the fate of Julius Caesar's assassins, of some fifty thousand other men, and of Horace's flirtation with company to which he had never belonged. He felt some fondness for his companions in battle — for Messalla, young Cicero, Pompeius, and others. But he was now taking a different path from them. They were fighting still. He was not.

Cicero was a rising officer for Octavian, recompensed in part for the savage death of his father. Although Octavian had had a pact with Antony that neither would stand in the way of the other's revenge, Cicero's proscription and murder, the severing of his hands and the piercing of his tongue, stood still as the greatest stain against them. It was Octavian in Rome who was still paying the price in senatorial anger. Promotion for the playboy son was a cheap response.

Messalla, the most literary of his wartime friends, was also with Octavian. Ahead of them was a massive naval battle against Sextus Pompeius around the Sicilian coast, Caesar versus Pompey in the second generation. Long forgotten was Messalla's past military status as Brutus's camp commander at Thasos, still farther away his past legal status as one of the proscripti, the very first to be outlawed with Caesar's assassins. Octavian had even, and very unusually, announced that this particular proscription had been the result of an unfortunate error.

Naval skills were much needed by Octavian. Sextus had already won victories in smaller skirmishes. In one of these the son of the divine Caesar escaped the son of the vanquished Pompey only by switching between small boats to avoid detection. Messalla was Octavian's rescuer then, and he was ready to be the same again, a commander within the massive force of heavy ships, with new heavy weapons, which Octavian's military chief, Agrippa, was secretly preparing in the smoking lakes around Naples.

Messalla's brother, Lucius Gellius Poplicola, was Antony's man, consul for 36 BCE, holder of Rome's highest traditional office of executive power. No form of traditional power was what it once was before the age of Caesar, but a consulship was not nothing. Gellius had plotted the assassination of both Brutus and Cassius before crossing over from Brutus's camp as the battles of Philippi began. He had read the signs well and was trusted now to mint the cash with which Antony paid his men, even to put his own face on the coins, and to hope, in the Roman way of reward, that he could make money as well as manufacturing it. He would now do what Antony required while keeping a close eye on the political winds.

There were multiple lines of authority at Rome. Alongside Gellius as consul was Marcus Cocceius Nerva, brother of the diplomat closer to Antony on the journey to Brundisium. Since 43, Sextus had been officially Rome's admiral of the high seas, its *praefectus classis et ora maritimae*. Antony and Octavian could also point to powers granted to them by the SPQR, the Senate and People of Rome.

It was a time for the powerless to be cautious. When Horace wrote a poem in which Sextus was a lawless pirate, he did not put the insult in his own mouth. He used a sideways blow, a rhetorical question. This was becoming Horace's way with politics. His art allowed him many such ways. He was careful — and ever more skillful.

Nor had Horace abandoned Brutus, no more than he had replaced him absolutely with anyone else. He stayed quietly loyal to the memory of the man he had followed to Philippi, while at the same time recognizing the reality immediately around him. He was out of his old problems but not yet safe among the new.

CHAPTER SEVEN

Hangers On

Horace was finally ready to let his first poems leave his desk. *I puer,* "Go boy," go and add these lines to my little book— and make it snappy. In this last line Horace was addressing his scribe, a trained slave, whose job was to finish the copies. In 36 BCE, six years after Philippi, Horace was a man in a hurry—and he wanted his distributers to hurry too, to begin the process by which his satires (though not yet his iambi) could be copied, recopied, boxed, and passed around the tiny circle of readers who would judge his success. This was his tenth satire. Vergil had written ten *Bucolica.* Ten seemed enough.

The final lines contained a list of people whom he wanted to impress. These included Bibulus, his friend from Athens; Gellius, the turncoat consul from Philippi; and Gellius's brother Messalla, recently forgiven. Others on the list of hoped-for admirers were Vergil and his friends Varius and Plotius, fellow walkers on the road to Brundisium.

This was a select band of writers of different kinds, including, tucked in the middle of a line so as not to be too obtrusive, Maecenas himself. Horace was keen to show that he would not be in competition with Maecenas's other friends. Varius could do the epics, Vergil the countryside, Pollio the history. Horace would write the humbler satires, and not too harshly. His assaults on witch torturers and old women in bed, his iambi, could wait awhile. He would be a good addition to the club.

Horace was saying nothing in these poems that an opponent might see as overtly political. He was more literary and confessional. He was jibing at other writers, past and present, and defending himself against anyone who thought he had been too harsh. His principal aim was to paint a picture in words of his own past, present, and maybe future. Horace's *libello*, "little book," the last word of his collection, was not praise of Octavian or Agrippa. Nor was it a direct accommodation with his own record in war. It was a calling card to join an exclusive club.

He had assembled his *Satires* with care. The first line of the first poem in his new book was aimed directly at the man he was calling. *Qui fit, Maecenas*, "How comes it, Maecenas?" It was a foretaste of the genial conversational style a patron could expect if he kept Horace around him, as Horace wanted him to do. Horace was already skilled at giving a taste of a literary meal, a slice of a story rather than the cloying whole.

Wasn't it odd, he mused in the next few lines, that no one in life was ever satisfied? Soldiers wanted to be in import-export, lawyers to be farmers, countrymen to live in the city. At the end of their lives those whose bodies were wrecked by war would say they would rather have been a trader at sea, those who for years had bought and sold would regret never having faced victory or death.

This eternal dissatisfaction was not, of course, a laughing matter. And yet somehow it was. People were so ridiculous, piling up money they could never spend or food they could never eat. How rare to find someone who would die content! Horace was suggesting that he might be that person — and might even help others to share his quiet wisdom.

But then he needed to stop, to switch direction. He was going to stop right there. Otherwise Maecenas might confuse his little book with the *scrinia,* the "boxfuls," by that bleary-eyed bore whom everyone knew, Crispinus, the anthologist of the dull, the kind of author Brutus used to like, always prattling on about *vivere honeste,* how to live honorably, and never likely to be brief.

He chose these critical words with even more than usual care, *Crispini Scrinia Lippi,* a man's name, the Latin word for a bookcase, the Latin for sore-eyed, a sufferer of that common ailment in the dust and heat of Rome. But *Crispini Lippi* had echoes of more than the pharmacy. The sound was the quiet undertone of everything, *Philippi.* From that faraway battlefield came the moralist rhetoric of Brutus, the shattered bodies of the soldiers, the pointless lust for loot, the general dissatisfaction that led to victory or death, the madness he was slowly putting behind him.

In these first poems Horace had the chance to explain who he was as well as what he did, not just to a man who already knew him but to readers and hearers even beyond Rome. He wanted hearers as well as readers because public readings were the way most men and women kept up with current events, and enjoyed poetry too. Julius Caesar's reports from Gaul, written to boost his reputation, had been read aloud in makeshift street theaters. Horace's attempts to write in the Rome of Caesar's heir might be read out too — to hearers whose own reading skills were as poor as their likelihood of affording a papyrus.

Among his new satires, fresh from the copyist, were dialogues, dramas, and poems which were themselves like speeches. They included his march to Philippi with Brutus, the courtroom drama in the city of the swans, the epic battle between two drunks, Persius, the seller of food and wine, and Rupilius the buyer—theatrical comedy, as his readers would surely appreciate. Now that he was with Maecenas, the final joke about the killing of a Caesar might not be so funny. The poem from Clazomenae had still to be worth the risk. There were all the *P*'s in the words: *Proscripti, Rupili pus, Persius, opinor, lippis,* perfect for the stage.

There were more details of his part in the diplomatic mission to Antony: bad food, intellectual entertainment, sleepless nights, another mock epic battle between two buffoons, this time a parody of the sort of street art likely to be performed when his poem was over. And then there was the girl who promised to share his bed but left him with only a wet dream. Horace sought the reputation of an honest reporter.

Maecenas knew it all already, but new readers and hearers would not. Yet neither would they learn anything about the embassy that Maecenas did not want to be learned. When the big political business between Octavian and Antony comes up in the poem, Horace is tending to his fuzzy eyesight, a metaphor as much as a medical condition, applying ointment for the same bleary eyes as at Clazomenae. He is lippus. He has to pop out for drugs. *Pila lippis inimicum ludere,* his "bleary eyes would stop him playing ball," even if he wanted to. The letters of Philippi again threaded through the line like a code.

Brundisium longae finis, "Brundisium was the end of a long journey," its last event a joke about superstitions of the Jews. Horace had brought another poem to an end before the politics began. He was becoming an artist of miniature pictures and fragments of great events, as well as a man who could be trusted to keep art in its place.

He was learning the poetic swerve, the switch in direction that kept readers and hearers alert. In the first forty-five lines of his sixth satire he continued the sort of chatting present in the first, keeping up the kinds of subjects that he thought might flatter and entertain. *Non quia Maecenas*, "Even though, Maecenas," he began, reminding readers of *Qui fit, Maecenas* at the start of the book.

Non quia Maecenas, Lydorum quidque Etruscos incoluit finis nemo generosior, "Even though, Maecenas, none of the Lydians who settled in Etruscan lands is nobler than you," you are not ready to despise the lower born. Horace was flattering and linking himself to Maecenas at the same time, both of them outsiders of different kinds. To some grander Romans, the Lydians who came to Tuscany in ancient times were immigrants from Asia, new arrivals who might even themselves have been former slaves: Lyde was a slave name. Maecenas too, for all his noble power, was a man who had made good.

Horace continued his conversation with some safe attacks on aristocrats who had let down their Roman lineage, naming them all individually even though he was not much interested in these no-good individuals, in Laevinus, Tillius, Barrus, or Novius, or expecting his readers to care either, or even always to know who they were. He named names because the good poet preferred the concrete to the abstract, a real person over a type, until suddenly he switched. *Nunc ad me redeo*, "Now, I'm going back to myself." He had begun his self-portrait. The subject of the rest of this satire is Horace alone.

This was the essence of his calling card to the new salons of Rome. He was, he said, *libertino patre natum*, the son of a man who had once been a slave. Everyone used to jibe at him for that. In case readers missed the point he repeated the words at the end of two consecutive lines. This heavy repetition was not what poets usually did, particularly those conscious of neatness and style. Horace was laying it on hard.

Yes, he had risen in the world since then. He was sometimes seen in public with Maecenas. He had once been a tribune of a Roman legion — in circumstances which he did not wish to highlight too much but was not embarrassed about either. He could deal with his past. It was part of who he was.

Maecenas was already well aware of Horace's pride in his father. This had been the subject of their first meeting. What Horace wanted his readers to know was that his was not the usual story of a man who overcame the handicaps of lowly birth, his schooldays hampered by the *magni quo pueri magnis e centurionibus orti*, "huge sons of huge centurions," the dark woods and bitter sun. No, the suspicious pride in his newly freed father was not something to be set aside or put behind him: it was the greatest example that any man could have, saving him both from countryside restrictions and the temptations of the city, inspiring him to be satisfied with a simple life.

His father's old priorities had not been forgotten. *Pudicum, qui primus virtutis honos,* "chastity, virtue's first grace" — that was his lesson from home, and Horace was writing that he could be relied upon to live by it. His iambi on the sexual preferences of older women were available only to a few friends and not yet in wide circulation. In this first published book he could put his best face forward, and if it raised a smile among the knowing that was no matter. If his little book was a success most readers would be unknowing.

His book revealed a few problems in his new life too, even if they were problems he was proud to have. In the penultimate poem came his first examinations of how his life had begun to change since his diplomatic trip alongside the great. People had noticed that he might be useful to them. *Ibam forte Via Sacra,* he began: there "I was, walking by chance along the Sacred Way."

In this poem he was not doing much; it was already part of his self-portrait that he often did not do much. Up came a man whom he hardly knew. Each said a few polite words. Horace tried to get away. The man persisted. He was a bore. He claimed that they were fellow scholars, and Horace replied politely again, quickening his step to escape.

It was a hot day. Horace was a short, tubby poet, with no fondness for unnecessary physical exertion, and sweat was soon dripping down to his ankles. The Sacred Way ran through the Forum, past the ancient house of Rome's kings and the last home of Julius Caesar. There was no shortage of subjects for conversation that he wanted to avoid.

Horace made up a story about needing to visit a sick friend on the other side of the Tiber. The man said he had nothing better to do than come with him. Horace's response was to feel like an overloaded donkey with damp, drooping ears, listening, against his will, while the man explained first how fast he was at writing poetry and then that he did, in fact, have business in the Forum, a summons to appear to face a lawsuit.

This second revelation was good news. The man would soon have to leave Horace alone and face his accuser. Roman justice was harsh against those who ignored court orders. But the man did not stop. He instead asked about Maecenas, noting that since Horace was now so close to the great man he must surely need an understudy, someone to provide poems when Horace for any reason was unavailable.

Horace saw no choice but to explain that this not how things worked. He had no greater horror, he said, than of those who wrote quickly and for advancement. The man did not believe him and said he would miss his meeting in court, with all the attendant risk, rather than an opportunity to meet Maecenas.

Another poet appeared, Marcus Aristius Fuscus, whom Horace saw as a close and dear friend. But Fuscus knew the bore too. He thought it hilarious that Horace was so trapped by his new social success. He rejected a quiet word in private because to do anything on a Sabbath holiday might offend the circumcised Jews, a joke that Horace did not find funny. There was no Sabbath holiday and, even if there had been, neither Fuscus nor Horace would have known or cared about it.

Jokes about Jewish superstitions were fine in their place. The travelers had shared one on the journey to Brundisium: Who besides Jews believed that incense could burst spontaneously into flame? But this was not the place or time. Fuscus, said Horace, was no sort of friend. He was a black sun on the day, deserving curses for cackling off and leaving him like a sacrifice with a knife above his head. Only the arrival of the bore's court opponent finally brought relief, the dragging of his adversary away amid shouts and screams, leaving Horace to feel as though he had been rescued by Apollo, the poets' patron among the gods.

This was a poet's account of a humorous encounter turned into poetry, as poets were able to do. It was also a serious sign of changing times. Horace was a man who could laugh at himself—and report the new realities too. The satire carried a message he was keen to convey to the patron whom every opportunist was now keen to meet.

In all his minor celebrity, Horace did not forget his origins and how easily he might have stayed in them. *Olim truncus eram ficulnus*, "Once I was a little fig tree," he wrote. As an insignificant fig, at the start of another poem from the end of his book, he could have turned out to be nothing but a log or, if he had been lucky, a carved wooden stool. Instead this fig tree had become a scarecrow with cracked buttocks and an enormous penis, a Priapus, tasked to chase birds from the fields and thieves from the cemeteries. This was promotion.

Horace knew many Greek poems in which objects spoke of their starts in life: bows as the horns of goats, statues as stones. He knew that Maecenas was beginning to clear up the burial grounds of the Subura and Esquiline Hill, where bodies lay in shallow graves, witches tortured boys for better sex, and sun-whitened bones were the closest urban reminder of Pharsalus and Philippi and the naval battle in Sicily in which Agrippa had just destroyed the hopes of Sextus Pompeius. Horace knew that Octavian was keen for Romans to feel the force of his beneficent regime. Horace was happy to mock himself as a wooden sex god, farting and flaunting his power to rape, scaring away his master's foes — and happy to keep being so.

While readers were unrolling the first copies of Horace's *Satires,* its first words, "Qui fit, Maecenas," formed a question beyond poetry alone. It was a question all political men were asking. How comes it, Maecenas? What's going on? Would the rival heirs to Caesar's legacy agree to divide it — or fight each other for it? Where was Antony? What was the next move? Was Rome really still in a state of civil war? Answers came much more slowly than the time needed to reach the final words of Horace's little book, "subscribe libello," the instruction to his slave to get the manuscript on the market.

If there were a trial of strength, Antony seemed to be in the stronger position. He had the bigger army, and it was still a fighting force. While Octavian was settling soldiers on the land, and risking revenge from the dispossessed, Antony was winning battles in Armenia and Parthia. He was losing battles, too — and news was scarce — but on balance, in the much-used military metaphor, the dice were falling his way.

They were golden dice if the stories from Alexandria were to be believed. The king of Armenia was Antony's prisoner, shackled in chains of silver and gold and dragged through the streets in a miserable splendor not seen since Pompey's triumph a quarter of a century earlier. But this triumph was not along Rome's battered Sacred Way, where temples tumbled to the pavements and Horace had met his bore; it was in Cleopatra's glittering capital. Antony had worn the robes of both Dionysus and Osiris, a glamorous Egyptian god. Beside him was the Egyptian queen herself, known to Romans from her days with Julius Caesar, mother of Caesar's son, now mistress of the man who she hoped would be the next Caesar.

Antony was winning support from local kings. Tarcondomitos from Cilicia in the northeast Mediterranean had once fought with Cassius. After Philippi he had changed both his allegiance and his name. He was proud to be Philantonius, "lover of Antony," in the Greek naming style used by the heirs of Alexander the Great.

For Cleopatra and her subjects Antony had gifts to cement his place in their favor, a range of fabricated titles within the Roman Empire for her children, the thrones of Libya and Media and places which were not yet conquered but would be soon. He was also wooing the Senate in Rome, suggesting plans to restore its old powers in a new republic.

Antony's successes gave Octavian problems — but also opportunities. Public opinion in Italy was critical to both men. Octavian's advantage was that Italy was his base. Many Italians might hate him — because of the proscriptions, the seizing of lands for soldiers, and the still strong sympathy for Sextus — but they might be led to hate Antony more. The volatile voters of Rome might remember Antony for his loyalty to Caesar and his bravery at Philippi, and admire his glittering progress through the East. Deeper in the countryside were conservatives for whom everything in Alexandria — its golden chains and thrones and most of all its ruling queen—were the opposite of everything in which they believed.

In Rome, in addition to Maecenas's restoration of the Esquiline cemeteries, Octavian ordered Agrippa to follow up his defeat of Sextus with a program of public baths and fountains, visible proof of why his fellow citizens' sacrifices had been worthwhile. He also succeeded in blaming Antony for Sextus's execution in Asia after the battle, suggesting that the death of the popular pirate would not have been his own choice. At the same time he began a new campaign of public announcements charging Antony as a power-crazed drunk under the control of an oriental witch. Octavian's sister Octavia was still in Roman eyes the wife of Antony, part of the diplomatic bargaining that had brought Horace on his journey to Brundisium. Octavian could play the role of outraged brother.

Antony responded with his own accusations, written from afar in strong soldierly language. He attacked Octavian's own sexual behavior, asking why he was so concerned about Antony's screwing the queen. This was nothing new, he protested; he had been screwing her since soon after Philippi. And, anyway, Octavian was himself in and out of every Tertulla, Terentilla, and Titisenia he ever met. And so what if Antony attended festivals as a god? Everyone knew that Octavian did more or less the same, playing the part of Apollo and inviting others in divine fancy dress to join him for dinners.

This was not the kind of barrack-room battle that Horace wanted to join. Poets were not Octavian's prime troops here. Antony's defense of himself on the charge of dissolute behavior, *de sua ebrietate*, on why he was not a drunk, was in prose. So were Octavian's replies.

Octavian had the power to send his personal manifestos throughout Italy—for display on the same white notice boards on which he and Antony had pronounced their jointly agreed proscriptions a decade before. The most important message was that Antony was the dupe of Cleopatra. Octavian's public anger was less against his old colleague than against a corrupting female foreigner.

Another big civil war battle would be unpopular, and Octavian was in a better position than Antony to grasp just how unpopular. A war against Egypt was, by contrast, a long-standing aim, rejected only because no Roman general should be trusted with the vast wealth that came from the Nile.

Maecenas was not assembling his circle of poets to engage in this sort of aggression. Octavian might possibly have wanted a bit more help: he had rich readers in Rome to convince, not just land-less farmers and former soldiers on other men's fields and the vast mass that was neither. Rich Romans did read poetry, but Maecenas did not sponsor poetry primarily for that reason. He had a real love of words that would last longer than a propaganda campaign.

Friendship with Maecenas did not solve every problem for Horace. Whoever was his friend, this was not an easy time to be a writer, and that was all Horace wanted to be. Moreover, he wanted to be a specific kind of writer: a wrapper of words within meter, a poet, not a historian or a pamphleteer, and even as a poet, a poet of a very particular kind.

Octavian, if he cared to be bothered, would be his ultimate arbiter. He had already noticed some of Horace's work, but all that Horace had learned from that attention was the likelihood of a vicious kick, as though from a temperamental horse approached from the wrong direction. Comments from Octavian were not easy to decode. The new Caesar had much less literary interest than the old, just as he was less of an orator and general. After Philippi, Octavian was still insecure. His perfect poem would probably have been an attack on Antony, his alcoholic excesses, and the lures of Egyptian sex. But Horace had not been asked directly for such a poem.

Nor was Horace close enough to Maecenas to expect detailed guidance from him about dealing with the man at the center of both their lives. Maecenas liked his new young client, but the success of any poet with the warlord of Rome was hardly his priority. Horace had not yet written much – and who could know what else might come from him, or even from Varius or Vergil, who had already done more?

Advice came to Horace from a grander older man of Rome, but it was absolutely what he did not want to hear. Gaius Trebatius Testa was one of Rome's top lawyers, a friend of the elder Cicero, an equal to him in discussing the finer points of life and art. Horace had never known Cicero; he had known only his much lesser son. Now he was in contact with a man in whom Cicero had greatly trusted, but the connection was not giving him the help he hoped for.

It was good that he could talk to Trebatius at all, a lawyer to the great but much more than that, a man at the heart of Rome's society of friendship relationships, of the *amicitia* which was so much more than personal friendship. For Horace a relationship with Maecenas might mean only that he was good company or useful as a poet. An amicitia with Trebatius was a sign of acceptance in a wider web of mutual aid. Trebatius took seriously the up-and-coming men, supporting Horace as Cicero had once supported him. But he did not lack confidence. He knew well the minds of his clients, was not averse to advertising his views, and did not expect to be ignored.

As soon as the first book of *Satires* was out for sale, Horace began writing his second book. He knew that it had to be different. Ideally, it would be more popular. Horace needed to say where he stood, to show where he stood, to write more poems in dialogue that might be read in public, not just in the seclusion that so few enjoyed.

Before writing them he needed himself to know more of where he stood within the new freedoms and new constraints of the age. Trebatius was the sort of man who could help, older than Horace, grander, but also born close to Horace's home in Venusia, a link worth exploiting if he could. Horace listened to Trebatius and then wrote a new poem about him, signaling mockingly that it was something of a one-sided debate, a legal consultation. All educated Romans, for better or worse, knew what those were like.

Horace began by pointing to his own work. *Sunt quibus in satura*, "There are those," he told the legal grandee, "for whom my satire" is too rough, and others for whom it is not rough enough. *Sunt quibus*, "There are those for whom." His readers would already hear the sound of a nervous client entering the legal arena, clearing his throat, wrapping his toga round his chest, pausing for breath before continuing.

The poem was in the form of a dialogue, a verbatim legal exchange. Trebatius's answer was succinct. He knew about satire, but he knew much more about Caesars. With Cicero's help he had become an officer under Julius Caesar in Gaul and made an enormous fortune there without having to take part in many battles. He was an acknowledged legal expert in libel, wills, and codicils. His opinion, and this was not just anyone's opinion, was that Horace should abandon satire altogether.

Quiescas, "Keep quiet!" Keep quiet! That was what Horace should do. Trebatius did not want talk about how rough a good satire should be. His advice was not to write it at all.

Horace's response was pained. *Ne faciam?* "You mean me not to do it?" That would be impossible. He quite simply could not keep quiet. He was shocked at the very thought.

Then came the silence of disagreement. Horace struggled for a better reason, one that a lawyer might accept. He found it in insomnia. He would not be able to sleep, he said, if he were not a poet.

Trebatius was unimpressed. *Ter uncti Tiberim*, if it was sleep that worried Horace, replied the lawyer, he should get *uncti*, "oiled up," then swim *ter*, "three times," across the Tiber, then steep himself with wine. And if that did not appeal, he should write a poem about the achievements of *Caesaris invicti*, the "unconquered" new "Caesar."

Epic appealed to Horace even less than exercise. He did not challenge the notion that Caesar was unconquered although his own experience at Philippi and the stories of every naval battle with Sextus bar the last suggested that it was mild exaggeration. Simply, he said, he could not write about dying Gauls, tumbling Parthians, or any kind of war. He was not that kind of writer. Only the wine appealed to him. Both men were enthusiasts for that.

Trebatius became impatient. He was a self-consciously civilized man, hugely wealthy at the expense of an earlier Caesar's dead Gauls, and famed for his witty jousts with Cicero about the meanings of words. He was friendly and obviously happy to help. He was not used to being ignored.

Nor was Trebatius a good enemy to have. When Horace came to turning his legal consultation into a poem he knew that he could not stray too far from what was said. Exaggeration or creative editing would be risky. Stylistic opportunities had on this occasion to be constrained. Horace stuck to his main point, the problem in an autocracy of being any kind of poet except a flatterer.

Trebatius reminded him that the great satirist Lucilius had praised the Scipios, not quite autocrats but about as powerful as a family could be in Rome before the Caesars. This was the moment at which Horace reported Octavian's record of kicking out like a bad-tempered stallion when poems did not suit him. Trebatius could be imagined nodding sagely at this point as though to say, "No further questions."

Horace was unbowed. He said that he was not like Lucilius, his rich and aristocratic predecessor. He was far beneath him in rank. He was an outsider. He did not want to use his pen like a dagger, but neither did he want to put it away. Whether it brought him good luck or bad, it was his weapon of choice.

Trebatius predicted that in that case Horace's life would be short, frozen from society if he were lucky, dead if he were not. As though in conclusion of his legal advice, he added a two-line warning about the law of libel when *carmina* were *mala*, when poems were "bad."

Ah, replied Horace, in his final lines, but what if the poems were good and Octavian said he liked them? Well, that would be totally different, said Trebatius. The case would collapse in laughter. *Tu missus abibis*, "You will get off and go home." Like any former slave, slapped around the head in the formal gesture of liberation, his slate would be wiped clean. He would be free.

Missus, "Sent away," free, his own man, far from the crowds. Horace had been born a free man, but the shadow of his father's slavery was always upon him. He had been his own man since the death of Brutus, but he needed help to be as independent as he thought a poet should be. Escape from crowds was already an obsession. The press of the dying at Philippi, the press of the living on the Esquiline slopes: both were weights that he wished to cast away.

So too was the press of his predecessors in poetry. He had not yet sent the copyist his angry homages to Archilochus, but his ties to the iambi of the old Greek buccaneer were weakening. He was writing differently now. No more older women would wonder whether his words for melting makeup and bestial preferences were directed personally at them.

He was freed as well from following the examples of Lucilius, the grand satirist of Rome, both Lucilius's attacks on his contemporaries and his travelogues through the Italian countryside. *Egressum*, as he had begun his own journey poem to Brundisium: he was "out of there" now in every way. From the past he had found the tools to describe his own life – and to fuse it with the world around him in ways which he already knew were new. But a secure life in which to realize his ambitions was not yet within his grasp.

CHAPTER EIGHT

Under Vesuvius

Horace sometimes traveled south on the same road he had taken as a schoolboy and diplomats' companion. The Appian Way was the start of routes from Rome not just eastward over the mountains to Venusia, Brundisium, and Greece but deeper into the south to Naples and its surrounding towns, Herculaneum and Pompeii. This was the area of the great gladiatorial arenas, the villas of the Roman rich, the finest vineyards, which grew on the ancient ash of Mount Vesuvius – death, drink, and carefully cultivated leisure, all side by side.

To see Vergil was always a reason for a journey. After the early loss of his lands, confiscated for soldiers in the same way Horace's had been, the author of the *Bucolica* now lived on the Bay of Naples and lacked for nothing. Although his most ambitious work, the *Aeneid,* was still an epic in progress, he had read enough of it aloud to have become the laureate-in-waiting of the new age. Along with Vergil were others who wrote poetry and liked to talk about poetry. Horace was now a welcome member of what the jealous saw as an intimate circle of poets, centered on Maecenas, sensitive to Octavian's ambitions for Rome.

Just outside Herculaneum, the richest of the resort towns, was one extraordinary house – a place for those seeking not only rest from Rome but the theory of rest, not mere pleasure but guides to the philosophy of pleasure. Its dominance of the shoreline was unchallenged. No visitor could miss it, though only a few could visit. Surrounded on three sides by vineyards, woods, and gardens, it tumbled like a waterfall over four floors from a broad terrace overlooking the sea.

Its owner had been the father-in-law of Julius Caesar, Lucius Calpurnius Piso, one of many failed peacemakers in his final decade in politics. Piso had died soon after the bereavement of Calpurnia, his daughter, on the Ides of March. His legacy to his house and his heirs included a delicate bronze of Mercury, the god whom Horace credited with his maddened escape from Philippi; a vast collection of other Greek sculpture; and, more unusually, a library of literary and musical theory and other philosophical texts written to help explain the modern world to those challenged by its changes.

Papyri lay in boxes on shelves from floor to ceiling, and in lower, two-sided shelves down the middle of the rooms. The philosophy of Epicurus – its reduction of reality to atoms and its rejection of divine interference in the world – was the library's guiding force. As a choice for Piso and his successors this must have sometimes seemed perverse since public life, which Piso embraced as ancient duty, was notoriously of no account to Epicurus. This was not just because Epicurus lived in Athens after the city had passed its greatness, but because he considered politics at any place and time to be an unnecessary disturbance to a life of pleasure and avoidance of pain, the way of tranquillity, the only way in which a man could escape the all-corrupting fear of death.

This new Greek philosophy had become surprisingly fashion-able among Romans, for whom politics was life itself. Calpurnia's credibility with Caesar when she warned of the omens before his death should have been much enhanced by her reputation as an Epicurean rationalist, though sadly for Caesar, it was not enhanced sufficiently. One of her slaves had a son called Twentieth, *eikadion* in Greek, after the date of the philosopher's birthday. Caesar had spent many of his last months of leisure in what was close to an Epicu-rean community.

When Epicurus was alive and speaking to his own community in his own garden, he had advocated life in obscurity, the enjoyment of small things, the happiness of the individual. He was a materi-alist in the tradition of Empedocles, with his theory of the four elements, but even harsher in excluding the gods from human life. Empedocles on his volcano believed that Love and Strife, son and sister of the god of war, controlled the flow of his natural elements. For Epicurus the world was material only, and human beings should not deceive themselves with any part of the divine.

Dead for more than two centuries, Epicurus still spoke across Greece to the bay of Naples. A new version of his thought in verse, *De rerum natura* (On the Nature of the World), had begun circu-lating at the same time as Cassius, a flexible Epicurean, was plan-ning Caesar's assassination. For Cassius the paramount search for tranquillity was incompatible with life under a tyrant, a conclusion with which other Epicureans could reasonably disagree. The works of Epicurus, and of Lucretius, his Latin interpreter, were useful for poetry, as well as for thinking about politics in difficult times.

This appeal was not for all. More traditional Romans, like Bru-tus, were distrustful of withdrawing from life in order to make life better. Their concern was not just for individuals but for the state as a whole. The avoidance of pain and pursuit of pleasure were luxuries in their view. Horace himself, as in so much else, sought a middle course. As a satirist he kept a mocking distance from all systems of belief, and his new place beside Maecenas did not need underpinning by any belief except the benefits of peace. This did not mean that all political discussion was off limits, particularly when in a suitably learned disguise.

In Herculaneum a discussion of Epicurus might range far beyond the ruler and the ruled. Many of the books in Piso's library were written by a poet-polymath who acted as a resident tutor and intellectual companion for the poets of Maecenas. His name was Philodemus, a citizen of Gadara, a Greek town southeast of the Sea of Galilee. As well as showing how the doctrines of Epicurus might be adapted for politicians and those at the political fringes, Philodemus wrote about words and sounds, how music and language worked together.

Philodemus poured out thousands of words on rage, sex, and free speech, more of them brutal than kind. Horace read his thoughts on the risks of chasing city women who had to wait till their husbands were out before asking their lovers to come around. Let a woman instead, Philodemus urged, be easily available, neither high priced nor slow to be ready when called. Philodemus's country mistress had flat buttocks, a long nose, short stature, and big feet, perfect for a witty poem at least. Time with the words of Philodemus — as well as a sizable papyri collection with uninterrupted views over the warm open sea — was more than sufficient cause for Horace to make the long trip south.

In Herculaneum, he could spend leisurely time with Vergil. Horace was still the junior writer among Maecenas's poets. Vergil was older, richer, and more shy, contemplating what was clearly to be a massive epic work. While Horace's thoughts were of adapting the forms of Archilochus, Alcaeus, and Sappho for the Latin language, Vergil was taking on the epic weight of Homer. Vergil was not translating the *Iliad* and the *Odyssey*, the task taken on by Livius Andronicus and studied by Horace at school. He was reworking the foundations of Greek literature, reversing the story's flow, putting travel before the travails of war, beginning with the odyssey of Aeneas's escape from Troy and arrival in Italy (not far from Piso's house) and moving on to the iliad of war to found Rome.

Vergil fitted squarely in with Maecenas's determination to give Rome a new history alongside what he hoped would be a new future. Horace never fitted squarely in with anyone or anything. Vergil had a consistent tone of high seriousness. Horace prized unreliability and the question of his trustworthiness — and not only as a narrator.

The two poets might joke together about wealth, wine, and perfume, about how, if Vergil wanted the best of anything when he visited Horace he would have to bring it himself. But no one on Piso's terraces would ever think of reading Vergil for an afternoon's pondering upon women, wine, and the poets — what they had drunk, whom they might have taken to their beds. Vergil's portrait of Dido, the passionate queen who tried to keep Aeneas in Carthage, was a study of fate not of a femme fatale.

Horace's poems invited easy discussions on sex and alcohol, on whether a poet could really drink as regularly and as much as in his poems Horace appeared to drink. *Nullam, Vare, sacra vite,* "Plant nothing before the sacred vine." That was Horace's advice to Varus, a friend who was planting out a garden. Those without wine, *siccis,* the "dry men," saw only the harshest miseries of the world.

But then drunkards, Horace went on, caused their own wars. Men should remember those half-human Centaurs high above the columns of the Parthenon, as wild from drink as were the Thracian tribes on the road to Philippi, none of them able to draw a line between *fas* and *nefas*, "right" and "wrong," once wine and sex had obliterated morality from their minds.

How did Horace work? Was he dry in the morning and not a drinker till later in the day? Horace's work was artful and, in the minds of some, complex to a fault: surely it needed steady fingers on the stylus, not ruddy cheeks and eyes. Was wine an Epicurean's retreat from pain, a politician's escape from the past, a sign of peace replacing war? Was wine only a sign, or was it as ubiquitous in a poet's life as in his poetry? A fellow guest might observe Horace and make up his own mind. No one would even think of asking such questions about Vergil.

When Horace read aloud (or sometimes maybe sang) his lines about promiscuous Phryne, brazen Glycera, faithless Pyrrha, and Chloe, mistress of disdain, his fellow guests might ask whose identities these names concealed, or whether they concealed anyone. Were they girls or boys? Did they deserve rose petals or gentle whips?

For Chloe, Horace began a poem with the premise that his days as a sexual combatant were over, that he was hanging up his kit as an offering to the goddess of love. *Vixi puellis nuper idoneus,* "I lived till lately fit for the girls." Was he serious? Was he simply temporarily out of action? Was the poem no more than a literary joke? The Greek poets were forever saying that their days as a soldier or sailor were past. What was Horace saying?

Whatever his intentions, the poem made clear, Chloe still deserved the whip for disdaining Horace's lust, *sublimi flagello,* "with uplifted lash," *semel,* "just once." Was the whip a stimulus for sex, thus proving that Horace's sexual weapons were not hung up at all? Was Chloe a future partner or a picture from the past? *Flagello tange Chloen arrogantem:* the listener would hear the cracking of the harsh repeated *G*'s. This was a short poem, packed with sexual paradox, perfect from a good guest.

Vergil did not invite such thoughts: his art was long and at the service of Rome, promoting and sometimes subverting imperial destiny but never making light of it. In courtly status at Herculaneum, Horace was a gifted newcomer but far from grand, hardly at the top table, still testing his ideas. When Philodemus wrote an essay on flattery, an art as necessary for survival on the Bay of Naples as, increasingly, everywhere, he dedicated it to Vergil, Varius, and two older critics, Quintilius Varus and Plotius Tucca. There was no place for Horace.

Octavian was himself a recipient of flattery — and skilled at returning it. He was a prolific writer of personal letters, but as his responsibilities grew, his time for elegant composition shrank. Horace, he thought, might make an excellent secretary, not for political affairs but for composing the kind of letter that he might want to send to congratulate a useful friend on a marriage or a birth.

This was a suggestion that Horace had very carefully to decline. He claimed ill health, an excuse which would have hardly impressed the always ill Octavian. But he managed his reluctance in such a way that Octavian took no offence, joking that Horace was a *purissimum penem,* an "amusing little fucker," in the sort of military slang that an officer might use of a common soldier. It was as if in their youth they had been marching to Philippi on the same side. Trebatius would have been proud of him — if perhaps surprised.

Horace's freedom, however, came only within the very gentle confines of Maecenas's world. His patron claimed, "If I do not love you, Horace, more than life itself, you can see your comrade as thinner than Ninnius." (Ninnius was a notoriously thin man, Horace just as notoriously tubby.) Horace and Maecenas could easily exchange jokes about bodily size, which was not a sensitive subject. But Maecenas was a protector only as long as Octavian ruled Rome.

If Antony were to take the city, a poet might be dealing with Fonteius Capito, another companion on the Brundisium road, or with no one at all since Antony had no known interest in art beyond the martial. The capital of the empire might not even bc in Rome since Cleopatra might insist on the greater glorification of Alexandria, at least according to Octavian's manifestos to the people of Italy.

Nor was Horace's freedom to write of concern to anyone except Horace himself, and maybe Maecenas's other poets, Vergil and Varius, and their very few readers and listeners. Artists were a luxury of peace. Traditionally, successful poets celebrated victors. Praise of battles won was not the kind of artistry that Horace saw as his own, but there were few others to whom his sensitivities or preferences mattered.

In 33 BCE Octavian's main man in the public eye was not Maecenas but Agrippa, victor over Sextus in Sicily, innovator of triumphant warships, and already the planner of the next war against Antony. In order to distract the people of Rome from the prospect of unpopular battles, Agrippa also took the junior role of aedile that year, the magistrate responsible for food supplies, clean water, and security in the streets. Octavian ordered massed displays of feasts and entertainments, free baths, free salt and oil, and chances to buy cheap clothes, far beyond what his critics and those sympathetic to Antony or the assassins of Caesar could expect.

In a satire on every kind of madness Horace mocked Agrippa's free issues of vegetables, his vetches, lupines, and assorted foods for both humans and animals. *In cicere atque faba*, "On chickpea and bean," he began. A chickpea, a *cicer*, was a reminder of his Philippi friend Cicero, whose father had died for abusing Antony, now somewhere abroad serving Octavian. The people were easily led, Horace jibed, as long as they were fed.

The barb was oblique, but it was sharp. War leaders were madmen, a complaint that it was safer to make by telling a story from Homer about how two great Greek leaders fell out at Troy, how Agamemnon preened himself (*rex sum*, "I am king") when challenged about not allowing his rival Ajax a proper burial. Ajax was mad, said Agamemnon: he killed a thousand sheep thinking he was killing his fellow generals. But then Agamemnon was mad too: he killed his own daughter in order to get the gods to shift the wind direction for his fleet. They were both mad. What was the difference between them?

Horace had an interest in the madness of war, the damage done to fighters and to the families of the survivors and the dead. But this poem was not designed to please Octavian, Antony, or the bean-giving aedile Agrippa. Any use of the word *rex* was a risk. Maybe Maecenas was more likely to be amused. Octavian was beginning to have a court, and in a court a gentle mockery of one man could be an encouragement to another.

Antony still had his supporters in Rome. Two of them, Gnaeus Domitius Ahenobarbus and Gaius Sosius, were set to be consuls in 32. Both were powerful men, with a recent history—in Ahenobarbus's case a rather long recent history—as critics of the family of the Caesars. Ahenobarbus had commanded the fleet of Brutus and Cassius at Philippi before transferring his support to Antony. Sosius had replied vigorously for Antony in Octavian's propaganda war in Italy. Lucius Calpurnius Bibulus, Horace's friend from Athens and Philippi, was also with Antony. For a man whose virulent hostility was to Caesar's family, not his cause, Antony was an easy choice to replace the loss of Brutus as leader.

Antony did not help the arguments of his friends when he divorced his wife, Octavia, and married Cleopatra in a luridly reported wedding in Alexandria. This was an act wide open to attack, not because Octavia was Octavian's sister but because she was popular in her own right and a Roman wife wronged by an Egyptian. But there were possibilities for a counterattack by Antony. Maybe together Sosius and Ahenobarbus might still legislate a reduction of Octavian's power. What, it might be asked by anyone neutral, was the legitimacy of rule by the two destroyers of the assassins if each was on the brink of destroying the other? There was no simple answer to that.

Agrippa accelerated the assembling of his fleet and the securing of supply bases in the Adriatic. Octavian watched and waited, mindful of the unpopularity waiting for a provoker of a new civil war. It was possible that Maecenas—and perhaps Horace too—would be part of what would ideally be a diplomatic and political clash as much as, if not more than, a military one. The possibility of the return of war was for Horace a horror, the prospect of his own part in it a reminder more horrific still.

Horace had no doubt where he stood. Why? Not for principle or for any kind of policy. He was on the side of Maecenas and Octavian because he was in the same place as Maecenas and Octavian. That was how he had begun the march to Philippi—because he was in the same place as Brutus. Every part of his life since then had come from that chance of geography. His mind had been forged by war and shattered by war. He wanted to be free of war. While Rome's would-be autocrats prepared their armies, fleets, and courts, Horace was preparing two new collections of poems, his early efforts inspired by Archilochus and the horrors of postwar Rome and a second set of *Satires*.

CHAPTER NINE

Town and Country

If Horace had been on the winning side at Philippi he would already have earned some land as a reward. Beneath a thin veneer of ideals the army of Brutus was no different from any other in the civil wars of Rome. The assassins' men would have needed recompense — and the prizes would have come from the losers, the friends of the losers, and the merely unlucky. As an officer he could have expected more than the twenty acres that the assassins' metatores, measurement officers, would have allowed for the men. He might even have kept his father's land if that had not been redistributed before the battle even began.

As a loser he had nothing until, as a poet, he gained much more than a fighter could have hoped for. Some six years after the journey to Brundisium, Maecenas gave him a small estate, a villa and several farms. This was not contested land. His neighbors were not fellow soldiers scrapping over who owned what, who would buy more from whom, and when they might have the opportunity to be soldiers again. The land was not in the middle of nowhere but in the Sabine hills, a region renowned for ancient austerity, some thirty miles northeast of Rome, rustic and even closer to Tibur, Rome's metropolitan holiday resort. His new home was balanced between town and country, and although the journey between the two was hardly safe, and whereas only a madman would do it at night, *hoc erat in votis*, as he began a satire for his second book, "this was a place of his prayers" and dreams. He could write there – and he could move beyond what he saw around him and begin to write about himself.

As ever, as though still traveling, he took a roundabout route to this poem's center. *Olim rusticus urbanum murem mus*, "Once upon a time there was a country mouse and a town mouse." Horace was adapting a story first told by the Greek writer known as Aesop from the same faraway age as Archilochus. Many fables of Aesop were familiar in Italy, although knowledge of the author himself, possibly a slave, possibly from Africa, certainly not a martial grandee, was scarce.

The art of Aesop was to speak truth to power while seeming to tell no more than tales for children. In some ways Horace, son of a former slave, was already becoming more like Aesop than like Archilochus, light and slanting rather than direct. His version of the fable was more subtle in style than anything in the ancient Greek: sympathetic, self-mocking, and sincere.

The country mouse, at the start of Horace's account, was entertaining at home. His guest was an old friend, a mouse who lived in a great house in town. The country mouse offered his best oats and seeds, the sort of food with which Agrippa was hoping to woo the masses of Rome. The town mouse accepted gingerly, with whiskered disdain. Horace was an observer as well as a teller of moral tales.

The town mouse at last could not refrain from giving his best advice. The two of them should recognize that life was short, that all pleasure was to be had in the houses of the rich. They should pack up and go. The country mouse agreed, and the pair scampered away toward the town walls, while *tenebat nox medium caeli spatium,* "night held the center of the sky." This was mock epic, the language not just of men but of heroic men: these mice were now promoted to miniature heroes on a mission at Troy.

In the big house was spread out the aftermath of a feast, the remains of the kind of food that Agrippa, Maecenas, and Octavian consumed themselves rather than giving their supporters to consume. The town mouse told his friend to stretch out on the purple couches while he found course after course, delivering each delicacy personally to his friend — always after a little careful tasting of his own. Horace now knew the rules of Roman banqueting as well as the behavior of the smaller rodents.

All was well until there came a terrible banging of doors. Two giant hounds, mousers of the house, began their own rampage through the scraps. The country mouse did not hesitate for an instant. He set off back immediately to his tree hole, chastened, grateful for what he had at home, looking forward to the satisfactions of the simple life. Thus the story ended in Horace's characteristic clipped narrative style.

Horace could now be something of a country mouse himself. He owned woods and fields. In Latin the word for a wood, *silva,* was the same as the word for the raw material of poetry. Horace had his new country home as well as his own readers in town. It was not luxurious by the standards of the rich, but it was leisurely. Before any verdict could be declared in the struggle between Octavian and Antony (or Octavian and Cleopatra, Rome and Egypt, as Octavian liked to see it), Horace had his great gift from Maecenas, his own place of peace.

Nothing, of course, was quite certain. He was still a civil war poet. In 31 BCE no ownership of land was wholly secure. A victorious Antony might eliminate Maecenas and grant the same farm to a fighter of his own who was not a writer for his adversary. But his was only a minor position, he might be able to argue. Horace was no outspoken propagandist for Octavian. He did not talk political tactics with Maecenas – whatever his critics might think. His was the art of the mild conversationalist and nothing more.

Horace was grateful but hardly a grandee. He still felt irritation – though sometimes a sweet pleasure, as he had to admit – when harassed for information and favor by those anxious about where Octavian might grab his latest lands for troops, by businessmen requiring the seal of Maecenas on some deed or other, by scribes in his former offices claiming important business but probably wanting news or a helping hand. He found amusement in mocking those who sought to repair lost fortunes with the wills of the newly dead. And if he seemed a bit smug, well possibly sometimes he was. Let others say so. Horace's father would have been proud that his son was even close to such criticism.

Horace was careful. He did not want to seem too close to power. He was a writer. He entertained. He did not advise. He did not know the progress, or otherwise, of the Dacian campaigns to stop Antony's invading Italy from the northeast. A poem about mice was the perfect way to let it be known that he was a poet, not a political aide. Perhaps, if the fortunes of war went against his new friends, the gift might slip by unnoticed.

In the meantime, *hoc erat in votis,* "this was what I prayed for," the solemn words with which his story of town and country began. Horace wanted *nil amplius,* "nothing more," than his new garden, its spring for water, and its woodland above, an idyllic description which diverted into a philosophical defense of his moderate desires – and then into the ambitions of mice. With a last jovial threat to make his city slave a farmhand (moves from town to country might be as devastating to a slave as slavery itself) and a defense of modest dining with his patron, his second book of *Satires* was almost complete.

While Antony was deploying his massive Egyptian fleet and army on the western coast of Greece (he was not, it turned out, on the Dacian route to Italy overland), and while Agrippa was fitting out Octavian's response, Horace was going back into his first work as a poet, preparing his iambi for the copiers. These vicious poems, the works of a much younger, angrier man, meshed uneasily with his new and gentler mood. Nonetheless he wanted them to be read – and from the new security of his farm in the hills he felt able to take the risk.

He had to look again at his war-damaged life after Philippi, his poverty in the dirt of Rome, his wild words on older women, his imitations of what he had learned from Archilochus when he first met Brutus, risks that went well beyond what Archilochus had risked for himself. So many had died. His friend Bibulus, the great hater of Caesar and great lover of poetry, had not lasted long in the service of Antony. So many tens of thousands had died. Horace added quickly two more iambi, appropriate for his place behind the lines of a new war for the future of Rome.

Ibis Liburnis, "You will go on the Liburnian ships." The stress was on "you" and the "you" was his *amice,* his "friend," Maecenas, at the start of the second line, about to go into battle. The ships were light galleys, Liburnians, faster than the giant ships of Egypt but dangerous for fighting at close quarters. Maecenas, for the apparent purposes of this poem, was set to share the *Caesaris periculum,* the "peril that Octavian and Agrippa" were about to face. Of the three only Agrippa was a fighter.

So Maecenas was going to Actium? So Horace too? What was the point of taking someone as *imbellis ac infirmus,* "unwarlike and weak," as Horace was? None except friendship. He would offer to accompany his friend anyway — and feel safer, even though in war, Maecenas, like a mother bird against a snake, would not be able to save him. It was a moving tribute which, while still more personal than political, was vivid in sense and intent.

The danger to Horace's new peace was as real as was his inability to forestall it. To any Dacian tribal leader or mercenary Greeks of the kind that had maneuvered at Philippi, Antony would still have looked the more likely victor. He had allies who had taken on new names to prove their love of him. As well as men called Philantonius he had Cleopatra's wealth, the bigger army — which wealth could buy — and more of the giant ships that would crush Liburnians in the wrong kind of combat.

The military balance — and the prospect of defeat — still held its chill. Horace never thought he would have to fight again. He knew that Maecenas would surely have bigger responsibilities than watching ships at war, but Horace, if Maecenas did leave Rome, would be with him. Meanwhile he had written a subtle tribute to loyalty.

Quando repostum Caecubum, "When can we bring out the best wine?" In the setting of the second of Horace's last-minute poems for his collection of iambi, the fighting between Octavian and Antony has already begun. Maecenas and Horace, predictably, were not themselves on the western Greek coast at Actium, not in a front-line ship nor even in one bobbing and rolling behind. But this little drama had its own immediacy anyway.

When, Horace asked, could they drink the Caecuban, the wine from the place where that pompous mayor had entertained them on the first journey they had shared, the vintages kept for the most important feasts? When could they be in Maecenas's luxurious house in Rome at a party like the one for Octavian's defeat of Sextus five years earlier? For the purposes of the poem, neither man knew much of what was going on. Initial reports seemed good. Caesar's former ally, now his enemy, *emancipatus feminae,* "enslaved to a woman," subservient to eunuchs, had fallen even farther. No one knew where Antony was. Horace's lines, as so often, conjured unfinished scenes.

Capaciores adfer huc, puer, scyphos, "Bring out the bigger cups, boy!" Bring Chian wine, Lesbian wine, Caecuban wine, bring any wine to settle that *fluentem nauseam:* those "heaving stomachs" that came from even thinking about a ship. Horace's first book, his *sermones,* had ended with a slave being sent to the copiers. His second, his *iambi,* was moving to its close with a call to another slave for the finest wine from the finest drinking vessels.

CHAPTER TEN

A Room of Mirrors

His faces stared back at him. He was in an inner room of what was now his house, his first home since leaving home as a child, red-roofed walls at the center of an amphitheater of hills, high crags topped by small towns, with some fifty acres of hillside below, all his to farm as profitably as freedmen tenants could, and to enjoy as he never had enjoyed land before.

He could see himself in the bronze plates on what were now his own walls. His image was stiller than in water, darker than in the daylight at Philippi, where a man might see a bit of himself in the back of his own shield – or the front of his enemy's. Horace had many faces now in the lamplit room in his home, where he could bring girls or boys or no one. He had many mirrors, on the wooden ceiling as well as on the mud bricks. Everywhere he stared back at himself.

Horace was short, fat in body as well as face, with blotches on his skin. But no one in a room of bronze saw himself quite as he knew he was. There were mirrors that might make a man longer and slimmer. A partial view might look better than the whole. A hand might loom large at the very moment it was pulling back. Blotches might fade. Sometimes the deception was deliberate, sometimes by the accident of manufacture. In metal every reflection was darker.

In the houses of Maecenas and the rich of Rome were mirrors which gave a brighter, sharper image. In the houses of the very richest were sheets of black glass, made of minerals quarried from the slopes of fire mountains, in which the image was in due proportion to reality, where a man's nose was the right distance from his forehead even if he looked like a ghost from Hades.

Horace was not himself rich enough for such domestic excess, but he was now the proud beneficiary of one of the city's richest and most powerful men. Mirrors, *specula*, were tools of speculation, self-examination, self-protection against attacks from behind, self-gratification of all kinds. His gift from Maecenas was a farmhouse in a wooded landscape of bright reflective springs, and inside the villa an inner sanctum of many faces, only some thirty miles from his patron but far enough away to be free.

Horace and Maecenas had to wait for news from Actium on which they could rely. Maecenas was securing Octavian's cause in Italy against the best and the worst that might happen. Horace was writing about his seasick stomach — from his experiences in the dining room, not the depths of the eastern Adriatic — and relied on titbits of fact as though they were food.

Reports came even to the best-connected absentees only slowly and in patches. The sea battle, it seemed, was won. It had barely been fought. Antony lost because of a failed strategy, not because his ships were too big. Agrippa held for Octavian the harbors and open sea that Antony could not capture. Antony was trapped. Lack of preparation made the difference between victory and defeat.

But Antony and Cleopatra were still alive, still in Egypt, and still able to continue the struggle. There was not yet security, either in Rome or in the countryside surrounding it. There were as many accounts circulating as there were hopes. But the outlines of the stories — and the outcome — were the same. There were old myths and new myths, both better suited to poetry than war studies, to ancient heroics than the tedium of strategic strangleholds.

First came the old myths. Before departing for Greece, Octavian had chosen a bit of bare city sand, called it Egypt, and watched while a priest hurled a spear against this territory of his enemy. This was said to be an ancient rite, although signs of its antiquity were scarce. Octavian was becoming ever more brazen in the use of "tradition" to disguise what was new. Maecenas was the master of such disguises.

Agrippa then launched the real offensive. Horace's friend Messalla, who in his last battle at Philippi had played philosopher with Gaius Cassius, became one of his commanders. The sea around Corcyra, the major Greek island between Italy and Greece, became the first site for fighting where no fighting happened. Antony and Cleopatra waited there to prevent Agrippa's crossing. Agrippa deceived Antony into thinking that his fleet was already in Greece, then seized Corcyra himself when Antony sailed some sixty miles south to Actium.

From Corcyra's harbors Agrippa's triremes could protect Octavian's troop transports as they sailed calmly across the Adriatic. With the speed that made him Caesar's true military heir, Agrippa also took other islands. He protected himself against the most unlikely threats. He was as much a perfectionist in physical force as was Horace in the force of words. Octavian landed his legions just five miles away from his enemies and took a position from which he could watch and wait.

The army of Antony and Cleopatra was the larger. The two had more ships. Their crews were better paid. Antony's tactical reputation stretched back longer than that of Agrippa. He had the seemingly stronger position, protected behind the straits that led to a bay of shallow water.

Then came the new myths. As every report confirmed, the bay was poor protection. Its waters swarmed with insects. Disease spread through the troops. There had been a vigorous argument about how to fight and with what; every gossip in Rome knew about that. Antony and Cleopatra could have forced an immediate battle on land. Or they could have marched away from the coast, as Caesar had done almost two decades before on his way to defeating Pompey, abandoning their own fleet but forcing Octavian and Agrippa too to abandon the coast.

Instead they stayed in the inland waters behind the narrow straits and looked out through the swamps to the sea. While Antony was away seeking fresh food for his army, one of his admirals broke out and was pushed back by Agrippa. This was perhaps genuinely the decisive point.

From then, as the stories continued, Antony's star started to fall. His own troops began to die, his mercenaries to melt away. Influential Romans, Ahenobarbus in the lead, switched their support to Octavian. By the time that Antony began what became known throughout the Roman world as the Battle of Actium, he had fewer ships and was forced to burn those he could not man. He had to make a miserable choice between giving up his army or his navy.

Even when choosing the navy, critics said, Antony saw his best chance as simply to get away. He had loaded on board his money chests; he had ordered sails, cluttering the decks and adding weight, the opposite of what an admiral would do before a battle at sea. Or, as others argued, his preparations had been a ploy, not an acceptance of defeat but a way to pretend defeatism. Arguments such as these were more intense than the battle itself.

On the early September day that both sides had chosen, Antony's ships slipped safely from the straits, three squadrons in a long single line. The assassin poet Cassius Parmensis was one of the captains, alert to the wind, ordering rowers, legionaries, and engineers. Gellius Poplicola, another survivor of Philippi, then representative of Antony at Rome, was also now fighting in his cause.

The sea was like the floor of a dance. Each side's sailors knew the other's well-rehearsed steps. Catapults fired flaming arrows. The wind fanned the few that found a target. Fighting was fierce in the few places where there was any, enough for Antony's line to falter.

At that point, for reasons that remained unclear, the ships of Cleopatra signaled the course of the future. Under full sail they left the lines of battle. This was not a feint. Antony followed with some fifty ships. Their sole destination was Egypt. Within a few minutes the battle was won. Within a few hours the army of Antony and Cleopatra surrendered to the heir of Julius Caesar. The sailors did the same.

The final part of the story was no more than a tying up of loose ends. Octavian suddenly had more troops than he wanted. An unnecessary army was an unnecessary danger. He sent as many men as possible as far away as possible. Their destination was not going to be around Rome. Horace's new neighbors were safe—from expropriation if not from many other uncertainties of the lawless countryside.

Horace himself was on the winning side, even if the war was not yet won. And if people began to think that he and Maecenas had been at Actium themselves, that was no harm. Once any battle was won, thousands of absent fighters appeared who would claim to have been there. Also among the new winners was Messalla, his Philippi friend. The young Cicero was even chosen to announce the victory at Actium in the Forum—and to fix the official notice to the speakers' Rostra, the place of both his father's triumphs and his severed hands.

Lollius could envisage a bright future too. He had not only come to know Octavian, he had found the man on Antony's side who had saved him at Philippi in a slave's disguise. He had saved his savior by asking Octavian to spare his life. There was a hardening coalition of the future. Among the poets only the assassin, Cassius Parmensis, was still on the losing side. Messalla's brother Gellius Poplicola, erratic and unknowable to the last, was missing, presumed dead.

It was ten months before Horace learned the final outcome of the civil wars that had marked his whole life. His new home was not quite yet a place of safety, but its position—and that of its owner— was stronger. He could look south to see where intruders might come from. The north side was sheer. He could see his neighboring mountains split by the valleys of three streams. There was cover from the clouds. For a sun lover there were the day's last rays.

But Horace had lost his complacency along with his innocence at Philippi. In the autumn of Actium his plum trees were bearing their fruit, his oak trees the acorns for his cattle. By the time the news was trickling in from Alexandria, the water levels in his streams were rising. Though so much was well, he took nothing for granted. Anxiety was everywhere, with every owl in the sky a possible harbinger of horror, just as his father and his neighbors had believed back in Venusia. The roads from Rome were still notorious for robbers. Uncertainty bred crime.

Horace's farm was idyllic when he sought a backdrop for poetry, but it was in the nature of any idyll that somewhere, as Vergil had written, a snake lay hidden in the grass. Behind every tree lurked something unseen. His first poems from his farm were filled with trees, a dozen or more different kinds, oaks to olives, reminders of renewal but also of dead wood in their hidden rings. Fallen leaves were like the leaves on the fields of Troy, signs of year after year of death in war.

So a rotten tree in one of his fields one day, just missing him as it fell, became a sign of much more: it meant nature was striking back, the countryside kicking at the new man from the town, even Rome's rural origins reasserting themselves over what Rome had become. A narrow escape from death by crushing, as Horace saw it, became the foundation of a potent poem, beginning in gentle abuse of the tree itself (an ode more like one of his iambi) before becoming an opportunity for a poetic journey into Hades, a scream of rage and fear softened by the songs of poets of the past.

Ille et nefasto die, "It was a black day," Horace began his opening line, that day when whoever he was first planted you. As so often, he was lightly laughing at himself at first. *Navita Bosporum poenus perhorrescit,* "The sailor" from Carthage, Horace continued, "is afraid of the Bosphorus storms," the soldier fearful of Parthian arrows, but the worst dangers come from nowhere, from a heavy branch falling on a man's head. The poem contained nothing yet but familiarity — and a wry smile.

The tree fell safely, Horace revealed. He did not die. But the rest of the poem postulates that he had. He takes his readers, or anyone who might hear him reading, on a journey to the underworld. Down there in the depths of gloom Alcaeus was still singing of his hardships at sea. In Hades the lovelorn Sappho was still moaning at the behavior of her Lesbian girls. The crowd of the common dead listened only politely, since still, sad to say, they preferred poems of war.

Poetry, Horace sang out, in tentative, repetitive lines as though by an artist in a new form, was also the way to absorb anger, to undo damage done. From the land around his farm he was introducing his readers to the old Greek poets in the world below who were now his inspiration. Horace could contemplate both the afterlife and the poetic life that was his commitment in the living world.

Every past poet was different. Since his time in Athens, Horace had been absorbing both the spirit and the meters of Alcaeus – and he had plans for the future if fate and falling trees allowed. He was more nervous at attempting to match the passion of Sappho, even if he ever felt it: her meter alone would work for him. But however good the stories from Actium he would certainly never write a war story himself. A few seasick scenes were enough.

It was Varius who wrote of war, Vergil who was writing a giant epic of the fight for Trojan Aeneas to found Rome. Vergil had already written of a perilous journey to Hades in the fourth of his *Georgics,* and the power of the original three-headed monster, Cerberus, whose gaping dog jaws had to be calmed by song before the traveler could continue on his way. Horace saw this as a model he might follow. Poetry, not drugs, might calm the dogs of war and the dead.

Falling trees and every other danger of the countryside stood for dangers for the whole country. Behind every bright light there was darkness. *O fons Bandusiae,* "Bandusian spring," Horace began, addressing the pool of chill water, so welcome to travelers, that he used to pass as a child beside the Appian Way. This was the spring that watered herds, but in this poem it was *splendidior vitro,* "more glittering than glass," deserving of flowers and the finest wine, ready instead to receive the hot "crimson blood," *rubro sanguine,* of a young goat for sacrifice.

Springs were familiar subjects of Greek poetry, homes of the

Muses, places for farmers and poets alike. Horace the farmer had springs on his estate, but Horace the poet returned to Venusia for the name of this spring to which he boldly promised the immortality of his verse, using sound and meter to match the "waters leaping and babbling down" the rocks, *loquaces lymphae desiliunt.* In the fons Bandusiae his past met his present — and stretched into the only part of the future that for Horace had any meaning, the place where art survives.

> O fons Bandusiae, splendidior vitro,
> dulci digne mero non sine floribus,
> cras donaberis haedo,
> cui frons turgida cornibus
>
> primis et venerem et proelia destinat;
> frustra: nam gelidos inficiet tibi
> rubro sanguine rivos
> lascivi suboles gregis.
>
> O Bandusian spring, more glittering than glass,
> worthy of sweet wine and flowers,
> tomorrow you will be given a kid
> whose brow is ready for battle and love,
> all in vain, since this child of the lively herd
> will stain your cool waters with its crimson blood.

The young kid, its life about to be cut off before it could begin, is a reminder of what was so nearly Horace's own fate. Horace's poem would make permanent the sacrifice in that place where talking streams tumble down. Any summer pool might be a faithful reflector of a man's face, better than a glass in a mirrored room; but a poet could also see danger coming up behind him. Below the surface of his country life lay death and blood. Horace was a war veteran whose wars were not over.

Then in July, 30 BCE, came the news that all seekers for certainty had been waiting for. In Alexandria, so it was reported, Antony had made Octavian a deluded offer of single combat, as though both men were ancient Greek heroes at Troy. Cleopatra, in the more reasonable manner of a monarch, had tried to negotiate for her treasure, threatening to burn it and her children, suggesting that one or more of them might retain her royal rights as a client of Rome. Octavian had stayed at a distance, receiving the surrender of the self-interested and the suicide of Antony and Cleopatra themselves.

The dynasty of the Ptolemies in Egypt, the last survivors of the heirs to Alexander the Great, was over. The treasure survived. This was no longer a political crisis, only a political drama. Octavian ordered the execution of Caesarion, Cleopatra's son by Julius Caesar; Antyllus, Antony's heir by Fulvia; and their army commander, whose family lost its perpetual export rights. He arrayed a mass of regalia for his triumph, hoping to outdo Pompey if he could. He promised an older poet, Cornelius Gallus, the responsibility of governing Egypt, and returned, rather slowly his supporters thought, to Rome.

Nunc est bibendum, "Now we must drink," now is the time to drink! *Nunc pede libero pulsanda tellus*, "Now we can freely dance." The news of the death of Cleopatra answered the question which Horace had so recently posed to himself. It was at first a crude response.

Before Actium, Horace had wondered, *Quando repostum Caecubum bibam?* "When could he — and Maecenas — drink their best wine?" Now, after the suicides at Alexandria ten nervous months later, this was the time for everyone to drink and dance. The queen who had threatened Italy, *contaminato grege,* "with her dirty horde," was safely dead, forced to flee from her burning fleet like a dove before a hawk. The propaganda of the period before the final battle became rousing poetry for the people of Rome.

Vergil was soon describing a shield for his hero Aeneas in which Octavian stood high on his ship above foaming waves, light pouring from his eyes while Cleopatra, crushed, blind to the deadly snakes of her suicide, was attended by a god dog. Agrippa led the fleet over golden waves. Vergil had not needed to be at Actium to write what he did, no more than had Horace needed seasick danger to write his very different poem.

The difference was everything. Horace had sympathy for the loser. After the rousing rhetoric of his opening lines Horace's message switched from contempt to compassion, antagonism to admiration. A line and a half was enough. *Fatale monstrum; quae generosius / perire quaerens,* "Deadly monster; seeking nobly to die," she did not fear the sword as women do. Neither did she run away to secret shores. Instead she dared see her ruined power with peaceful face, to clasp fierce serpents to her veins, more ferocious in the death she chose than as a warrior, as though scorning to be led away in her enemy's ships no longer as a queen but *mulier triumpho,* a mere "woman in a triumph."

This understanding of the newly weak was recognizably now Horatian. It was the kind of political clemency that can go only to the humiliated, but its poetic clemency came from the mind of a man who knew about being down. For Horace it was also a new style of poetry, one of his first carmina, his odes, maybe the very first in the meter of his Greek lyric model Alcaeus; for Maecenas it was perfect.

———

When the Senate held its first meeting of 29 BCE Octavian was still away from Rome in the East. The men of the old Roman elite did not know how they should treat him. Nor did the new poets among Maecenas's friends. There was uncertainty about what sort of power he would take on his return. The senators restricted themselves to awarding lifetime titles to the victor (Octavian would forever have the supreme power of Imperator) and ordering the closure of the gates to the Temple of Janus, the traditional symbol that the city was at peace.

Maecenas met Octavian soon after his victorious friend was back in Italy. With Octavian at Atella, north of Naples, was not Horace but Vergil, the senior member of his circle of poets, who read to him from work in progress. The *Aeneid* was barely begun, and Vergil read from the *Georgics,* his four-part poem celebrating the glories of Italian culture, from soil to citizenry.

At the end of the first Georgic he looked back to the recent past, conjuring the molten rocks and Tiber floods that followed the murder of Julius Caesar. He dispatched Philippi to much more distant history, imagining future farmers on the battlefield with piles of excavated spears and helmets rusting into the land. Each in its own way marked the beginning of a new golden age in Vergil's eyes. Horace was somewhat less convinced, avoiding rather than embracing the idea, hopeful but less naive.

In Rome, Octavian bought time and popularity with cash and gladiator shows. He commissioned Varius to write a tragedy, *Thyestes,* for a festival to celebrate Actium and paid him a huge fee. He encouraged historians to see the glorious past of his family, just as Brutus's family had done. He ordered a new platform for speakers in the Forum to be made from the prows of ships, the *rostra,* captured at Actium. The Rostra built from previous great naval victories, once used by Cicero and Antony, were part of the past. Mythology was already being made in wood as well as words. There were plans for new myths in stone too. Almost complete was a magnificent temple to Apollo, a war god who loved the arts, a neighbor to the more modest house of Octavian himself on the Palatine Hill.

Details of the division of powers between the old and the new, the Forum and the Palatine, were rather less clear than the architectural symbols. Maecenas was *atavis edite regibus*, "born from ancestral kings," in the words with which Horace began the first of his *Odes*. But those kings, if they ever existed, were Etruscans, Lydians, migrants from Asia. Maecenas had no more stake in the old senatorial aristocracy than did Horace himself. He was said to favor an unapologetic display of Octavian's autocracy, the very outcome that the assassins of Caesar and the fighters at Philippi had failed to prevent.

Others argued for greater care. In whatever way the truth of power might develop, the story should be of restoration and renewal not of revolution. In 27 BCE, Octavian held the consulship with Agrippa and made a grand show of handing back all wartime emergency powers to the Roman Senate and people, the SPQR. Agrippa was celebrated in newly carved statues that had once held the head of Mark Antony. Octavian took new titles, most dramatically that of Augustus.

This was a name not seen before except in the early epic poetry of Rome, the kind that Horace had firmly set himself against. It was two hundred years since Ennius, Rome's writer of Roman history in robust verse, had described how famous Rome was founded with *augusto augurio*, "august augury," the certainty that the holy prophets were on the city's side. The move was slightly more subtle than Octavian calling himself Romulus, as some had advised, but not much. A great shield became a lexicon of the approved vocabulary, *iustitia, virtus, clementia, pietas*, "justice, virtue, clemency, piety," by which the new regime would be harmonized with the old.

For those who held offices alongside the new Augustus these were testing times. Were they supposed to behave as their predecessors had done, or was their independence pure pretense? After Philippi, Messalla had fought against Sextus in Sicily and also against the tribes of the southern Alps. He had fought in the propaganda war and the real war against Antony. He was experienced in the new age and was soon off to distant Syria, where the responsibilities of a Roman governor would not be so different from those in the past.

Cicero had been consul in 30, a job that was absolutely not what it had been when his father held it three decades before. Antony's poet son Jullus received clemency but no office. The assassin poet Cassius Parmensis received no clemency, only the arrival of an assassin from Rome at his Athens retirement house.

Maecenas may briefly have had ambitions for Horace to join the race for these offices whose powers were so ambiguous and risks so great. There were many poet-politicians whom he might join, Gallus in Cleopatra's palace at Alexandria being only the most prominent. Horace's now evident subtlety, the aggression of his iambi well behind him, might have usefully served the cause. He used his subtlety instead to evade all calls to service. If he were to serve it would be on terms of his own, using the poets he had read between leaving home and arriving at Philippi.

Alcaeus and Sappho, the singers in Hades, wrote songs in complex metrical patterns whose power was hard to unlock in Latin. That was Horace's aim. To be the first to bring these masterpieces into Latin was the art that he recognized as wholly his own, already taking root in his poet's farm, with its fountains of fresh water and its hills of sun and shade.

The life of Alcaeus, inseparable from the factional wars which were fought on the island of Lesbos around 600 BCE, was already the one with which Horace could identify more than with Sappho's. Alcaeus wrote about sex, war, and politics — and most of all about wine — as though he were a man of leisure, even though there was little leisure in his life. His meters were a means of imposing chains in order to fly free. And Alcaeus's work had lasted, still in rolls to be read, little imitated, challenging for any successor.

After an autumn of Actium and a summer of final victory Horace set out a winter scene. *Vides,* "See!" That was the ringing first word. As in every poem but in some louder than in others, Horace raised his voice and demanded his listeners' attention.

Vides ut alta stet nive candidum, "See how white it stands gleaming under the thick snow." The sight was the isolated peak of Mount Soracte, north of Rome. After *alta,* the fifth syllable, came a slight pause. That was the rule in the first line of the meter to which Alcaeus had left his name.

And the same rule applies in the second line. *Soracte nec iam sustineant onus,* "Nor can any longer they bear the weight." They? The pause fell again after the fifth sound, then came a long syllable and two short, a long, a short, and a long.

And then to the shorter third line, the core of the four-line stanza that Alcaeus had bequeathed to any who dared be his imitators, the answer to those who could not bear the load, *silvae laborantes geluque,* "the struggling woods and the ice." There was no pause in this third line, only a stately slowing before the fourth, *flumina constiterint acuto,* "how the rivers have stopped in their flow," again with no pause and the sound of words like a current running back.

Horace extended the winter scene in two more stanzas, inviting the boy who was Master of the Party to dissolve the cold with wood on the fire, uncork some good local wine, and let the gods look after the world outside. And then came the third stanza and the point. To drink while contemplating Mount Soracte was to grasp the present as the rarest luxury while knowing how brief that present was.

Quid sit futurum cras, "What will come tomorrow?" Another pause, then *fuge quaerere et,* "beware of asking." Beware of asking what tomorrow will bring and *quem fors dierum,* "what will be the fortune of your days." Just be grateful *cumque dabit lucro,* "and put everything down as a profit."

In the third line, with no pause according to the Alcaic rule, came the slow switch—from philosophy to pleasure. *Nec dulcis amores sperne,* "Don't set aside sweet love affairs." And in the fourth came the pressing of the point to the "boy" with the wine cups. *Puer neque tu choreas,* "Don't turn down parties while you're young."

The fifth stanza set out the sorts of places where whispering lovers might meet. These places were all in the city, far from the wintry slopes of Mount Soracte, but nowhere specific until the startling scene that came as his sixth stanza and last, a boy in pursuit of a girl.

For "now," he wrote, a noise is the "betrayer" of their "secret place," *nunc et latentis proditor,"* the "welcome laughter of the girl in her corner," followed by a teasing struggle, *intimo gratus puellae risus ab angulo,* "a token seized from her arms," *pignus dereptum lacertis,* "or from her hardly reluctant finger," *aut digito male pertinaci.*

After *Vides* and that first raising of the voice, the essence of the poem was its sound, the stresses that the words would bear in ordinary conversation and then their linking in the new tight chains of verse. Horace's choices were between forms but even more between the failures of first efforts in a peculiarly difficult task. Every arrangement heightened the sense of the place, the familiar party philosophizing, the vivid assignation with the girl in the last words, hardly reluctant, *male pertinaci*.

To his listeners and readers this did not sound natural. It was not even exactly like the Greek of Alcaeus. It was poignant, stately, like nothing they had ever seen or heard.

CHAPTER ELEVEN

Treacherous Ground

While Horace was tightening his control over the meters of ancient Greek, Maecenas and Agrippa were managing Augustus's grip on Rome. Agrippa had the authority of a military victor, a route to respect that had been long understood. Maecenas was more of a novelty, not a soldier or an orator, his descent from Etruscan kings irrelevant, except to Horace, his power only that he acted in the name of the man who was now Rome's king for every purpose that mattered.

The Senate was purged of Antony's supporters. Both Agrippa and Augustus wore bronze breastplates under their togas for the first day of the new lists. Triumphs were awarded, the traditional parades through the streets by which generals had long displayed their achievements and measured their support. When Messalla led his Gallic prisoners along the Sacred Way it was to confirm his final rehabilitation after Philippi. Marcus Licinius Crassus, the grandson of Julius Caesar's banker, had fought for Sextus and for Antony but was allowed his day of triumph for his victories in Thrace. Lollius, supreme survivor, was about to be governor of Galatia, from where, with the backing of the new regime, he might move even higher.

Augustus prized loyalty and the service of those who knew their place. He was planning new military expeditions to ensure the security of Spain and Gaul. Senators, even those newly confirmed for loyalty, were not allowed to leave Italy without his permission. Young Crassus, whose notoriously rich grandfather had died seeking a triumph in Parthia, wanted an additional honor for having personally killed an enemy king. This was denied. Augustus would never be able to claim such an achievement himself, and exceeding Augustus was not to be allowed.

Horace was no more than an observer, more confident than before the victory at Alexandria but knowing that caution was still appropriate. The new politics was like a magic trick in which reality had changed, but everything was supposed to look the same. Augustus was exercising dictatorial power without risking the opprobrium of being a dictator. The plan might work. Or it might not.

Thanks to Maecenas Horace was among the few who also knew that during these readjustments to the rule of Rome, Augustus had again fallen ill, maybe seriously ill. Illnesses of Augustus were ever more serious now for the empire. The man who had missed the First Battle of Philippi as an invalid behind the lines now missed the elaborate games to celebrate the victories of Alexandria and Actium. Horace's friend Varius had earned a fortune far exceeding a small farm for his verse play to mark the occasion. But when the mythical king Atreus was preparing a pie filled with flesh of his brother Thyestes' children — and looking forward to the father taking the first bite — Augustus was not in the theater. For this ancient warning of the evils of civil war, revived for the new Rome, the son of the Divine Julius Caesar was in bed.

There was no safety from infection in his house on the Palatine

Hill. The lower-lying Subura, across the Forum, might be more dangerous, but everywhere the water and air of Rome were fierce on the frail. Augustus was physically weak and still had enemies. There was the risk of his joining his heavenly father well before Rome achieved the stability that Julius Caesar had helped destroy. Maecenas had authority to order the execution of anyone with ambitions to speed this progress to the gods — and he used it. His targets included Marcus Lepidus, the son of the Lepidus who was Octavian and Antony's now almost forgotten ally in the time of the proscriptions.

Horace looked backward in his own anxiety. *Motum ex Metello consule,* begun "when Metellus was consul": thus he opened a poem addressed to Pollio, the literary general who was embarking on a history of the civil wars starting in 60 BCE. That was the year of Horace's fifth birthday, when Metellus's formal consulship meant less than his absence from the informal Three-Headed Monster alliance of Crassus, Pompey, and Caesar. Horace's message to Pollio was *incedis per ignes suppositos cineri doloso,* "you are treading over fires hidden beneath treacherous ash" — *doloso,* "treacherous," the fall of the stanza's final word. The volcano could erupt again at any time.

Horace liked every year at his farm to mark with a party his escape from the falling tree. He did not want to sound too serious; who likes going to a serious party? But he chose the day when Romans celebrated their married women, decorated his villa with flowers from his garden, and did have serious things to say.

He gave Maecenas an answer to some comic questions that his distinguished guest might ask when he arrived: "What is a bachelor like me doing on Mothers' Day?" *Martiis caelebs quid agam Kalendis* and "why the flowers?" *Quid velint flores.* The answer was the need to remember, in some appropriate party way, how close to death he had come, not on a battlefield but in his own fields, "almost done for by a blow from a branch," *prope funeratus arboris ictu.* He imagined Maecenas smiling. This was an intimate poem, a memory of gentle joking between poet and patron.

This party at his farm was Horace's version of the Matronalia festival for married women, which may have been another bit of levity. Had he ever told Maecenas about his mother? Unlike his father, she had not appeared in the bachelor poet's work so far. None of Horace's women were *matronae.* His friends might joke at the numbers of girls – and boys – who came through the rooms of his farm. There were no girls in this latest poetic scene. His party was to celebrate an escape from rotten wood. The missing ladies simply offered a vivid way to begin it, to invoke what friends would say when arriving: What's going on here and what are all these flowers in aid of?

Once the dead tree story was over, the main point of the poem arrived: how to avoid the stresses of the time, how much wine was needed to suit the seriousness of his own near disaster, and how Maecenas needed to relax, to think about his own writings in Greek and Latin, stop worrying about the Parthians (always squabbling with each other), the Spaniards (now finally crushed), and the poor of Rome (always with us). The key was to note that death could come from anywhere – to Augustus, to anyone. Maecenas should escape into the moment, the only certainty there was. *Dona praesentis cape,* "Seize the gift of the present."

Escape was a widening theme for Horace. The story of the tree had become his latest memorable deliverance. It might not have been much in itself, but it was part of his story. A brush with death was certainly something to celebrate. Escape was a part of what he was.

Looking back at his life, he had escaped from home by being a good student, by being worth the expense of a Roman education, by burying himself in words from the past. He had escaped from his libraries by following Brutus as an officer in an army. He had then escaped from Philippi by means that his mind barely now comprehended, by luck, by methods and madness now forgotten, in clouds of dust and dreams, by deals and pardons, distinctions barely made and hard to disentangle.

Back in Rome he had escaped the slums of the Subura, where witches tortured children and old women taunted his sexuality. He had wrapped his rage within the sounds and subjects of poetry made respectable by the Greeks. His poetry made possible his escape to Maecenas. The journey to Brundisium was his greatest flight to freedom since Philippi. His escape from a falling tree was as nothing compared to his past, but it stood for much of what had gone before. In celebrating his good fortune on his own farm he was marking all his fortunes.

Horace also wrote a poem about a different escape. Its recipient was Marcus Aristius Fuscus, the friend who had once so lamentably failed to protect him from the hanger-on seeking favor in the Forum. He and Fuscus had a bantering past together; Fuscus had on that occasion made feeble jokes when Horace had wanted firm help. Fuscus now received some light self-mockery, twenty-four lines in Sappho's meter that sounded at the start as though Horace were now the bore himself.

"A man of upright life and pure of sin," he wrote without obvious irony, *Integer vitae scelerisque purus,* needs no defense when he goes out into the wild world. "He needs no Moorish javelins or bow and quiver filled with poisoned arrows, Fuscus," *non eget Mauris iaculis neque arcu nec venenatis gravida sagittis, Fusce, pharetra.* What was this about? Doubtless to Fuscus's surprise, Horace was claiming to be just such a virtuous man himself.

Why? Because when he was out walking beyond the boundaries of his farm, singing quietly about Lalage, his latest love, he was confronted by a wolf, not just any wolf but a monster, "such a prodigy as neither the forests of warlike Daunus nor Juba's land would ever rear," *quale portentum neque militaris Daunias latis alit aesculetis nec Iubae tellus.*

So then what happened? This beast was bigger than any from around his southern homeland under the rule of the mythical Daunus – or from the Africa of the current king, Juba, recently restored by Augustus. Yet this mighty wolf turned away from him and fled – even though he was distracted and unarmed. Let Fuscus not forget that Horace was, indeed, a protected species. The Muses would somehow always save him wherever he went. He did not even need to be virtuous. Love itself was enough, as he explained to Fuscus in four final lines of escapism, well worthy of Sappho's meter, words that any rival poet might with reluctance have praised.

> pone sub curru nimium propinqui
> solis in terra domibus negata
> dulce ridentem Lalagen amabo
> dulce loquentem.

> Put me beneath the chariot of the sun when it's too near
> In a land denied to human homes
> And still I will love my sweetly laughing Lalage
> Love her sweetly talking.

This was Sappho in perfect Latin.

The second of Horace's poets imagined in the underworld already had a much greater status in Rome than Alcaeus. She was famed for her love poetry, especially the love of young women for each other, and was talked of as the tenth Muse, the fittest human companion to the nine Muses believed to live on Mount Olympus.

She was a pioneer in describing the physical sensations of jealousy—the agony when she saw a man with her lover, her broken tongue, fiery skin, buzzing ears, and blindness. This kind of poetry, far from sport and war, was unique to Sappho. A century before Empedocles died in a volcano's flames, she was seen as a pioneer poet on a volcano, a volatile artist with her own kind of mania, seeking her own kind of perfection in art and life and, on failing, hurling herself to her death.

Facts about her were scarce and unimportant, just as for Empedocles, but she already had a story: her arrival in Sicily from Lesbos at the end of the seventh century BCE as a refugee from the same civil wars that had exiled Alcaeus, her descriptions of the despairs of love, her clifftop suicide. Some of her poems had come to Rome before: Catullus, Clodia's lover and aristocratic critic of Julius Caesar, had produced what was almost a translation. Horace, however, was less interested in translating what Sappho said (in his view, high passion was to be controlled, not communicated or encouraged) than in using how she said it. Sappho's favorite meter, identifiable even to the unscholarly by its lilting third line running uninterrupted into a short fourth line, was becoming a favorite.

For Horace's party invitation to Maecenas these short fourth lines fixed the poem's important points, first *arboris ictu*, "by the fall of a tree," then *consule Tullo*, "when Tullus was consul," closing the third stanza with the vital vintage of the wine, 33 BCE, then *clamor et ira*, "riot and rage," what they were supposed to be escaping. The date, 33, was one that mattered and merited the place the meter made for it. This was not an old wine; it was first poured into its two-eared jar in the year Horace received his farm. His life was laid out in indelible dates, 60, when Metellus was consul; 44, when Caesar was killed; 42, the horrors of Philippi; and finally 33, when some sort of countryside peace returned.

Horace also used Sapphics for sexual subjects, a taunting of an old woman who had once rejected him, whose lovers "did not so often now rattle her window bars," *Parcius iunctas quatiunt fenestras.* Less and less did she hear the plaintive words, "Lydia, are you asleep?" *Lydia dormis?* Those were again the last two words that closed the Sapphic stanza in a way Horace loved – the backward pull, the closing of the thought. This was a return to the stories of older women that he had told in his first poems written in Rome after Philippi. But the tone was calmer, the art greater, the vivid detail of a street with its once attractive prostitute, the language that recalled a sexual life lost, *iunctas,* "joined," but now only as a closed window was joined.

His new poems, even a party invitation, were the art of his own life. When he looked into his mirrors, he saw many new faces of himself. He was a changed man from the one who had once, perhaps twice, lost nearly everything. But among the possibilities that were new were still the shadows of his past. Politics was not his priority, but neither was Rome secure. In Athens, Horace had opened papyrus rolls and read poems by Sappho, whose themes extended well beyond the rage of sexual feelings – to hymns to gods, to anxieties about the safety of her brother. On his Sabine farm he used her meter to show both sexual insecurities and his public anxiety.

"Now enough!" *Iam satis!* The *Iam* was almost a shout. Enough was enough! "The father of the gods has sent down enough grim snow and hail," *Iam satis terris nivis atque dirae grandinis misit pater.* Horace was addressing, at what would be unusual length, the necessity of calm political weather and of the only father who could deliver it. Again each stanza bequeathed by Sappho ended with a banging home of his theme in its shortest line, "the city's terror, the temples of the hearth-goddess Vesta, the songs to Vesta, the need for the prophet Apollo," in the first stanza, *terruit urbem;* in the fourth, *templaque Vestae;* in the seventh, *carmina Vestam;* in the eighth, *augur Apollo.*

Until there came the twist. Maybe there was a divine savior already in Rome, Mercury disguised as a young man, "Caesar's avenger," *Caesaris ultor.* And then there came two more stanzas and the final Sapphic closure, "while you Caesar are our leader," *te duce Caesar.* With those three words, in his favorite form, Horace set an end to the second phase of his life, the first the period from Venusia to Philippi, this second from Philippi to his farm in the Roman hills and his place in a new regime.

There was a sense of transition here — and this poem, by his new standards, was not a work of perfection. It was long, perhaps unnecessarily long. It was filled with echoes of Vergil, almost homages.

Rome's savior, Horace wrote, should pass to heaven only after curing the ills of the city. That was probably a safe statement to make — or at least as safe as such a near prayer ever could be. Disguising Mercury as Augustus was bold but still a bit clumsy. Augustus as the god whom Horace had made his rescuer at Philippi? Augustus as any god? It was not clear in what way Augustus would allow either or none.

In some places Mercury's silver statues were already disappearing, melted down to make more splendor for the Temple of Apollo. Agrippa's new temple would be named the Pantheon, a place for all the gods. In Egypt the poet Cornelius Gallus, a literary governor of the kind Horace never wanted to be, was thought to have too greatly enjoyed being worshipped in the traditional Egyptian way. Suicide was Gallus's way out of enjoying something that Augustus might have enjoyed — or might not.

Certainty for officials was no more easily found than for a poet. In the same year, 26 BCE, Messalla took the job of city prefect, in charge of policing Rome and enforcing civil obedience. The survivor of Philippi who had governed a province and won a faraway triumph became quickly less certain of his place close to home. He gave it up after only six days. He was not sure where his power began and ended – and what his responsibilities were supposed to be.

Young Cicero was now in Syria in Messalla's place, able to mint his own coins. He was still no sort of writer but was gaining an image of himself in silver that his father never achieved. Messalla himself, it was rumored, remained a republican at heart, organizing dinners at which men read aloud poems attacking proscriptions and praising the older Cicero – and Brutus too. He was creating his own circle of poets, which included Albius Tibullus, a writer of elegant love elegies with no political themes of any kind. Horace knew Tibullus. He joshingly suggested Tibullus abandon his miserable moanings about his mistress and follow Horace's way. Did he want to write like the long-winded assassin of Caesar, Cassius Parmensis? Surely not. But maybe Tibullus did – and maybe politically, not just as a poet.

On his farm Horace was secure as long as Maecenas and Augustus were secure. He was able to rebuff attempts to bring him closer to town while being at the same time wholly dependent on the town. As a country mouse he was safe. In his room of mirrors he could see his many faces, the many shapes that a body can be when a man is staring into bronze. He was not the only Roman with such a room, a place to make his stomach smaller, his head higher, his skin clearer. Partners for sex could come and go, girls and boys by their thousands, he suggested with a poet's boast: slaves (ideally other people's slaves), freed women, professional women, maybe even wives, though preferably not.

The best place was a place for dreams. Reality was the blood of war and the mud of town and country. He was never a fighter or a farmer or a man of fashion. He had put the mud of life behind him – or hoped he had. His future identity would be formed by working together as a poet with present and past, with Maecenas now, with Brutus in the near past, with Alcaeus and Sappho in the past that seemed less distant than once it had been.

Horace had a healthy accord with Maecenas. He needed peace with the spirit of Brutus and those who had fought with him. He sought the immediacy of Sappho, who had thrown herself off a cliff when the pain of love and rejection was beyond bearing. He had his pleasures and his demons, but they were linked to a solid sense that the future was for balancing the two, keeping both in due proportion, as the philosophers taught, which was always so hard to achieve.

CHAPTER TWELVE

Odes and Eels

In the middle of Horace's journey to Brundisium, ten years earlier, Maecenas and his entourage had spent the night at the house of Lucius Licinius Murena, a relation of Maecenas's wife, Terentia. There had been a friendly distribution of the duty to entertain the diplomatic party, Murena providing the beds and Fonteius Capito, Antony's man, serving the dinner. It was the last stop before the poets Vergil and Varius joined the expedition, a night followed by a "most welcome" morning, *gratissima,* as Horace recalled.

Another member of the same well-connected family, Aulus Terentius Varro Murena, was now providing more than beds for the night along the Appian Way. He had a career in politics, and he wanted it to stretch ahead, however uncertain the road. He was one of many aristocratic sons whose advancement, once won in foreign battles and Forum debates, now hung on the whim of the victor at Actium.

Seen from the wings by a would-be star, the new stage was full of corpses and men who were only shakily standing. A leading family member of the previous generation, the elder Lucius Lucinius Murena, had needed the finest rhetoric of Cicero to fend off charges of electoral corruption in the consulship elections for 62 and, worse in some eyes, of being a dancer. "Hardly anyone dances when he is sober, unless he is insane," Cicero had airily told the jury. Members of the new generation would now gain preferment, whatever their style of life, not by oratory or entertainment, but only if it suited Augustus that they should.

The name Murena meant a sharp-toothed eel. It did Aulus Murena's hopes no harm that he had a family link to Terentia, whom Horace praised (perhaps a bit too personally) for her sparkling eyes. Terentia was close to Augustus as well. Some said that she was as close to Augustus as to Maecenas himself, sharing Augustus's bed when required. As Antony had pointed out in his propaganda battle before Actium, the club of every Tertulla, Terentilla, or Titisenia in town was not a hard club to join. But Aulus Murena was certainly in the inner political circle in a way that Horace was not — and never could be. He knew what was going on — and also that he might be part of it.

After the triumph at Actium everyone looking to the future kept a close eye on Agrippa. While Maecenas was an adviser and enforcer who wanted to be little more than that, Agrippa was both Augustus's military commander and the rebuilder of Rome. While Maecenas had cleansed the slums of the Subura, Agrippa was extending the temples, bathhouses, and markets into the vast empty spaces in the Campus Martius behind the Capitoline Hill.

Maecenas was an aesthete who wrote bad poetry but bought up great poets. Agrippa was a man of action who wrote books of geography, bought up architects, and was happy to criticize Maecenas's poets when he thought their style too fancy. Thanks to Agrippa there would soon be roofs on a hall for voting in elections: if the people's votes mattered less than they had in the past, they could, at least, be cast in the shade.

The magnificent new Pantheon would have new parks and baths for its neighbors. Marble was assembled as though it were a critical war material. The mudbrick Rome to which Horace had returned after Philippi was disappearing fast. The man responsible might even become Augustus's successor, the ambitious might think. That succession might even be soon.

To Aulus Murena, or to anyone in his family looking forward, this was no idle thought. Augustus's frailties were known to all who were close to him or who knew someone close. He was away at war in Spain—and seemed likely to remain in the dangerous role that had won him power. On foreign battlefields no one was safe. Augustus was advancing his few close descendants into traditional positions of power, but he and his current wife, Livia, had no children of their own, and the idea of a dynasty was as alien as the elevation of a king.

Horace was no Murena. He was not looking ambitiously into the future. By contrast, he had only one thought about Agrippa—that he did not want to write about him. "You will be written about by Varius," *Scriberis Vario,* was how he began the sixth of the odes that he was putting in order for his next publication. *Scriberis Vario fortis et hostium victor:* Varius is your poet, "you mighty victor over our enemies." There was some ambiguity here over whether being a mighty victor was a mighty good: Augustus might want the victory wholly for himself now that someone else had won it. There was no ambiguity about Horace's literary view, borrowed from Callimachus of Alexandria, that any big book of warfare was a bad thing.

The meter that Horace chose for this poem—based on the pattern long short short long—was named after the Greek erotic poet Asclepiades, a writer much favored by the Egyptian Ptolemies, whose rule had come to an end with Cleopatra. But there was little erotic about the Agrippa poem, not until the very end. Meter was yet again not a guide to a poem's subject but a cage for Horace's poetic discipline, not a set of rules as in a prison but a means of concentrating force. He was already planning an opening sequence of nine poems, each in a different Greek meter, a parade of his versatility. This variant of how Asclepiades had written his verse was one of many he had to master – and to show his mastery to the few who would recognize and admire it.

Nos Agrippa, "I, Agrippa," he began the second stanza, the first-person plural, *nos*, able to stand in Latin for *ego*, the singular. *Neque haec dicere nec gravem Pelidae stomachum*, "I can't speak of the things that you do any more than I can speak of the anger of Peleus's son Achilles," or any other epic themes too grand for me. This was the convenient modesty that Horace was beginning to make his own. If Agrippa was expecting any more praise of himself from Horace he was clearly going to be disappointed.

But equally, if Varius was expecting more detailed reasons from Horace why this glorious commission, maybe as profitable as his Actium tragedy, should come his way, he too would be disappointed. Varius was a fellow veteran of the journey to Brundisium, a friend, a respectable writer of official plays, but perhaps not a very admired fellow poet.

The rest of the poem was wholly about that first word of the second stanza, *Nos*, "I," about Horace himself and why he was not fit for this sort of military task. His preference was for battles fought against men by "cruel girls with their nails sharpened," *sectis in iuvenes unguibus*. Let Varius write about how Agrippa had saved Rome by saving Augustus in his battles against Antony and the son of Pompey. Varius was welcome to these risky subjects, which were useless for the poet that Horace saw himself to be.

——

While others might be looking to their futures, Horace was concerned with adjustments to the past. The return to Rome of his friend Pompeius, a fellow survivor of Philippi, gave him a good opportunity to confront demons still lingering from those days. Pompeius was not a grandee like Messalla; he was one of Horace's mates. The difference between Horace and Pompeius was that while Horace had somehow escaped immediately in the direction of Rome, Pompeius had been sucked back into the continuing conflict, fighting for Sextus in Sicily, losing again, before eventually finding himself back in the city transformed by their war.

"O often with me," *O saepe mecum,* Horace began his poem inviting Pompeius to a reunion dinner at his farm. The two men were not just chance acquaintances. They had been through hell together, *tempus in ultimum,* "into deepest danger," the first line fell to its end.

How were they going to deal with subject of Brutus? The now dangerous name came at the start of the second line: *deducte Bruto,* "led out by Brutus." Or was that led down and astray? At the end of the line followed *militiae duce,* "leader of our army." *Duce* was particularly difficult. When Horace had ended his poem that cried out for peace, "Iam satis" (Enough is enough!), the words *te duce* stood for Augustus, the man whom Brutus had wanted to destroy.

This new poem to Pompeius was a gentler work, a call to reminisce, to remember the wine of lazy days waiting for the war to happen, the laurel leaves that had perfumed other parties. Together they had collected their scents in Syria along the way, and the luxuries of Antioch had made bearable the battlefield.

"Philippi with you," *Tecum Philippos,* the second dangerous name began the third stanza, followed immediately by what happened on that fateful second day of battle. "Rapid flight," *celerem fugam sensi*, "I experienced." Then "I dropped my shield, not a good thing," and ran: *relicta non bene parmula.*

Horace was making poetry from a poem by Archilochus that he knew, that some of his readers knew, and that he knew they knew. He was welding it to his own memory and that of his friend, maneuvering his way past the political obstacles of his time but not being silent about his past.

He re-created the Philippi scene, "when menacing men touched their chins to the ground," *minaces turpe solum tetigere mento.* Horace's poetic account of that day was in one way almost lighthearted, a memory of men biting the dust; but in another way it was dust he could still taste. He had no idea how he had escaped himself: he was out of his mind, as if a god had whisked him away, as though they were all in that epic war at Troy. His friend's fate had been more prosaic, the sucking waves of real seas that had brought him to fight again.

Whatever the truth of their shared past, his invitation was to put that past—at least briefly—out of their minds. Pompeius should join him *sub lauru mea,* "under my own laurel tree," where they could fill cups with wine and seashells with scent. Whatever their shortcomings as soldiers, or as pickers of winning sides, they had both been men of wine. Horace could already imagine the scene of their reunion, the calls to bring on the bacchanale, to bring out the best, *oblivioso massico,* the "wine that obliterated."

Pompeius might want to share Horace's room of mirrors, to take all the pleasures of his house. There were many ways for a man to see himself, his past and future and, most of all, his present. Pompeius might decide to abandon his loyalty to Brutus or merely push it to the back of his mind. He might or might not have political ambitions like Messalla and others from the defeated side at

Philippi. Whatever the future might hold, Horace was going to welcome him now to his own new world.

What Pompeius had seen at the Battle of Naulochus in 36 BCE was not as well known as the story of Actium. It was less in Augustus's interest to promote its memory, harder to present Pompey's popular son Sextus as a foreign foe. Naulochus was a rehearsal for Actium, militarily if not for poets, and Augustus had wanted to concentrate on what, from his perspective, was the real thing. For Pompeius the details of his defeat were six years in the past before he needed to share them with Horace. But in outline they were still clear enough.

Agrippa had prepared meticulously before the fighting began. Sextus, once ruler of all Sicily, had been unable to follow up his successes, which had so often embarrassed Octavian before, and had been left controlling no more than the beaches opposite his huge fleet. Commanding in his blue coat of Neptune, he had then either to risk a sea battle between a thousand ships on the island's northeast coast or give up his headquarters and his hopes.

For Octavian, there had been a different risk. Antony would have quickly taken advantage of any failure. Antony and Sextus could have been allies as Octavian, son of Caesar, and Sextus, son of Pompey, could not. This was a battle story as significant as any in these wars.

Octavian had Agrippa's heavy ships and their weapons of grappling hook and gangplank combined, the *harpax* and the *corvus*. But these were little tried. Sextus was master of the older naval arts, the darting triremes that slid behind an enemy's line and dipped their prows beneath the waves to crush and destroy.

Each man had taken his risk. New prayers to the gods rose to the sky in the smoke of sacrifice. Such a battle did not happen by accident. The auguries had to be right — for both sides. It had to be planned, its timing, if not the tactics, all agreed in advance. It might have been a war of darting through wind and wave or one of grinding hulls. The early moves were the key.

Sextus's sea god was against him. When each side formed in a long line, from the shore side out into the waveless waters of the bay, Agrippa's tactic of harpax and corvus had been devastating. Pompeius and his fellow sailors, whenever they successfully came up behind Octavian's ships, faced downward fire from a catapult launching long iron harpax hooks. Hundreds of them, Romans and freed slaves alike, were reeled in like the local tunnyfish.

Agrippa's soldiers stormed over the gangplanks as he stretched his line and came around and behind, a classic military tactic for Roman armies on land. Sextus's ships were driven toward the shore, where their maneuverability and speed meant nothing, where the battleground was an undulating floor of wood. At the end of that September day in 36 BCE, Sextus had only seventeen ships able to flee.

Naulochus Bay, never less justifying its Greek name, Ship-shelterer, was strewn with smashed hulls and small boats seeking survivors worth a ransom. Pompey's son had gone even before the sea was clear. With him went Cassius Parmensis, the poet assassin. Pompeius, who might have been treated as a relative of his commander (even if he was not), was one of the luckiest survivors of the last battle for Caesar's killers and those who supported their ideals.

Horace himself had long since reduced the battles between Octavian and Sextus to a complaint about uppity ex-slaves who made Roman sacrifice pointless: war, war, what were they fighting for? After the decisive verdict at Naulochus, careless of his own slave-tinged status in the eyes of rivals and critics, he had enjoyed a party with Maecenas and put it in a poem.

Octavian had put Naulochus behind him too — even more quickly. He had paused for no official celebration, brutally avenging what he saw as mere slights to his authority, deporting hundreds of men, returning slaves to prison fields powered by slavery. Slaves without owners were impaled to discourage future insurrection: death on the stake might, depending on the skill and intent of the executioner, take a day or more. When Horace wrote his poem to Pompeius, his old friend was back from a long exile after horrors as searing as Philippi.

Eleven years on from the defeat of Sextus, six years on from Actium, Augustus was back from his war in Spain, battered in body and an even greater anxiety to his supporters. There was talk of raising him to a new role that would put him above the laws of Rome, but, unlike Julius Caesar, he did not need or want such protection. Instead, he wanted protection for his new form of government after what had seemed to be his imminent death.

Marrying his only daughter to his sister's teenage son Marcellus was unlikely to be sufficient to secure that. Rome was not ready for a young ruler of its empire. Agrippa was discontented that his own service had gained too little reward. Senators were nervous about the early advancement of Livia's sons Tiberius and Drusus. Anxiety spread beyond the circles where Horace played his part and out into the city streets. A cash handout bought time — but it was unclear how much.

Horace had opportunities to observe the government closely. He had what seemed to be a standing invitation to spend time on the Palatine. He would be welcome, Augustus wrote, just as if he had accepted that secretarial job offer — though Horace, like many recipients of such letters from the great, might have reasonably wondered how welcome he would genuinely have been. He was completing three books of the carmina, his odes, which, to new readers, would be so different from what he had published before.

These new poems were self-portraits, not portraits of others, whether the great or not. Some were extraordinary responses to present life and past art, a distinction that Horace tried to blur as much as he could. Would buyers like them? Surely no one who read his poem to Pyrrha, slim, fair, slave girl or ex-slave (who could say?), could fail to appreciate what he had achieved. It began with a question that in his best teasing way needed no answer.

Quis multa gracilis te puer in rosa, "Which slender boy on a pile of rose petals is pressing himself upon you now?" *Cui flavam religas comam,* "For whom do you tie back your blond hair, you who are *simplex munditiis,* "simple in your elegance"? How often will he who enjoys you weep with disillusion!

> heu quoties fidem
> mutatosque deos flebit et aspera
> nigris aequora ventis
> emirabitur insolens
>
> qui nunc te fruitur credulus aurea,
> qui semper vacuam, semper amabilem,
> sperat, nescius aurae
> fallacis.
>
> Alas, how often will he weep at your faithless ways
> and the changing gods and wonder
> at seas rough with black winds and storms,
> all innocent as he is,
>
> he who now too trusting enjoys his golden times,
> who hopes you will be always be open to be loved,
> ignorant of the treacherous wind.

The sound matched the sense. This Pyrrha, whoever she was or was not, changed her partners as the weather changed over water. He himself had weathered the storm and to prove it had hung up his sailors' clothes in an offering to the great god of the sea. The pattern of the words was perfect, *credulus, nescius, fallacis,* "too trusting, too little knowing the truth," unlike anything in Latin before. The poet appeared to be in the story (Horace was a far from slender rival) and then, in another view, not there, in a poetic fantasy of sex and flowers. Horace placed this as the fifth in his opening parade.

In 23 BCE, when Horace was putting the last touches to his *Odes,* Lucius Sestius, a wealthy winemaker's heir, once a minter of coins for Brutus, and a survivor of Philippi, became consul. It was a special consulship, for the second half of the year in which Augustus had held the first half. This was the first time that Augustus had not been consul since the defeat of Antony and Cleopatra.

The move was formally to show the return to normal politics. Sestius had never given up his reverence for Brutus and kept a bust of his former commander in his house to prove it. But Sestius was equally no threat. His life in politics, beginning with his boyhood appearance in court on behalf of his father, had left him more contemplative than active, something of an Epicurean, no sort of rival, a reassurance to those around Augustus who surveyed the fragile stability of the empire.

It was a time of plague. For months it had seemed again that Augustus might die. His sickness in his fortieth year was more serious than his many sicknesses of the past. His sister's son Marcellus, newly married to his only daughter, Julia, was no longer even a thread on which a dynasty might hang. Marcellus was already dead. Throughout the spring and early summer Agrippa had held the signet with which Augustus sealed his letters. When Horace wrote his poem to *beate Sesti,* "blessed Sestius," his old friend from a faraway battlefield, he began with the beautiful familiarity of springtime, seasonal symbol of peace, before descending into a terror that was universal, stalking every time and season.

Solvitur: the first word is the key word, the relaxing of a hold. *Solvitur acris hiems,* "It is a harsh winter that is setting the land free," the welcome west wind is back, and the rollers can run the dry ships back to the sea. *Iam,* "Now," the goddess of love is leading out the dancers under the low-hanging moon. *Nunc decet,* "Now it is right to wreathe" heads with the new greenery, *nunc et,* "and now" right to sacrifice to the god of the flocks. *Nunc, nunc,* just like *Nunc est bibendum,* in a happier time, when it was right to drink to the death of Cleopatra.

The repetition of "now" was a reminder of the only time that was ever present. *Pallida mors,* "Pale death," he reminded Sestius, finally mentioning his name, stalks the hovels of the poor and the turrets of the rich with the same tread. *Vitae summa brevis,* "The very shortness of life" forbids us from starting distant hopes. *Iam te,* "Now" night will crush "you" down in the place of which many tales are told but from which there is no return.

Then came Horace's last words of hope. There will be no return, *beate Sesti,* to the world where you admire beautiful Lycidas, that boy for whom *nunc omnis,* "now all the young men," have a passion and soon the girls will lust for too. The underworld is forever. Meanwhile there was the real world where Horace was living in 23 BCE, his farm, its trees, springs, and mirrored room, the parties where Sestius was welcome to join him and where fears of death and for the state were as far away as they could possibly be.

pallida mors aequo pulsat pede pauperum tabernas
regumque turres. O beate Sesti,

vitae summa brevis spem nos vetat inchoare longam.

iam te premet nox fabulaeque Manes

et domus exilis Plutonia: quo simul mearis,

nec regna vini sortiere talis

nec tenerum Lycidan mirabere, quo calet iuventus

nunc omnis et mox virgines tepebunt.

Pale death beats with the same foot on the hovels of the poor

as on the towers of kings. O blessed Sestius,

the very shortness of life forbids us to begin long hopes.

Soon night, the fabled spirits of the dead

and the cheerless house of Pluto will press upon you.

Once you get there, neither shall you draw lots

for the rule of the wine jar nor wonder

at tender Lycidas, the boy for whom all the young men

are now hot and soon maidens will warm.

This was the fourth poem in the first book that Horace was about to release to his readers, part of his opening parade of virtuosity in Greek meters, one once used by Archilochus. It was not a poem which any reader, sensitive to meter or not, would easily miss.

One short poem in the second book, about the virtues of moderation, seemed particularly suitable for a friend from the family named after a killer eel. *Rectius vives, Licini,* "You will live rightly, Licinius," it began, if you steer a middle course in life, avoiding both the wide-open sea and, in the emphatic last line of his Sapphic stanza, *litus iniquum,* the "treacherous shore." *Sobrius aula,* "Soberly" you should shy away from the "halls of the great," Horace ended the second stanza. *Turgida vela,* "Swollen sails," he ended the poem, needed to be shortened when the favoring wind was too strong.

Rectius, at the start of the poem, was a strong word for Horace, taken from everyday speech, the kind of language that Agrippa might have approved but Vergil much less. Aulus Murena was one, it seemed, who did not get the message. He appeared in court in what might have been a routine case. He was defending a provincial governor against a charge of exceeding his authority in Thrace. But the governor claimed he had Augustus's authority for his actions, and Augustus, in a rare intervention, spoke personally to deny this. Aulus was on the wrong side of the only line that mattered.

Horace's arguments for moderation, whether platitudes or warnings, were as nothing after that. Aulus was accused of joining a plot against Augustus to finish what the plagues of nature had failed to achieve. Terentia warned him that he was a suspect. Whether she had learned this from Maecenas or from her pillow talks with Augustus was not clear, nor whether there ever had been a plot.

Whatever the truth, Aulus Murena was at first able to escape – and was tried in his absence. But despite arguments in his favor, he was found guilty, hunted down, and, amid much disquiet, executed without further legal intervention. It was a murky episode. Some wondered whether his guilt had been his part in a plan to assassinate Augustus or his zeal as a defender when Augustus was for the prosecution. The case was a matter of much popular debate. The tip-off from Terentia became a bigger issue than the conspiracy itself. Maecenas divorced his wife, and it seemed that his relations with Augustus might never be the same again.

CHAPTER THIRTEEN

Horoscopes

Horace did not choose his publication date well. Twenty-three BCE was a bad plague year. Succession and inheritance in every family, not Augustus's alone, were vulnerable to the vicious vagaries of disease. It was a delicate time for readers to respond to poems that ranged from loyalist praise of one-man rule to sympathy with the survivors of Philippi. The implications of Marcellus's death were still unclear. There were the unpredictable sensitivities of Agrippa. Maecenas was not as reliable as before as a guide to what was good and what was not.

Only the second poem in the first book of *Odes* was directly addressed to Augustus. Was this too little attention or too much? Horace received a letter of thanks for the emperor's personal copy, *quantuluscumque,* "small as it is," hardly a response of clear enthusiasm. His old adviser Trebatius Testa would not have found this reaction very comforting — somewhat ambiguous, even, on its best interpretation, and too frail for Trebatius the careful lawyer. To call a book small was high praise among literary critics who followed the "big book, big evil" advice of Callimachus in third-century Alexandria. But was it praise from the man who controlled Alexandria now?

Augustus also took the opportunity to make jokes about the poet's weight and waistline, quipping that Horace might in future like to "write on a pot so that the circumference of your volume may be rounded out like that of your belly." It was a friendly note, intimate in its way. Horace probably did not laugh very much.

Did his poems suit the new present? In advising on how to live safely he had praised *auream mediocritatem,* a "golden middle way," but where were the extremes and what was the middle? It was hard to know. His advice had in any case failed to help Aulus Murena stay alive.

Horace's poems included the uncontroversial, or the probably uncontroversial. One offered some gentle advice from an older man to a younger friend, unidentified, his name disguised, who had fallen in love with his slave. That poem could surely bring no harm. But nothing was, in truth, very sure. Even poems about the changing weather and the fickleness of sexual partners might be misinterpreted.

Weather was close to health. Health was close to political calculation. The mists of plague rose and faded over what had once been the swamps of Rome, where, close beneath the surface, there were still swamps. The marble of Augustus's temples showed the shining path that he wanted the city to take, but many paths were still untaken.

Horace had no nostalgia for his city days. He was safer than ever on his farm. He was familiar with its fields and woods and his own life among them. He had everything he needed: his own wine, his own oil. He had partners for sex and places to write. The shade followed him throughout the day.

No one would have denied him the mirrored room in which his height might seem higher, his skin less blotchy, and his waist reduced. Such rooms were common enough. Large pieces of glass were rare, but it was not hard to assemble a mosaic of small panes, a means to expand those parts of the owner's body which he wanted to seem larger, minimizing flaws. Augustus might laugh at Horace's body and liken its shape to a wine cup, but no one else would take that liberty. He was the man in charge here, and while Maecenas might sometimes visit, Augustus surely would not.

Even before the death of Aulus Murena, probably not so serious a fall for Maecenas as his enemies hoped for, Horace's patron affected to look forward to his own death. He often believed himself ill. This was something the two of them could talk about. Hypochondria or horoscopes? Self-obsession or a search in the heavens for signs of future fatality? Either was fine. Horace did not mind that kind of conversation, although he might write a complaint about it.

In his second book of *Odes* he included a poem specifically about the perils of future watching — in the meter of Alcaeus. Patron and poet were shown sitting at the farm together, discussing how their stars were aligned *incredibili modo,* "in an extraordinary way," and how they would die on the same day. Horace must have written it seven years previously, soon after the tree had nearly fallen on his head.

"Why," he asked Maecenas, "do you kick the life out of me with your complaints?" *Cur me querelis exanimas tuis?* A bad horoscope was worth nothing. Horace trusted little in the alignments of Jupiter and Saturn. But the conceit was a pleasant one. Pleasing his patron was a pleasure.

Horoscopes could in other circumstances be less a way of enjoying a conversational afternoon than a bar to enjoyment. "Do not ask," *tu ne quaesieris,* he told his lover Leuconoe. Just eight lines, the shortest poem in his first book, were an injunction, a firm order, that she not "risk the Babylonian horoscopes" about when she might die: *Babylonios temptaris numeros.* It would be "not right to know," *scire nefas,* even if it were possible.

He had a message for Leuconoe, philosophical and carnal at the same time. The present was unique. The past could not be brought back, although Augustus's historians could fabricate and imagine it. It was not possible to know anything in the future, although a poet could boast and hope. So, live in and for the present.

Tu ne quaesieris, scire, nefas, quem mihi, quem tibi
finem di dederint, Leuconoe, nec Babylonios
temptaris numeros. ut melius quidquid erit pati!
seu plures hiemes seu tribuit Iuppiter ultimam,
quae nunc oppositis debilitat pumicibus mare
Tyrrhenum, sapias, vina liques, et spatio brevi
spem longam reseces. dum loquimur, fugerit invida
aetas: carpe diem, quam minimum credula postero.

Do not ask, it is not right to know, what end for me and what for you
the gods have given and do not risk the Babylonian horoscopes,
    Leuconoe.
How much better it is to endure what will be, whether Jupiter has
    granted us many winters
or whether this is the last one that now wears out the Tyrrhenian sea
    on the cliffs.
Be wise, strain the wine, cut back long hope into our short space.
Even while we are talking, envious time has fled away:
seize the day, trust least in the future.

This was the message. *Sapias,* "Be wise"; know the score; know the only thing that can be known. This was not an invitation to study knowledge, to discuss Epicurean doctrine, not the sort of talk he might have with Maecenas. There was little that was deeply philosophical about this poem. *Vina liques,* "strain the wine." *Dum loquimur,* "even while we are talking" about horoscopes we could be having sex. *Carpe diem:* "seize the day." These perfect eight lines were a way of inviting sex now, immediately, the only real time there was.

As the months moved on in which Horace's friends and enemies might (or might not) be reading the *Odes,* it became no easier to select the right reaction. Augustus's health grew stronger, and anxieties for the present eased, but these three books were works in which distinctions among politics, art, and life were hard to grasp and too often seemed to change. Horace was more secure than he had ever been in his life, his poems rather less so.

His *Odes* were difficult. The words *carpe diem* had never been used in that way before. Plucking fruit was a common enough idea. Plucking time, seizing a day, was not. Other novelties were even more demanding on his readers. It was in the essence of the Latin language that the words of a sentence could run in almost whatever order the writer wished: each individual word contained a marker that connected it to another and to the whole. But Horace's art of molding the sounds of the Greeks to the language of the Romans stretched what was possible toward what for many was beyond the possible.

Those addressed in the poems, or drawn by their political message, encountered other difficulties. One of Julius Caesar's once loyal commanders, Lucius Munatius Plancus, was given more to think about than he might have hoped. Consul in the year of Philippi, he had gone on to win a dubious reputation for dressing as a mermaid and slithering across the marble floors of Alexandria at the parties of Cleopatra. He had long before that founded cities for Caesar. He had joined Cicero in seeking an amnesty for Brutus and Caesar's other assassins. He had fought for the assassins, then for Antony and Cleopatra, and only then, just before Actium, for Octavian, finally finding the winning side. It was at Plancus's nomination that Octavian took the name Augustus.

Plancus had traveled widely, throughout both the war zones of the Mediterranean and the political pathways of his time, operating always at a level far above Horace. The two men need never have met and probably never did until both were at Augustus's court, Plancus working at the center, Horace playing at the edge. Even in 22 BCE, Plancus was one of Rome's censors, with the job of judging whether a man had the virtues necessary for the Senate. Horace was nowhere near the Senate, still the son of a onetime slave and the friend of the rather less influential Maecenas.

But what was Plancus to think of the seventh poem in Horace's first book of *Odes?* "Other people will praise," *Laudabunt alii,* it began, followed by a long list of cities loved by grand tourists: "glorious Rhodes," *claram Rhodon;* "or Mytilene," home of Sappho and Alcaeus, *aut Mitilinen;* "or Ephesus," the main city of Roman Asia, *aut Epheson;* or many more, from Athens to "hardy Sparta," *patiens Lacedaemon.*

This must hardly have seemed like an auspicious start to a poem for Plancus — a list of places that other people will praise, but Horace, presumably, will not. The meter, one that was again paraded to show Horace's range, was borrowed from a writer of erotic poems in ancient Sparta, Alcman, a contemporary of Sappho's. It was a form Horace had used once before — for his bedroom memories of the woman best suited for an elephant.

Again, there was nothing very erotic about this poem, or even much about Sparta, except as a tourist destination that Horace was not going to talk about. Nor had there been many recent tourist opportunities for a man like Plancus. Romans in Rhodes were as likely to have been helping Caesar's assassins extort cash for Philippi as sightseeing at the remains of the Colossus, statue of the Sun God, its former Wonder of the World. Sparta was a place whose four-hundred-year-old military reputation mattered less than its ability to provide troops for Antony and Octavian.

These were ambiguous sites of war more than peace which Horace was suggesting to Plancus should now be put behind him. The list was a reminder of the soldier's place in the conflicts of recent times, much more equivocal than that of the poet. It was far better, Horace said, to celebrate the safety of Tibur, the hill town between his farm and Rome, where the river Anio fell through ripening orchards in its justly famed waterfall.

This was a familiar theme, although the idyll was not to be set in Horace's farm (no invitation to Plancus there) but at Plancus's own home among the apple trees and sparkling springs. Wine was the best dispeller of cares, whether Plancus were in uniform or under a shady tree. That was the message, familiar, albeit cleverly wrapped up.

But then the poem became much less familiar. Horace ended it with an ominous war story. *Nil desperandum*, "Despair of nothing," he wrote, putting the words in the mouth of an unfortunate Greek returning from the Trojan War. This man was called Teucer, and his father, far from welcoming him home like a hero, had ordered him straight back out to sea and out of his sight.

Teucer had thought he was safe at home in peace, but the war for him was not yet over. He had to tell his tired sailors to drink their wine while they had the chance. "O brave men who have suffered worse," *o fortes peiora passi*, "tomorrow we will again set off over the vast sea," *cras ingens iterabimus aequor*.

There the poem ended, abruptly and, like so many of Horace's stories, without an outcome. Plancus, like every other reader, was left with the question of what Horace meant and why this poet from nowhere, even under the protection of Maecenas, thought he could lecture his betters in such a manner.

Teucer's failing, in his father's eyes, had been to return from Troy without his war-maddened brother Ajax, who had taken his own life in shame at not being awarded the arms of the dead Achilles. In the very recent real world, thousands of Romans had returned home without their brothers from the wars waged by Julius Caesar and his adopted son. Plancus himself had lost his brother in the proscriptions, possibly by his own betrayal.

The death of Ajax, felt far beyond his family, had rippled out into the lives of other exiles. It was hard for those who were damaged to find peace. Horace had been lucky, but he had not wholly escaped, even in the peace of his farm. Nor would Plancus find it easy, Horace warned. Like Teucer, he should bind his wine-flushed forehead with flowers and drink yet more while he still could.

Another veteran of compromise had his own poem. Horace had a message that was even starker for Quintus Dellius, Antony's fellow party lover, a man who knew well the threats of death and exile in the decades of civil war, and had been notoriously successful at avoiding them. Whether every day was a party or a misery, death was always close, Horace warned. The waters on which Dellius was soon to sail were not the great Mediterranean Sea but the river across to Hades and *aeternum exsilium*, "exile without end."

Dellius had begun his career of fun and fighting with Caesar's louche enforcer, Publius Cornelius Dolabella. After Dolabella had tortured to death one of Caesar's leading assassins, Dellius switched sides to Cassius, the joint leader of the assassins. From there he switched again, to Antony, and enjoyed, with Plancus, the luxury of Cleopatra's court before falling out with the queen and joining

Octavian. Messalla, whose own career was only a little more consistent, called him *desultor bellorum civilium,* "the circus rider of the civil wars," jumping from one horse to another as the march of history passed by.

"Cultivate a calm mind," *Aequam memento,* Horace advised Dellius in the third poem of his second book of *Odes.* Maybe the recipient interpreted his poem as a piece of platitudinous elegance, advice to gather his rosebuds while he might. Or maybe it had a nastier edge. *Moriture Delli,* "Dellius about to die," ran the end of the first stanza.

Augustus had too many distractions in the present to give much attention to poetry and the past. Soon after the publication of Horace's *Odes,* he left Rome for the East, aiming to secure the loyalty of local kings and hoping to bring back from Parthia the standards lost by Crassus — ideally by diplomacy, if necessary by force.

The kings in their small kingdoms might not need much persuading. In Cilicia the self-styled lover of Antony, Tarcondimotos Philantonius, had not lived long after Actium, and his son had not survived long after that. The wise preferred now to be Philokaisor, lovers of Caesar.

Parthia was tougher. The catastrophe at Carrhae had been the biggest wound to Rome in Horace's childhood, worse because it was wholly self-inflicted. Although Crassus and his army had not died fighting fellow Romans, the failed invasion across the Euphrates stemmed directly from rivalry between the heads of the Three-Headed Monster.

Horace had seen both the mass of hopeful troops tramping down the Appian Way in 54 BCE and the survivors a year later, straggling back with none of the rewards they had been promised. So too, had the citizens of Rome. It was the kind of defeat that could not be concealed by propaganda. It had to be avenged, and it was part of Augustus's newly cementing settlement of the past that vengeance be swift.

His campaign did not begin well. Augustus had barely reached the borders of Parthia before he had to return to Rome. The plague that had almost brought about his own death was not abating. Plague in the city brought the smell of burning flesh over his new baths and temples. In the countryside it brought empty fields and famine. In the ports it brought soaring prices. Horace was far enough away, and high enough in the hills, to escape the worst. Most were not.

Ruling Rome was a struggle for the loyal consuls left behind, Lollius and the man who had saved him at Philippi and whom he had saved after Actium, Quintus Aemilius Lepidus. Theirs was an unusual bond of war from a conflict that still cast a long, ragged shadow over Roman life. But bonds of war were not enough to meet the challenges of peace. For Lollius, governing Galatia had been much easier than having responsibility for Rome. During his time as consul he repaired a bridge – and put up a plaque to prove it. But administration required more than the special loyalty of those whose lives had been spared.

When the hungry crowds were rioting, it was not a hostile protest against Augustus but a plea that he take more power and solve their problems. No consul could deal with that. Julius Caesar had become dictator for life. Why, people asked, should his son not do the same, or at least take the consulship for life, or at the very minimum take direct responsibility for the corn supply and keeping Rome fed?

Augustus returned and obeyed only the last of these popular demands. Dictatorship had led to death for Caesar and more than a decade of war. Augustus's plan was for a more fundamental shift beneath the surface of the political landscape.

The third book of Horace's *Odes* began with six poems which, more than any others, showed the direction of that shift. Like the beginning of the first book it was a parade, this time not of virtuosity but of virtue, not of metrical skill (all six were in the meter of Alcaeus) but of an even harder demand on a poet, the fusing of a plausible personal sensibility with the politics of an empire.

These public poems about Rome were written as though to be read aloud to the citizens as they gathered for their entertainments. He might have read the lines aloud himself, perhaps outside the Palatine Temple of Apollo, perhaps in places less exposed. Like so much of what Horace published in 23 BCE they were a surprise.

The first words were a shout that was itself hardly a people pleaser: *Odi profanum volgus et arceo,* "I hate the common crowd and keep away." The thought was borrowed from Epicurus, who preferred philosophical reflection in his garden, but that might not have been the first association made by those who read or heard it. This was the cry of a man who knew both what was going wrong and what was needed to fix it. Romans needed to remember what had made them great before they had so nearly thrown greatness away.

There followed in this most prominent of his poems a discussion of luxury's lures, the foolishness of forgetting the shortness of life, the importance of due proportion in everything. *Desiderantem quod satis est,* "He who wants only what is enough," began the second set of six stanzas, that man has no worries from even the harshest weather. Personal greed had sapped the state. *Contracta pisces aequora,* "The fish feel the shrunken waters," the poem went on, moving the focus from the general to the very specific; fish feel the needless expansion of human homes out into the ocean, the builders, their slaves, and the foundations that spurn the land and sprawl out in the deep.

Augustus was hostile to property development unless he himself were the developer. He disliked the fashion among the Roman rich to extend their holiday homes without buying more land. The sea god Neptune, he claimed, had been his ally against both Sextus and Antony. Elaborate piers were an act of impiety to all the gods of the sea but, worse than that, an act of show aimed at inspiring envy. A fancy beach house, Horace warned, saved no one from the gods of "Fear and Threat," *Timor et Minae*.

What was the point here? Not easy politics or popularity. Certainly not easy poetry. Spurning the people while close to the greatest populist Rome had ever produced, criticizing luxury outside a luxurious palace after rehearsals on the Bay of Naples: these were paradoxical necessities for healing the state. Horace had embraced both the poetic challenge and the healer himself.

Along with his world, the survivor of Philippi was a changed man. These poems were not to the taste of all. They may not have meant much to the visitors to his mirrored room, or been read much in Augustus's armies, but in Rome they set a new tone in the poetry of politics, a wail of disdain, a sigh of relief, a whiff of hypocrisy, and a way forward to the national renewal that in some way or another was surely to be desired.

The second in this parade of political poems began as a recruiting call for Augustus's latest campaign. *Angustam amice pauperiem pati robustus acri militia puer*, "Let the battle-hardened boy learn gladly to suffer hardship," and harass the fierce Parthians. Let cavalry training be the key to victory. Thus did Horace announce an official program in a poem, doubtless conscious, as he had never concealed, that he had avoided those tests in his own robust youth.

Dulce et decorum est pro patria mori, "Sweet and right it is to die for one's country," Horace continued, conscious again that he had never himself fought for his country, only for an unsuccessful ideal of Rome promulgated by the assassins of Julius Caesar. Pleasure and propriety were often contrasted by philosophers, but Horace brought the two together in a way which was a risk to good taste even at the end of the first century BCE.

At this point the poem was teetering on the edge of embarrassment, pulled back only by the fusion of a public virtue with one which he could convincingly claim for himself. *Est et fideli tuta silentio merces,* "Safe is the reward for faithful silence." Horace had been silent in the service of Brutus at Clazomenae, and with Maecenas on the road to Brundisium, and he was still silent now. Augustus approved of silence from his court. Not for nothing did he have a riddling sphinx on his signet ring.

Horace's art did not depend on revelations of the secrets of others. Whenever he told a story, he joined it late and left it early, focusing on accidental facts. Moving on quickly in this poem from the praise of brute soldiering and the sweetness of young death, he made the tact of silence his own virtue, one he could sincerely set beside the virtues necessary for the ever-more centralized state.

Out in the East, Augustus had no immediate need of a recruiting sergeant: he had too many would-be soldiers, not too few. He wanted the ideal of fighting and suffering for Rome in the future, and he wanted this ideal cemented in a program that the leading men of Rome would remember. It was not the propaganda of poetry that mattered to Maecenas but its permanence, not the immediate impact of the second rate but the lasting importance.

Back in the deserts of Parthia, Augustus did a diplomatic deal with the neighboring king whose power was closest to that of his own. He agreed on borders for the first time between the two empires: when Crassus had invaded Parthia he was never sure whether he had begun his invasion or not. Augustus negotiated the return of the legionary standards lost by Crassus and also by Antony – all without needing his soldiers to endure any sweet and proper death.

In Rome, Maecenas appreciated the propaganda value of the standards' return, but it was the standard of public behavior that concerned him more. The patron, like his poets Horace and Vergil, took a longer view than the politician. That was still Maecenas's role.

Augustus had to watch closely from afar the day-to-day politics of the city: the people who wanted him to be a dictator were reacting to his refusal by electing men whom he did not control. There was one successfully elected reformer in particular, Marcus Egnatius Rufus, the pioneer of Rome's popular and much-needed fire brigades, whom the Senate condemned to execution. Augustus had to rate the risky popularity of men such as Rufus higher than the risks of poetry. Horace could say what Augustus could not. He could say it repeatedly. *Odi profanum volgus et arceo*, "I hate the common herd and keep away."

Iustum et tenacem propositi virum, "The just man of clear purpose," is shaken by nothing, Horace thundered out at the beginning of his third ode on the state of Rome. "The fiery enthusiasm of citizens decreeing depravity" will not shift his purpose: *non civium ardor prava iubentium*. Such was the ideal – and Horace developed his theme over another seventy elegant Alcaic lines, criticizing excessive greed, exploitative mining, and other activities detrimental to the best spirit of Rome, if not to its immediate economic prospects.

In the fifth and sixth poems he fused Augustus's plans to invade Britain and repair Rome's temples with lectures on sexual morality, particularly the behavior of married women, and on how Romans should live up to the standards of their ancestors. He decried the wives who chose lovers randomly at parties when the lights were out. Augustus was planning controversial new laws against adultery. He wanted to impose rapid compulsory remarriage for merry widows. Horace was not a married man, but he got the message.

In the fourth poem Horace set out the obstacles in his past life that might so easily have barred him from this high moral tone for the public good. *Non me Philippis versa acies,* "The broken battle line at Philippi did not stop me," the *non* and the *me* being the words with emphasis. Nor was he thwarted by the tree that once fell on him at his farm, nor by his shipwreck in the seas below Mount Etna. This finest of the political parade poems, like all the odes in different ways, was about Horace himself, whether he was inviting guests to his bed and table, enjoying wine, sex, and countryside, or setting his adventures in philosophy at the service of the state.

The mention of Philippi was no longer about the embarrassment of being on the wrong side but the magic of his escape under the protection of the goddess of poetry. *Descende caelo et dic age tibia,* "Come down from the sky and play your pipes," this poem began in a summons to the Muse Calliope from Augustus's temple steps. *Auditis?* "Do you all hear" her too? he asks the crowd. Poetry was everything. If Calliope were with him, he wrote, he might even follow Augustus to the wilds of Spain, where men drank the blood of horses, or to the even more barbaric Britons. The horrors of any new battle were wreathed in pleasant fantasy. Those of the old too were subsumed, if not ever wholly erased, by the power of the poet he had become.

Success was also a strain. He was beginning to feel old. To celebrate Augustus's latest triumphant return from foreign war, he wrote like a master of ceremonies, shouting out who should stand where for the procession of the grateful. He harked back to the Spartacus rebellion, whose reverberations had filled his childhood, a civil war of a kind for the son of a former slave: yes, some vintage wine from those distant years would be good. He would like to celebrate with a girl at his farm, but his body and face in his mirrors told him that he was not the lusty youth he had been *consule Planco,* the emphatic two-word fall of a Sapphic stanza. The year when "Plancus was consul" was the year of Philippi, 42 BCE, the date that had long marked his life.

CHAPTER FOURTEEN

Death of Vergil

Brundisium was the port of the stag. From its inland harbors and houses stretched two prongs of water, like antlers, out toward the sea. Brentesion was the local name for the horns of the deer that stalked the hills behind, Brunda the name in Latin. Some of the town's founders were Greek, some claiming that their Trojan War hero Diomedes had been the founder. Brundisium was a vital link between Rome and its eastern empire, but like so much of Italy, it was Roman only as Philippi was Roman, a station on an imperial way.

The start of any journey to Greece was deceptively calm, a long slipping by of wooden wharfs and mud flats before the slap, the sullen sound as the hull hit the swollen waves of the Adriatic. The local Messapians who lived in the town were sailors. The oarsmen were slaves from anywhere. Romans were the passengers. It was rare to find a Roman who relaxed as his ship reached the end of the harbor walls and found the sea.

This nervousness came in many forms. There was no longer the fear that major enemies might strike, neither pirates nor the Roman fleets of civil war rivals: Pompey, Caesar, Antony, and Octavian himself. Augustus still had hostile opponents but none of them had navies. Italy was connected safely to Greece as it had never been before. Yet for those who lived beside the antlers of Brundisium their status as citizens of Rome's most strategic port was still a mixed blessing at best; they were a rich place for trade, an open wound for trouble coming in on the tide, no place for calm.

Good harbors were rarities. Few places by the sea were safe for large ships, especially with large numbers of people, to land or leave. A harbor was a metaphor of the supernatural too. A harbor, for Empedocles, was where the earth was formed of air, fire, and water. For Philodemus, philosophy itself was a harbor. For the Athenian playwright Sophocles, four hundred years before, a harbor, for most men, was something not be relied on in any way — and a metaphor for death, the final destination. And there was always for a Roman the horror of the sea itself, almost the sacrilege of leaving the zones of mortals for those of jealous gods. Brundisium was where men left home.

Horace's older friend Vergil was no more a seaman than most of his compatriots. Like Horace, he sought inspiration in Greece, but unlike him, he would often travel to find direct inspiration. Horace had expressed anxiety in the past about Vergil's safety in seas beyond the walls where winds were competing tyrants. "One-half of my soul," *animae dimidium meae,* was how he had described the poet in the third ode of his first book.

This poem was addressed to a ship leaving harbor, and its position in the publication in 23 BCE was its importance. Only Maecenas and Augustus stood ahead of Vergil in Horace's parade of virtuosity and gratitude. Vergil had introduced Horace to Maecenas. Without that help he might still be fending off older women in the Subura.

In 19, there was hardly less cause for anxiety than there had been earlier. Vergil was leaving again for Greece. He was taking with him the unedited text of his epic *Aeneid*. Like Horace, he was a perfectionist. He tested every word in its metrical frame. He had read parts aloud — to Augustus and his family, and to others. He was a shy man but a powerful reader when he needed to be. He had made Augustus's sister swoon with a passage in which Aeneas met her dead son, Marcellus, in the underworld.

Vergil stood high in the Augustan sky. He was unique in his powers. When a rival was accused of borrowing one of his lines the plagiarist replied that the theft meant nothing: hearing the great man was what mattered; anyone could borrow but not everyone could be what Vergil was. At one point Vergil had even planned a poem directly about Augustus before he instead returned to Homer, to Aeneas, a minor hero whom he would make major, a young man whom he would make a very different kind of hero, dutiful, loyal, a worthy ancestor in Augustus's house.

When Horace felt the need to praise Octavian or preach the necessity of the emperor's survival he used the language of propaganda more lavishly, less subtly, than Vergil did. When Vergil strayed into lightness he was never as effective as his younger friend. When Vergil fell into excessive grief at the death of a mutual friend, Quintilius, Horace was there with a poem that gently used the arguments of Epicurus to bring him back within reason's bounds. "What is the decent limit on loss?": *Quis desiderio sit pudor?* Only patience can lighten what we cannot change.

Horace was a very different poet. He had no more desire to follow his elder into the sweep of epic than to follow him to Greece. He found all his inspiration on papyrus or in his head. And his work, as it seemed at this time, was over. In the final poem of his third book of *Odes* he had begun, bombastically as it had seemed to some, with the words *Exegi monumentum aere perennius*, "I have made a monument more lasting than bronze." Neither rain nor time would destroy it.

Horace had looked forward then with equanimity to his death. When he died, he wrote, "a great part of me" would avoid "the goddess of the grave," *multaque pars mei vitabit libitinam.* He would grow in fame "for as long as the priest, with the silent virgin, climbs the Capitoline Hill," *dum Capitolium scandet cum tacita virgine pontifex.*

Horace was not ill in 19 BCE. He had no need yet to fear the grave goddess, Libitina. He was no more facing death than any other man who visited Rome. Thanks to Maecenas he did not need to visit Rome very often. But he had seemed to be signing off, his last words both a boast and a taunt.

The taunt was to his critics. He already knew who they were and what they said—that he was pampered, too much protected, extraordinarily lucky in his patrons. Horace had no doubts about his virtues as a poet, but his self-confidence was brittle. His poems were difficult for his readers and hearers alike. His command of structure, rhythm, and word order was ambitious from the start because it had to be. Without his confidence he would have been nothing. But his words were rarely easy.

Exegi monumentum aere perennius
regalique situ pyramidum altius,
quod non imber edax, non aquilo impotens
possit diruere aut innumerabilis

annorum series et fuga temporum.
non omnis moriar multaque pars mei

vitabit Libitinam; usque ego postera

crescam laude recens, dum Capitolium

scandet cum tacita virgine pontifex.

I have made a monument more lasting than bronze,

higher than the royal pyramids,

which neither biting storm nor the powerless north wind

can destroy, nor the uncountable years ahead and the flight of time.

I will not wholly die and a great part of me

will avoid the goddess of the grave.

I shall grow, ever fresh from praise, for as long as the priest,

with the silent virgin, climbs the Capitoline Hill.

That was the boast. But then he needed the justification, his unique service to his homeland by the Aufidus River and its mythical king.

Dicar, qua violens obstrepit Aufidus

et qua pauper aquae Daunus agrestium

regnavit populorum, ex humili potens,

princeps Aeolium carmen ad Italos

deduxisse modos.

I will be spoken of where the wild Aufidus roars

and where poor, dry, Daunus has long reigned over his rural people,

spoken of as a man powerful from low birth,

the first to bring Aeolian song to the poetry of Italy.

Vergil's epic was very different. It spoke for itself. It was metrically more simple. It came with a patriotic story. The past-tense claim of "Exegi monumentum" suggested that there was no more work ahead for Horace. For Vergil, the older man, with most of his epic work unpublished, almost everything was still ahead.

Meanwhile, Augustus was back in the eastern part of his empire and showing no desire to return quickly to Rome. Although in Italy he had to measure carefully praise from such as Vergil and Horace, abroad, in places long schooled in autocracy, he was more free. In Rome the people wanted to pile upon him more honors than he thought was wise. In the East he could play the role of monarch without worry.

After his own success in Parthia he arranged a success for his stepson, Tiberius, in the not too difficult task of installing a pro-Roman king on the empty throne of Armenia. He freed some cities from taxation and punished others. He set up court in Samos, a Greek island famed for fine wine and as the birthplace of Epicurus, receiving embassies from as far away as India, receiving a present of a slave boy with no arms and prehensile feet.

In Athens an Indian ambassador threw himself on a funeral pyre in his honor. This was a very different reception from the one the Athenians had given to Brutus when Horace was a student. Autocracy, even if not called tyranny, was the order of the day. If anyone spoke any longer of the tyrant slayers Harmodius and Aristogeiton, it was more quietly, and the words were less heard. During his ceremonial days in Athens, Augustus heard that Vergil was on his way across the Adriatic — and with him the unfinished text of the epic poem that had long interested him more than anything else produced by the entourage of Maecenas.

The two men met. Vergil, seeking peace in which to write poetry, set off again for the Isthmus of Corinth. The sea journey was hard. On land again he sat out in the sun as Horace loved to do but he himself was better not doing. Augustus sent word that he was about to return to Italy and that Vergil should join him. There was no choice but to obey.

The short trip had left no time to solve the final problems of the *Aeneid,* to complete the many unfinished lines or the plot. The opening of the poem was almost perfect: Aeneas was shown buffeted by winds and waves at sea, forced to land, finding three stags in the hills, one for each of his ships that had survived. Shooting stags began a theme of war and peace, hunters and hunted that lasted throughout the passion of Dido and descent into Hades until the poem's less finished ending.

Vergil was a poet of grand themes, a vivid describer of the glories of nature. Every student of the Greeks in Italy knew a story (not always the same story) of how Empedocles, divider of the world into air, water, earth, and fire, had thrown himself into the flames of Mount Etna to choose the time of his death. In the third book of the *Aeneid,* when Aeneas was approaching Italy for the first time, Vergil made his readers feel as though they were inside the eruption itself, in the avalanches of ash under smoking skies, amid the vomit of rocks, beneath the balls of fire that licked the stars.

These early books were intense, already acclaimed by his friends, but on his voyage back to Italy, the artist had to face his own mortality and the problem of preserving what, if anything, was important from his life. By the time the imperial fleet slid back into the port of the stag, Vergil was dying. He knew he was dying. He told his fellow travelers that the twelve books of the *Aeneid* had to be destroyed.

Vergil landed safely at Brundisium, the harbor from which he had embarked, the destination eighteen years before of the embassy of Maecenas and his poets to Antony; but he never left it. Horace did not immediately hear that his sometime fellow avoider of ball games, the man he once described as *animae dimidium meae,* "the half of my soul," was dead. He was not among the mourners when Augustus led a funeral march over the mountains to Naples, or when Vergil was buried near his adopted home as a noble prophet of the new Rome.

Vergil's tomb was close to Aeneas's landing place in Italy. His life in death was immediately political, committed to the fusion of present glory and heroic past. His orders for the destruction of his text were ignored. Without a living poet to argue otherwise, it was easy to stress the positive in Vergil's vision and push away what was brutal and less helpful to the national cause. Varius and Plotius Tucca took on the job of preparing the poem to fulfill its purpose.

There was no literary place for Horace here. Varius was a writer of epic himself, sympathetic to the poetry of storms and stress and struggles to found a new city. Tucca was an editor and critical friend from the terraces of Herculaneum. Their territory was the large and grand. For Horace a big book was still a big badness, the lesson he had learned in Athens before Philippi. His own poems were miniatures, political in parts — sometimes uneasy parts — but tiny scenes, not grand narratives that started with stags. He was useful and admired, but if he were being hard on himself he might have reflected that his own best-known animals were a town mouse and a country mouse.

For the next four years Horace retreated and wrote what were mostly very different poems — melancholic, contemplative, with a powerful sense of passing time and an equally powerful belief that his poetry could mitigate time's decay, whatever people thought or said about it. Behind these lines, and sometimes clear on the papyrus pages, was a stubborn belief in Augustus's regime as a bastion against decay in the real world.

He wrote letters in verse, one of them to Maecenas, full of anger and resentment, just reliant enough on Greek precedent to put some distance between himself and his feelings. He could appear to be quoting rather than pronouncing, but just as in his early iambi on the witch women of the Subura, those who listened could hear the reality of his protest. Literary knowledge might give him some protection against the charge of oversensitivity: he was highly sensitive nonetheless.

He attacked what he saw as his superficial imitators, his hypocritical critics, the rivals who envied his seclusion, the fickle mob who, as in his first days of fame, preferred a poet it could see and harass in the streets. He had no school, no disciples for sharing fixed ideas. He was eclectic in his choice of whom to follow in philosophy and art. Small poems were still the best kind. Like a master in mosaics or glass, Horace was a perfectionist. He knew the pressure on a poet seeking the highest standards, and destroyed more lines than he completed, knowing that only through the bad lines came the good ones. He mourned Vergil, whose fame was rising from his death, but a Vergil was not what he wanted to be.

He wrote letters to young men, seeking a friendlier audience or one that would appreciate his avuncular advice. He asked his friend Bullatius about his travels in the tourist towns of the Aegean, in Samos, Lesbos, and Smyrna. Had he had a good time? Men who "rush across the sea," *trans mare currunt*, "change their sky, not their mind": *caelum non animum mutant*. Bullatius would do better at home.

Did Bullatius enjoy himself even in Lebedos, the tiny desolate spot, neighbor of Clazomenae, the town of the swans? Both were once staging posts on the assassins' march to Philippi; both were now returned to peace and rebuilding their prosperity. Of all these fashionable places it was Lebedos for which Horace had his only yearning, where he thought he might live in peace, "forgetting my friends and by them forgotten," *oblitus meorum, oblivisicendus et illis.*

But it did not much matter where a man lived as long as he was of balanced mind. Horace looked back to his first trip out of Rome with Vergil and Maecenas, at the damp, frog-ridden towns of the marshes on the Appian Way. He could live even there.

Greed was among the greatest enemies. *Fructibus Agrippae Siculis,* "The profits of Agrippa from Sicily," was the start of another short letter to Agrippa's man Iccius, the steward of great southern estates that were even greater after the victory at Naulochus. The slaves who had fought for their freedom at sea were now producing corn and colossal profit for their conqueror.

Horace had warned Iccius five years before about being driven by desire for jewels and attractive slaves to join a dangerous expedition to Arabia. Horace's sympathies had been wholly with the slaves, among them the sad boy once *doctus . . . tendere,* "trained to be an archer," now waiting tables while waiting to be taken to a Roman's bed. In this new letter he again criticized Iccius's obsession to be more than a mere steward of Agrippa: he had money and time to take physics lessons from Empedocles on the very island where the poet of love and strife had plunged into the volcano. What more could he want?

Horace wrote an unusual prepublication letter addressed to his own next set of poems, reminding his *Epistles* that he had never promised them appearances before a big public in the bookselling streets. Like a beautiful smooth-skinned boy, he predicted instead, each papyrus would set off into the city and be thumbed and soiled by vulgar hands before it lost its fashionable youth and found itself in the back of a mothy cupboard far away.

But before his poems met that all too likely fate, if anyone any-where by any slight chance were to ask the papyrus about its au-thor, it should reply first that Horace was libertino natum patre, "the son of a man once a slave," then that he was like a bird with wings too wide for his nest, favored by the foremost of Rome, and finally that he was in his mid-forties, short, prematurely gray-haired, apt to fiery rages but always able to be appeased. Horace was writing his own publicity paragraphs, the kind of reluctant boasting that was not yet the duty of every ambitious writer.

He was mockingly prostituting his collection. The words *ut prostes sosiorum pumice mundus,* "so that you can sell your body smoothed with the pumice stone of the booksellers," were all from the vocabulary of the pimp. Sellers of both boys and books liked to offer a product without hair in the wrong places. Pumice, the rough gray stone of the volcano, was the tool of bathhouse and publishing house alike.

Horace was also defending his poems, most of all from charges that he had copied meters from the Greeks and might not thus be considered an original. Had not Sappho sometimes done the same? Was not art built upon other art as well as life? If the vulgar did not understand this, that was their problem alone.

Whatever his hopes and sometime certainty of popular appeal, Horace was happy to retreat as an elitist, to have his work held in the hands and read by the eyes of the discriminating. He preferred hands and eyes to ears and eyes. He was read in performance. He sometimes performed himself. But better was the eye of one who could read and reread, rolling out the columns of text, rolling back, recognizing craft and art.

Horace's own choice for holiday reading was Homer, *Troiani belli scriptorem,* the "Trojan War writer." He wrote to a young rel-ative of the now notoriously wealthy Lollius, whose life had been entwined with his own at Philippi. This young Lollius Maximus was fighting for Augustus in Spain, and Horace used Homer's epics to assault the horrors in times of all war, "faction, treachery, crime, lust, and anger," *seditione, dolis, scelere, atque libidine et ira*. He played the role of the old conservative that Orbilius, the tutor chosen by his father, had once played: Homer was a better teacher of ethics than any modern tutor, he intoned, the *Iliad* for the avoidance of folly, the *Odyssey* for the pursuit of virtue. *Sapere aude*, Lollius should "dare to know" the truth, to read, to study, and, if he was successful, to be wise.

Horace summed up for Lollius his own experience of what was already a new kind of court around Augustus. An ambitious young man now needed different skills for the household on the Palatine Hill from ones he might have once have deployed in the Forum below it. Flattery was a vice, but truculence was a danger. Horace sounded the way Trebatius Testa had once sounded. Lollius should humor the powerful, even wealthy eccentrics who liked to re-create the Battle of Actium in their country fishponds. At some point he might wish to withdraw altogether to a quieter life of contemplation. It was as though he were addressing himself when young.

Horace's collection of letters set off to the booksellers, each copy in its own case, each like a slave primped and pimped, as their author put it in his text inside. But he was not ready yet himself for quiet contemplation. No sooner was his writing table clear than he was again harping on his confused and angry themes, how civil war had torn him from the "groves of Academe," *silvas academi*, how Philippi had left him like a bird without wings, a beggar without any of the land he had left behind, how only "poverty emboldened and impelled" him to write, *paupertas impulit audax*. There was some truth in the first two complaints, only ironic self-pity in the third.

The recipient of this random rage, identified at the beginning of its first line, was the young aristocrat Julius Florus, *Floro bono claroque*, a would-be courtier who had also received a letter in the first book. Perhaps, he told Florus, dear old Horace should just imagine that people liked his poems, that he was an acclaimed success. What was so wrong with self-deception?

The letter closed with a story about a mad rich man from Greece who liked applauding an empty stage in an empty theater. He imagined he was watching wonderful tragic actors until his friends cured him with drugs. The man was furious. His manic illusions were his greatest pleasure. He did not want to be cured. He wanted them back.

CHAPTER FIFTEEN

Game Show

Augustus declared that in 17 BCE there would be the long-delayed week of *Ludi Saeculares*, Centenary Games, the city-wide party of sacrifices, feasts, and shows that had been postponed thirty years earlier in the dangerous days of Julius Caesar. By a very flexible tradition these games were supposed to happen every *saeculum* of a hundred or so years. No one, it was agreed, should have the chance to go to them twice, but the last one had happened in no one's memory, in the year of the destruction of Carthage almost 130 years before. The gods had been displeased at the postponement, it was said: and the horrors of Philippi and the wars after Caesar's death had been part of the result.

New oracles were now produced. The saeculum was redefined as 110 years. Achieving this result was no problem for Augustus. The role of the priests who climbed the Capitoline to consult the Sybil's prophetic books and decide such dates had long been political and was no less so now. Julius Caesar's position as the chief priest, pontifex maximus, purchased for him by Crassus, was the basis on which he first built his power.

Augustus had barely succeeded, against more than usually determined opposition, in passing moral legislation promoting marriage and punishing adultery. He now felt secure enough to fix his Centenary Games a year earlier than his organizers had first suggested, his new date fitting neatly with the renewal of his formal powers as Rome's autocrat; while not always necessary for getting his way, these were a weapon against potential critics and worth adding to the reasons for a party.

Only the demands of these games forced Horace back to a theatrical stage in Rome that was also the most political stage of his life. In the months following Vergil's death, architects, artists, and lawyers were summoned to a massive operation of military planning and precision. Gaius Ateius Capito, one of Augustus's most flexible lawyers, ensured that every priestly pronouncement was appropriate for the show ahead. Lollius, never one to miss an opportunity, was prominent in the *quindecimviri,* the board of fifteen men coordinating every aspect of the event. Marcus Cocceius Nerva, once Antony's man, brother of Lucius Cocceius Nerva, who shared that long-ago journey to Brundisium, was a member too, another of the many whose pardon by the victor had propelled them into new power.

If Vergil had been still alive, the role for poetry at the festival might have been different. But the *Aeneid* was now on a separate path to promote Augustus's vision of past and future. Messalla's poet Tibullus had also just died, at almost the same time as Vergil. He had never written about Augustus. He was part of a circle that had taken a different route out of Philippi, vital loyal service by Messalla in public, private performances and readings of a kind closer to the old world. Tibullus had been famed for erotic, not political works. He was a minor rival minus the aptitude and skills that were of most public use to the new regime. But his death had left Horace even more necessary — and more alone.

Augustus wanted to bring this once-in-a-lifetime festival out of what he saw as Rome's primitive darkness into the light of day. It would take place as May turned to June. The night sacrifices would be not to the gods of the underworld but to the fates that controlled the earth and the sky. In the daytime rituals the goddesses of childbirth would have precedence over the gods of the dead. All would happen as the helpful books of the Sybil had commanded. There would be a *Carmen Saeculare*, a sacred Song of the Century, sung by a choir of boys and girls with their faces to the future.

This was Horace's first commission directly from the state, a very different kind of challenge to his present intertwined senses of himself as servant and artist. Issues here of poetry's service to politics were more fundamental, but also simpler, than he had faced before. Once he had accepted the assignment he also had practical issues to confront. This was the most important public event of his life, of anyone's life. That was the point. Nothing could be allowed to go wrong.

There was no surviving model from previous games. He could make his own rules. But his song had to be easy to learn. That was clear from the start. His normal lyric poetry was not easy, as his critics were not shy to complain.

He had to choose his form with care. Learning it would be simpler if each stanza were separate, if no sentences ran from one to another. The Sapphic stanza ended naturally and dramatically with its short fourth line, so that was the form he chose. *Tempore sacro*, "at this holy time," was the first dying fall; *copia cornu*, "the horn full of plenty," one of the last. He was already used to making the meter of the most sexual Muse into a chaste servant of a moralizing regime.

There would be fifty-four members of his choir, twenty-seven boys and twenty-seven girls, the numbers chosen by the priests with the organizers' help. Some two hundred years earlier the aged Livius Andronicus, favorite of his schoolteacher Orbilius, had used twenty-seven girls for a hymn to Juno aimed at curbing natural disasters. This was the kind of numerical continuity, not too specific or demanding, that the occasion required.

The selection of the individual performers would be based in part on ability but more on parental status. All the singers had to have fathers and mothers who were alive. This had to be a choir stressing the continuity of family life in the aristocracy of Rome.

What was the song supposed to say? He had some freedom, but like all freedoms in the new age for poets, it came with constraints. The ideal of the Roman family—fecundity, purity, and chastity—was central to the purpose of the games. So too was the need to show a rebirth of Rome itself, a revival of the virtues that came before the corruption of the old republic. The place of the recital would be the Palatine and Capitoline hills, beginning at Augustus's new Palatine Temple of Apollo.

There were potential obstacles. Some might be expecting praise of the imperial family, with a central focus perhaps on Agrippa and Julia, Augustus's widowed daughter and his military chief, on whose marriage any succession then seemed to depend. Though able to avoid the most flagrant eastern flattery, Horace still struggled to find his way.

Not even Horace could make vibrant poetry out of laws on marriage which were so far from his personal taste. Moves to outlaw extramarital sex and stop women lamenting too much at their husbands' deaths risked ridicule—and his words, twisted uncomfortably into their Sapphic lines, risked betraying his real views.

The fundamental form of the poem was an address to Apollo

in his own temple, to Diana, and to the goddesses of childbirth in their various forms. "May you advance our decrees on women's sexual behavior," *Prosperes decreta super iugandis feminis,* was the best he could manage. For Horace this was hardly poetry, even if it was good politics — which it probably was not. Direct praise of the new, cleaner Rome, purged of witches and poisoners in plain view, was no basis for poetry. Nor was a law exiling adulterous wives and their lovers to separate barren islands. He was better at the glancing cut than the blow to the stomach.

Horace wanted to recognize the loss of Vergil, while adjusting those of his friend's themes that either he could not stomach himself or were unsuited to the needs of the new saeculum ahead. Vergil had created the idea that Rome was built on seven hills. Horace was happy to go along with that. Vergil had harked back to a Golden Age that had gone, a time when humanity and nature were as one. Horace was doubtful. Augustus himself was not hostile to a lost age of gold, but he preferred to look forward.

Vergil had made Aeneas the lover of a Carthaginian queen who had almost prevented the foundation of Rome. He would not have been able to give his hero a sexual purity to match Augustus's ambitions for their city. Horace had no such commitments. He did not own an Aeneas. He did not write narrative, not since his days on the road to Brundisium. He was able easily to create a modified character for his choristers, *Castus Aeneas,* "pure, chaste Aeneas," whose other virtue was that he had "built a road to freedom," *liberum munivit iter.* This was not the freedom for which Horace had fought at Philippi, but a freedom in a veiled autocracy that he increasingly well understood.

Horace's greatest inspiration came from the idea that the games be held in the day and the night and to show the contrast between future and past, heavens and underworld. He knew that the poem would first be heard beneath a giant bronze chariot of the sun outside Apollo's temple. He wrote a stanza beginning *Alme Sol*, "Gentle Sun," that may have, unusually in this poem, satisfied his ambitions as both poet and political assistant. "Nothing greater than the city of Rome let the sun ever see," *Nihil urbe Roma visere maius.*

This Song of the Century, like the festival itself, was more than a re-creation of the old. It was a new song for a new show. It was not a processional hymn. It was something separate from the processions, adapting, explaining, and teaching.

The copiers set to work. Each of the singers needed a papyrus roll. The poem was difficult for a new reader, as so much of his work was difficult. It was modern and unfamiliar, and there had to be no mistakes. Augustus, Agrippa, and the whole organizing committee would be there. The people of Rome would be there. It would be the climax of the greatest games of everyone's lives, the last performance before the last sacrifice, the last show before the plays, the chariot races, and the hunting. By then Horace would not be needed. He would be gone.

And so it happened. On a sulfurous summer night, twenty-five years after Philippi, fourteen years after Actium, the third of three sultry nights and days, Horace's choristers climbed to their places on the Palatine Hill. Lines of torches lit the way through the Forum, signing the path to the Field of Mars, where the festival had begun two days before. The light was needed even though the heat was not. The slaves of the rich sprinkled water to dampen the dust. The poor coughed only a little more than those whose air had been cleansed. Under awnings against the fading sun the Song of the Century was about to be performed.

An audience of citizens stood exhausted by festivity. On the first night Augustus himself had sacrificed nine female lambs and nine she-goats to the Fates. A slight man, his head uncovered, he had still been easy to see. There had been blood and rejoicing, then a whole day of plays and performances before a second night of three kinds of sacrificial cakes for the goddesses of childbirth, twenty-seven cakes in all, the same number as made up each of the sets of singers, no blood but no less excitement for the numerologists of ritual.

This was permanently diverting entertainment. Augustus had made his first sacrifices in a corner of the Field of Mars known as the Tarentum. An ancient buried altar had to be exposed to rare view. Each night 110 married women arranged chairs on which various goddesses might rest. Any who were mourning dead husbands were ordered to restrain their grief. Augustus's wish, with new force of law, was that all widows should as quickly as possible marry again. Heralds in long cloaks and feathered helmets delivered orders backed by the threat of a winged wand of wood. Augustus himself was everywhere, in the people's minds even when resting out of their sight in his house above the temple stage for the choir.

Horace had only a small place in the proceedings. Poets were used to being a small part of any party to which they were invited. This was true of all times; even the greatest tragedies of Athens were presented among the smoke of sacrifice and the blare of military parades. Horace had no illusions that the art of his song was important for most of the people in the Forum, or even that they would catch all his words.

He knew that his was hard poetry to hear and understand, hard to remember and recite. His carefully constructed hymn was important for the performers, as every performance was, important for Maecenas and those with their minds on the future, important for Augustus, too, but maybe not as big a matter as the goddesses' chairs or the pregnant pig he was about to sacrifice to Mother Earth on this third and final night. More people would notice a mistake with the sow than with the scansion of a Sapphic verse.

Before the performance began, Horace told his singers of his own importance as a poet inspired directly by Apollo, and how important they themselves were as children of the stag-hunting Diana. The girls, when they were married women in their turn, would proudly recall, he said, that they had learned their singing from Horace the poet. More immediately, lest they forget the lessons of their rehearsals, he reminded them to remember the Sapphic rhythms and watch the beat of his thumb.

Phoebe silvarumque potens Diana, "Apollo and Diana, queen of the woods!" With those words the song began. It hoped for eternity for Rome. It gloriously hymned the sun. It directly praised marriage. It less directly praised Vergil. It thanked Augustus, obliquely but clearly, for his victories in war and peace. It thanked the organizing committee. And within a few minutes it was over.

The young choristers, with their forty-eight-year-old conductor in tubby attendance, walked down from their platform on the Palatine to the Forum. Those in the crowd who had missed the minutiae of Horace's lyric would quickly have another chance. The choir had to process through a hundred yards of Roman history before performing their song again on the Capitoline Hill under the temple of Jupiter Optimus Maximus, the Best and the Greatest.

Heralds handed torches to the crowd. The smoke of sulfur swirled. Lights flared over the house of the pontifex maximus, once Julius Caesar's official home, over the site of his funeral pyre, over the Rostra where Antony had roused the crowd in Caesar's memory. The line of flames lit the side of Caesar's basilica, his place for offices and meetings, not yet completed by his adopted son. They showed Romulus's cave, where every February half-naked men with whips began a famed fertility race. Mark Antony had once notoriously run this Lupercalia, "race of the wolves." The lights stretched as far as the second platform for the choir, on the hill where Caesar's assassins had met after their deed was done. Not all of Rome's history was about Julius Caesar, but he dominated so much of what the choir could see.

For eyes looking farther back there was the hole in the ground where a legendary enemy had fallen in a long ago mythical war. There was the temple to twin gods who had fought for Rome in another war, for which no account survived. There was also an archway through which, some sixty years before, Pompey's triumphant chariot, drawn by elephants of too great size and too little discipline, had failed to pass. There was to be no ambiguity, and no sly mockery of failure, in future accounts of these great games of the century.

Augustus had plans for the writing of Rome's ancient history, just as he had for the city's future. He was pleased that Vergil had done some of the work. He had historians and antiquarians who would do more. In the meantime he had Horace, his poem, and his choir — all about to be presented to the people for the second time. Then there would be his knifing of the pregnant pig and the theatrical hunting of boars and stags. He would have his own official account of his celebrations recorded on a tablet of stone.

CHAPTER SIXTEEN

Poet on a Volcano

Within months of the great games its principal players were far away from Rome and from each other. Agrippa was in the East, not fighting but solving awkward diplomatic issues such as what rights Jews should retain in different parts of the empire. As an administrator he had a free hand — and felt he well deserved it. Augustus was on the other side of the empire in the West.

Horace had long ago suggested that Agrippa's deeds in creating the Augustan age should be celebrated in poetry — as long as someone other than himself would take on the job. No one of note had accepted the challenge. Agrippa was writing his own autobiography, including descriptions of the places he had known and made, in plain Latin prose. He had nothing in common with the leisured art of Maecenas and Horace except their slightly fraying links to Augustus. The three men made a shifting triangle in support of their leader, Horace like Agrippa from a background outside the nobility, Horace like Maecenas with a shared sensibility for art, Agrippa like Maecenas central to the history of Augustus himself and what it was now reasonable to call his throne.

Any throne needed an heir whom subjects could see occupying it when the incumbent was gone. Twenty years before, building and leading the fleet that destroyed Sextus Pompeius, Agrippa had been Augustus's most likely heir and successor. Now the official heirs were Agrippa's sons from his marriage to Augustus's daughter, Julia—the boy known as Gaius Caesar, aged three, and Lucius Caesar, newly born in the best spirit of Horace's hymn to childbirth, both of them now also Augustus's adopted sons.

Horace had little good to say for heirs. The next generation was part of the unknown future, a cloud whose most common function, in his poet's mind, was to hinder pleasure in the present. Sometimes he referred in his poems to the future owners of power and property but always to disparage them. An heir was someone who would drink the best wine next year that the owner ought to be drinking now.

To think about succession was to waste time. Horace had no children himself and even less likelihood of having them than had Livia and Augustus. When he died the greatest part of his wealth would revert to the men in power who had given it to him. His poetry would be the part of him that would survive, just like Agrippa's buildings, but would last longer than those, he hoped. His heirs were his lyrics, their words like mosaic stones intricately laid and lasting like nothing else.

Augustus, however, lacked the luxury of carelessness he had created for his poet. To maintain stability for his supporters he had to offer stability in the future – or try to. His older stepsons, Tiberius and Drusus, were the likely heirs until Gaius and Lucius came of age, a status which required them to be kept busy and ideally out of town and a long way from Agrippa. Keeping the candidates occupied and apart was his tactic, if not quite a strategy. Some critics in the Senate had still to be reassured that power would return to themselves and that there was no succession strategy at all.

Augustus himself was no more making war in the West than was Agrippa in the East. But he was watching closely the need for wars to come. His favorite, Lollius, fresh from his role in the Centenary Games, was a commander on the Rhine, where the river boundaries were less secure than those of the Euphrates. Worries circulated about the truculence of the tribal peoples of the Alps. Gossips also said of Augustus that when he was away from the Palatine he could more easily enjoy the company of Lycymnia, as Horace called Maecenas's former wife, Terentia, in his poems of appreciation.

Horace was able to withdraw to his farm. His contribution at the edge of politics was over. He had done his bit. Rome was under the control of two consuls, both from Augustus's wider family, neither important to Horace. Rumbling dissent from Senate and people about the lack of old freedoms continued. Lectures on morality had not increased support from those whose behavior was not as moral as their language. But none of this was beyond the power of the consuls to control — or within the concerns of a poet once his official job was done.

Horace wrote his longest letter — and longest poem of any kind — to a father and two sons of the Piso family, the wealthy politicians and would-be writers who had once entertained him and Vergil so welcomingly at Herculaneum. This must have seemed to them a very strange offering, a departure from the principles of the brevity he so prized in poetry. At the same time it was a highly discursive lecture on how and why poetry should be written. It was far from showing the balanced mind that their guest had once so prized in his conversations.

The youngest of the Pisos had ambitions to be a playwright, and Horace, who had written dialogues but never a play, declared confidently what the rules for the stage should be, advising brevity and other virtues at very great length. The letter contained good suggestions, couched in terse, memorable phrases. *In medias res,* "into the middle of the action," he urged as the place where a drama should be launched, recalling to his friends the technique of his satire of Brutus in the Clazomenae courtroom. A late entry into a story gave the best result – and often an early exit too. A good writer pruned his work, clipping superfluous parts, concentrating the reader's mind.

Ut pictura poesis, "poetry is like a picture," he usefully explained, experienced differently according to where the viewer or reader is standing. New words are necessary – like a river on parched land. Old words are like minerals mined from the earth. Common words, joined in new ways, can have new power. Maybe the Pisos, in their seaside pleasure palace, might create their own carpe diem. This was all good advice.

But Horace also gave his views on the numbers of actors (never more than three onstage at once), the numbers of acts (five) and the use of stage machinery (rarely). He urged an old man's caution in publishing juvenilia, at least anything written before boys were nine. He displayed much mastery of the schoolmasterly obvious, intoning the need to avoid vulgarity and to say the right thing at the right time. He praised the eloquence of Messalla, his friend from Philippi – no longer a controversial view. He offered advice on music and art, comedy and tragedy. It was as though he were providing the kind of intellectual entertainment once required for the journey to Brundisium – but this time to a class of children. He mixed good words with good sense in the best methods of his early teachers.

Then suddenly, as though the children had departed and only

Vergil and the dead poets were listening, the letter leapt in a new direction. Horace began to pour out his feelings about his own poetry as he never had before. He wrote about the precariousness of his place in society, the perils of seeking perfection when no one noticed or cared, the madness, alienation and despair that were necessary for the only art that mattered. In an instant the Pisos of Herculaneum, studying drama in the peaceful shade of Mount Vesuvius, were face to face with a mad poet of Mount Etna, their friend Horace as a modern-day mystic Empedocles staring down into hot ash.

Horace was suddenly raging against his life. When children see a poet, he taunted, they do not sit quietly and listen, they pursue and mock. Men dread touching the maniac for fear of catching the mania themselves. And when the mad poet raises his head, sticks his nose in the air, and stalks off spluttering his verses, does anyone care if he falls into a ditch or down a well? No, they will say that his death was his own wish.

And perhaps they would be right. Empedocles, poet and philosopher of the greatest age of Greece, was famed for his doctrine of four natural elements ruled by Love and Strife (*Eros* and *Eris*, almost the same word in Greek) but was said to have wanted a different immortality too. In one way or another (and who really knew?) he wanted to be remembered as an immortal, not merely as someone who had left a lasting legacy. He had stood at the edge of the volcano, looked down into the smoking darkness, and let his body follow his eyes. All poets should have the right and power to destroy themselves. Anyone who saves a man against his will is no better than his murderer.

Horace was now railing at his fate at ever becoming a poet. What had he done to deserve it? Had he pissed over the ashes of the ancient dead? Had he dug up a dark patch of holy land? The answers did not matter. His madness was manifest to all. He was no more than a caged animal, and if, like a bear, he were strong enough to break his bars, he would terrify his listeners, the learned and unlearned alike, by the lash of his recitals. If he held a man in his arms, he would read him to death, clinging like a leech till he was gorged with his victim's blood.

The poet as a madman on a fiery mountain: this was Horace's picture of himself for the Pisos. The poet as bear and sucking leech, the wild beast, the bloodsucker, maybe a financial bloodsucker as well as a thief of life. That was stranger still. These pictures were savage and satirical in the strangest way, not what anyone reading would have been prepared for. It was hardly a letter likely to encourage the young Piso boys to become writers.

At the start of the letter he had used the example of a mad painter who joined a woman's head to a fish with feathers, a jocular warning in his art theory against breaches of unity. It seemed then as though his readers would be due for more good advice, all of it as gently expressed as they were used to. Instead, four hundred lines of classroom theory later, when even the keenest student might have been nodding, Horace was back to madness in different, harsher ways, first presenting his mad poet in a pit, abandoned by everyone, assumed to have wanted to die.

> ut mala quem scabies aut morbus regius urget
> aut fanaticus error et iracunda Diana,
> uesanum tetigisse timent fugiuntque poetam
> qui sapiunt; agitant pueri incautique sequuntur.
> hic dum sublimis uersus ructatur et errat,
> si ueluti merulis intentus decidit auceps
> in puteum foueamue, licet "succurrite" longum
> clamet "io ciues," non sit qui tollere curet.

Poet on a Volcano

si curet quis opem ferre et demittere funem,
"qui scis an prudens huc se deiecerit atque
seruari nolit?"

Just as though an evil itch or sickness weighs on him,
or a religious mania and a raging moon,
men of right mind run away and fear to touch the maddened poet;
careless children chase and taunt while he goes roaming around
with his head in the clouds, belching out his lines,
and if, like a hunter looking for blackbirds, he falls into a pit,
however much he shouts "Help me, citizens!," no one will pull him out.
And if anyone does bother to let down a rope, well,
"How do you know that he hasn't thrown himself down on purpose
and doesn't want to be saved?"

The mad poet was a warning from and to Horace himself. And that was not all. The horror would become worse, not just the poet as a stupid bird-hunter or even a suicidal old philosopher but as a caged bear and, in the letter's last word, a bloodsucking leech.

. . . dicam, Siculique poetae
narrabo interitum: deus immortalis haberi
dum cupit Empedocles, ardentem frigidus Aetnam
insiluit. sit ius liceatque perire poetis;
invitum qui seruat, idem facit occidenti.
nec semel hoc fecit nec, si retractus erit, iam
fiet homo et ponet famosae mortis amorem.

nec satis apparet cur uersus factitet, utrum
minxerit in patrios cineres, an triste bidental
moverit incestus: certe furit, ac uelut ursus,

obiectos caueae ualuit si frangere clatros,
indoctum doctumque fugat recitator acerbus;
quem uero arripuit, tenet occiditque legendo,
non missura cutem nisi plena cruoris hirudo.

So I shall speak. I will tell now of the death of Empedocles,
the poet from Sicily, yearning to be considered immortal, who, coolly
leapt into the fires of Etna. Let poets be free to perish!
Anyone who saves a poet against his will is a killer.
He hasn't done it just once. Just because he's rescued, he won't be
brought to his senses and stop craving a famous death.

It is just not clear why the poet keeps on writing, whether
perhaps he has been pissing on sacred ground or been cursed
for some other crime against the gods. No, he is mad, like a
bear that has broken the bars of its cage, a repulsive reciter who
makes everyone run away, learned or not. If he catches a
reader, he grips him tight and reads him to
death, a leech that never leaves the skin until swollen with blood.

An entertainer in his patron's cage, a leech on his patron's body, a dependent, a parasite: this was a poet's lowest sense of himself. A comic end to a literary letter? Hardly.

Gradually Horace took up again his old challenges. At the end of his third book of *Odes* he had boasted of building his monument "more lasting than bronze," *aere perennius;* "higher than the royal pyramids" of Egypt, *regalique situ pyramidum altius.* This had seemed like the end. Now he was beginning a fourth book, back once more working into Latin what, in the distant days before Philippi, he had learned from Alcaeus, Sappho, and Asclepiades. His old idealism and anger were still not far from the surface. He could be as crazed as he had been when reporting from the bedrooms of the Subura. His first words of his new book were a prayer to the goddess of sex not to give him too hard a time.

"It has been a long while, Venus," he wrote. *Intermissa, Venus, diu.* "I beg, I beg," *Precor, precor,* he continued, in the second Asclepiad line; "I am not what I was" when ruled by my dear Cinara, *non sum qualis eram.* He left ambiguous whether he was referring to erotic lyrics or erotic acts, his mirrored mosaics of words or his room of mirrors. The two had become so linked that it hardly mattered.

In the shortest poem in this unexpected book he saw a sad future for a reluctant boy lover, one who refused him now but would one day look in the mirror, see stubble where once there was soft, downy skin, and ask himself why he had not been a more enthusiastic sexual partner when he had the chance. By then he would be the pursuer, not the pursued. His best time would have passed. The mirror would have new faces.

"You cruel boy, still potent with the gifts of the love goddess," *O crudelis adhuc et Veneris muneribus potens,* "Damn! you will say in future when you see the reflection of the new you," *Dices heu quotiens te speculo videris alterum.* Why did I not do then what I want to do now? Why are my old pink cheeks not mine when I need them?

This was a familiar tactic for encouraging young boys to submit to sex. It was a powerful expression of a classic literary theme from the libraries of Rome as well as Athens. It was a staple of life. It was also a deeply felt complaint against the passing of time, an imagination of a future looking back at the present and wondering what might have been.

More cheerfully, he imagined a more specific figure in his life as she looked back in old age at her life in these years. This was one of the choristers who had sung his Song of the Century. He began by again praising Apollo, "O god whose power the children felt," *dive quem proles,* before bringing back the memory of himself bidding all his young singers to stick to Sappho's meter and watch his thumb as he beat out the time.

To one of them he made a vivid prediction of her future pride. *Nupta iam dices,* "As a married woman you will say" that you joined the sacred song, skilled in the rhythms of "Horace the poet," *vatis Horati.* The word *vatis* was a boast, meaning not just a poet but a prophet, a man inspired by the gods. Vergil had been a prophet too. This was their new literary status: mediators with other worlds. This was also the first time that Horace had used his own name in the lyric poems that meant the most to him. *Vatis Horati:* the reference, though bold, is characteristically indirect, only glancing, edited to almost nothing in the memory of a married former virgin of his choir.

When Horace begged the goddess of love to leave him alone at the beginning of his book, he urged her to visit instead the home of his new friend Paullus Maximus, uniquely in the *Odes* using both names. There, he said, she would be hymned by a choir and entertained by the dancing of boys and girls. In this new phase of Horace's life — as laureate poet and appreciator of peace — the place of Philippi in his mind had been taken by Augustus's great games, and the place of Philippi's survivors by younger men who had made their pacts with the new politics.

The second poem was addressed to a son of Mark Antony and Fulvia, Iullus Antonius, a recipient with a peculiarly dangerous pedigree in Rome's recent past. Iullus had survived the purge after Actium that had cost the lives of his brothers. He was now himself a poet who had married a daughter of Augustus's sister Octavia and was firmly placed in the new regime.

Pindarum quisquis studet aemulari, "Whoever seeks to rival Pindar," Horace began, warning of the risk of a watery grave to anyone who strove to match the mighty poet famed for flattering the great of Greece some four hundred years before. Such ambition in a poet, like that of the mythological Icarus, son of Daedalus of Crete, would mean flying far too close to the sun.

Horace was in a quandary here. What Iullus wanted was for Horace to be the one facing the fate of Icarus and to be writing a new poem in praise of Augustus's glory — some military equivalent of the moral message of the Song of the Century. In the past Horace had replied directly to that kind of request, pointing out his inadequacies and the preeminence of others. But this request might be different. If Iullus, now so favored in Augustus's house, was asking for a poem, Horace could not be sure that the request was not, in fact, from Augustus himself. Iullus might be just the messenger. This time it might be insufficient to say that he was not an epic poet and to suggest a replacement from one of the many who liked to see themselves as the Roman Homer.

What Iullus wanted was not epic but lyric praise, a matching of Pindar, the panegyrist of politicians and charioteers. Horace was well capable of writing a poem in Pindar's style. Everyone knew that he was capable. Horace had somehow to turn the request back to the man making it — and, while he was protecting himself, give Iullus some flavor of what a choral poem of praise to Augustus might be like.

He wanted Iullus to take on the assignment himself. He had to make clear that his desire to be supplanted was sincere. But he also wanted to warn Iullus against dangerous aspirations to flatter too much. He should not aim slavishly to follow Pindar. *Pindarum quisquis studet aemulari, Iulle, ceratis ope Daedalea nititur pennis vitreo daturus nomina ponto,* "Whoever seeks to rival Pindar, Iullus, is on wings of wax, however much they are made from the magic of Daedalus, and soon will give his name to the glassy sea" in which he will drown. Horace's young friend should praise Augustus as best he can but be cautious. The bad past was never far behind. There was a thin line along which every courtier had to walk, a firepit beneath every piece of apparently solid ground.

Throughout the fourth book of *Odes,* as it took shape in these years, sounded the continuing sense of uncertainty, fear of a fall, the continuing cry of that caged bear trying to escape – and the desperate tread of marching time. The contrast between nature's permanent renewal and our inability to renew was intense. Horace was ever more a poet on a volcano.

In his first book of *Odes,* when he addressed the return of spring it was by vivid descriptions of nature followed by philosophical observation. Only after the changing rivers and trees came the reminders of the shortness of life. His opening words, *Solvitur acris hiems,* "Fierce winter loses its grip," were the start of two separate poetic strands.

In the spring poem of his new fourth book Horace tied the twin strands together. *Diffugere nives.* "The snows dissolved," and the march of the seasons was itself a devouring of time, a proof against any hope of immortality. *Immortalia ne speres monet annus,* "The changing year itself warns against thoughts of life beyond death." *Et almum quae rapit hora diem,* "and every hour steals the daylight." Nature's constant eating and renewal of itself stood in stark contrast to any human fate. Horace's advice? To enjoy for oneself whatever one might be tempted to leave to an heir. This poem of dark beauty was a gift to Manlius Torquatus, a young man related to the consul in the year of Horace's birth, from a family famed for opposition to Caesar, whom he was advising to gather his rosebuds while he might.

Horace offered another poem to Lollius, who had shared in the success of the Centenary Games before suffering a distant disaster that was, sadly for him, the latest talk of Rome. As a commander on the Rhine, he had barely left the festival singing and smoke before an army of three German tribes crossed the river and crushed his Legion of the Lark, once famed as Gallic fighters for Julius Caesar and Mark Antony, proud conquerors of elephants, with shields to prove it, now losers of their eagle standard in Rhineland mud. Horace needed to respond. His friend, he said, need not worry because he had a poet to protect him, a promise that was probably less than Lollius would have liked from a friend close to the center of power.

Ne forte credas, "Do not believe." In his poem Horace promised Lollius, somewhat archly, that his other great exploits for Augustus would avoid *lividas obliviones,* "envious oblivion." They would never be forgotten while he had a poet for a friend since no one would ever have heard of Helen of Troy or Agamemnon without Homer—or even lesser figures like Teucer, hero of Horace's poem to Plancus. Lollius, he said, could reasonably expect Horace to remember him as favorably as Plancus, despite his spotty record over the years, and without harping on about the lost eagle of the Lark.

CHAPTER SEVENTEEN

Captor and Captive

Poetry and politics were ever more inseparable. Two border tribes in the Alps, emboldened by Lollius's defeat, were now becoming a threat to the empire. Or at least the Vindelici and the Raeti could be so perceived if it suited Augustus to do so. Horace could not now keep as far away from heirs and would-be heirs as he would have liked. At the end of the summer of 15 BCE Augustus wrote to Horace from Gaul to ask for a poem to celebrate a great victory that his stepson Drusus had just won – or which Augustus had just decided he had won.

Augustus was manipulating a propaganda campaign among his family that was much more complex than the military campaign itself. The Alpine war was one of simple brutality. The battles, far from the sight of any writers, were less what Horace had witnessed at Philippi and more a village-by-village campaign of burning, enslavement, and transportation. Horace had never been to the Alps or anywhere near the Alps. This was a literary assignment purely in the service of politics, far from the war that was its seeming subject.

Horace's job was like that of a courtroom lawyer, rhetoric with a calibrated purpose. Both Livia's sons had to be encouraged but not too much. Drusus's victory had to be primarily a victory for Livia's family (distant glories were the safest) and for Augustus. The young victor had to be praised but not praised so much that it frightened either the Senate or the sons of Agrippa.

Augustus needed permanent public support for himself—and for whichever successor he chose, the very dynastic outcome which Brutus had died to prevent and against which Horace had once fought. For those looking forward rather than back, to potential heirs and their supporters, not to dreamers of life without Caesars, the nuance of every one of Horace's words would count. Drusus was a popular young man, but, with Agrippa and Julia's children, the young Gaius and Lucius, still their adopted father's favorites, he and Tiberius, the older members of Augustus's wife's family, feared a fading future.

Horace took on this unappealing assignment in two parts. The first was borrowed from Pindar, the grandiloquent poet whom he had warned Antony's son of trying to match, not one of Horace's favorites for his personal poetry but perfect for this. Pindar required endurance. So did Horace's homage. *Qualem ministrum fulminis alitem*, "Just like the winged bearer of lightning," he began in a sentence which stretched over four Alcaic stanzas, describing the eagle of Zeus in the sheep pen and a young lion in pursuit of a goat. Finally Horace reached his point: just like these kings of beasts, he intoned in words written to be recognized rather than believed, was Drusus as he attacked the ax-wielding Raeti.

The second section praised Drusus's ancestors in Rome's war against Carthage two centuries before. Taken together, which was probably easier when the poem was read aloud to devotees, the two halves of the poem achieved its complex aims. He then had to repeat the exercise in praise of Tiberius in the same campaign. Here he took the unusual initiative of addressing Augustus directly, *Auguste,* as part of his aim that the father be not diminished in the panegyric of his sons. On Augustus's return from Gaul after clearing up the mess left by Lollius he poured out his relief. *Divis orte bonis,* "Our leader, sprung from the noble gods," give back the light to your country!

Horace had also to respond to Augustus's request for an epistle addressed to himself. The emperor, it seemed, wanted to counter any future suggestion that Horace had avoided the task of writing one. The request was maybe just a suggestion but, even if so, hardly an ordinary suggestion. It was common enough for a poet to address a patron with unsolicited pleas or praise, less so to respond to a patron's request which had the clear status of a demand. For this task, one even more sensitive than hymning Tiberius among the axmen of the Alps, Horace wrote a long letter to Augustus about poetry – in the same style as his letter to the Pisos but without the human bird and the mad poet.

He began conversationally, almost apologetic about wasting Augustus's time. *Cum tot sustineas et tanta negotia solus,* "Since you alone are bearing so much weight of work and expectation," he wrote before moving swiftly on to add Augustus to Hercules and Romulus in a list of Rome's semi-divine benefactors, all of them insufficiently rewarded in their own lifetimes. After more than 250 meandering lines he ended, as a gentle jester hoping that in death he might avoid the pomp – and bad poetry – of a Roman funeral.

In the main part of the letter, however, Horace was still something of the madman, declaiming as though to his whole world that no one understood him and his art. He too was an unappreciated master of Rome. He despised, he said, the Roman preference for appearance over content, the dazzling shows which overwhelmed all words. If this was his only reference to the Centenary Games it was hardly tactful. Nor was it very clear. In some ways, he recalled, those games had been magical, and how could they have happened without a poet?

Critics of poets should remember that. It was unfortunate, he went on, that people so often remembered what they hated more than what they liked. He himself was not grandiose or greedy, but he got no credit for that. He was a miniaturist (except in these letters) and a modernist, and if readers did not like his work, so be it: better by far than to be writer of poems for the waste bin.

This was an almost manic defense of his work, defending at some length all modern poetry against those who were envious of its practitioners and who, as result of that envy, were obsessed with the old Latin writers alone. The pioneer Latin poets whom he had read before his education in Athens were crude and obscure, he said. The comic playwrights wrote only to put a coin in their pockets. Most of those who now claimed to like them were mere pretenders, followers of antiquarian fashion. How long would it take for Horace to become an appreciated ancient? Now he was only the unacknowledged future.

This was bravado, also bold. Augustus himself was known to watch the old Roman plays and to encourage their production. Horace's knowledge of this imperial preference did not inhibit his flow. He did not, he said, regret studying Livius Andronicus under Orbilius; he was just amazed to be told now that Andronicus was beautiful and faultless. Italians were rude mechanicals. Greeks were elegant and subtle. Horace was reminiscing, exaggerating, and distorting like a dinner table entertainer, well ready to offend if offence was the way to attract attention.

Rome might have conquered Greece, he proposed, but in reality the recently conquered nation had defeated the conqueror — and brought art to rustic Italy. This was a ringing line: *Graecia capta ferum victorem cepit et artis intulit agresti Latio,* "Captured Greece captured the fierce victor and brought art to rural Rome." It was also, at best, a distortion of the truth. Horace and Augustus both knew that the influence of Greece on Roman literature predated its conquest by centuries. Both cultures had their men of brilliance and their bumpkins. Romans were entwined with Greeks from their city's start.

None of this argument mattered much. Literary history was not Horace's real purpose in this epistle. His subject was himself, his success in his own mind, and the uselessness of his unskilled competitors, too many of them, too obsessed by scribbling, whose *insania,* madness, was all too clear.

Horace was as insecure as every man of bombast he knew. His added insecurity was that he had never produced a poem that thanked Augustus as Augustus would have liked. His achievement might not have been enough (he was excellent at saying no to orders for epic praise). It had also been widely misunderstood. He had brought the most sophisticated Greek lyric poetry into Latin and made something new. Was that not enough?

Greece had helped to make Rome, helped Rome make itself. Horace had twisted bright new threads in an old coat, no small thing, surely a proper cause for pride among the many achievements of the new age. But in this, his only letter to Augustus, Horace was less celebratory than anxious—about himself, about poetry, and about Rome itself.

Everywhere was need for caution. Nothing could be guaranteed. In art, as in politics, the good could revert to bad. In his longest address to the man who had dominated his life since the death of Brutus he recalled an incompetent court poet for Alexander the Great, Choerilus, who received "royal money," *regale nomisma,* for staining the royal reputation with his uselessness. The coins were called Philippi; *rettulit acceptos, regale nomisma, Philippos.* The totemic word hung heavily at the end of its line, as though waiting for the recipient to respond.

The tone of these poems was bright but often wearying – as was their author. In the final ode of his fourth book he praised the peace achieved by Augustus almost mechanically, as though the list of defeated tribes and cowering countries were about to be carved in stone on the newly planned Altar of Peace. *Canemus,* "We will sing," he promised in the last word of his last poem in the meter of Alcaeus. *Canemus,* We will sing of the noble heroes of Troy and their Roman successors. That promise was for the far future. He was not singing now. His fourth book of *Odes,* published in 13 BCE, contained only fifteen poems, half the number of book 3, filled with protests at the passing of time and proof that his best time had passed.

More significant for Augustus, Agrippa's best time had passed too. His last act was to persuade the Pannonians of the Danube that they would be unwise to fight a Roman army if he was its commander. No one else had that status. Tiberius was moving along the Rhine suppressing mountain tribes. Drusus was pacifying Germans. But Agrippa, Augustus's commander and second-in-command as far back as the death of Julius Caesar, was successfully uttering threats while suffering swollen feet, exhaustion, plague, and coughs.

Early in 12, Augustus rushed south to his side, but arrived too late. The greatest general and co-ruler of the empire was already dead. Always taller, stronger, and fitter than Augustus, still unhymned by Horace or Varius or any other poet of note, he failed to outlive the man he had brought to power. At the time of his death, his third wife, Augustus's daughter, was pregnant with another child. The birth of a boy, the next Agrippa at Rome, named Postumus in his father's memory, added to the truth that the question of Augustus's heirs and successors could from this point be avoided by no one.

CHAPTER EIGHTEEN

On the Esquiline

Horace retired again to his house and farms. He also took another house that Maecenas had put at his disposal in nearby Tibur, the town famed for apple trees and waterfalls, where the unceasing sound of the river Anio was thought beneficial for diseases of the mind. This time his retirement was real. There was to be no fifth book of odes – or any further ceremonial duties when, in 10 BCE, Augustus joined Drusus in Gaul to dedicate a giant altar to the imperial ideal, the closest he considered prudent to the idea of an altar to himself as a god. Horace had his limits as a praise poet, and this might perhaps have been one of them.

On the same day as the dedication, Drusus's wife, Antonia, daughter of Augustus's sister and Mark Antony, gave birth to a second son. A new range of heirs was emerging. Augustus, Tiberius, and Drusus began a joint program of marking their various military achievements by traditional parades and marches rather than victory poems. Drusus was just about to receive his own personal *ovatio* from the troops when suddenly he too was dead, at age twenty-nine, the brother long favored by so many as the heir. There was much grief at this loss but no further call on Horace to pick up his theme of the young eagle plunging from snowy crags.

Some said that Drusus's mind had been moving against the idea of anyone being Augustus's heir. He was thought to favor a return to the politics of the years before the ascendancy of Julius Caesar. Among the deepest mourners of Drusus's death were those who hoped still that Brutus and his followers had not died in vain at Philippi. There was suspicion that Drusus's brother Tiberius might have been a poisoner as well as a terrorizer of Alpine tribes. The surviving family stood together, however, celebrating the twentieth anniversary of Augustus's notional abandonment of his emergency powers. The eighth month in the Roman calendar was renamed Augustus. Parades were again preferred to words.

In late September 8 BCE Maecenas died. He had never wanted to be a brake on his friend's autocracy; he had no fondness for the republic that had perished in ceaseless civil war. But even in times of estrangement, he had for thirty years been a brake on Augustus's bad instincts. Without Agrippa or Maecenas on the Palatine Hill the stage was clear for family members warring to succeed.

Maecenas made Augustus his heir. This was becoming a formality. Augustus appreciated the idea that no one but himself should drink the wine that rich men had left undrunk — or, if he would not drink it himself, decide who should be the drinker. The minister who claimed descent from Etruscan kings was buried at his estate on the Esquiline Hill, the area of Rome that he had transformed from slums of prostitutes and witches to slopes worthy of his own grave.

The much greater legacy to Augustus from Maecenas was the work of Vergil and Horace. Maecenas's will included instruction as well as gifts to Augustus: *Horati Flacci ut mei esto memor,* "Remember Horatius Flaccus as you remember me." Maecenas meant the best memories of the turbulent years he and Augustus had shared.

The rebuilt aggrandizement of Rome had made the Subura cleaner but had not stopped the almost annual surge of disease from the Tiber and the sewers below its streets. Less than two months after Maecenas's death Horace himself fell suddenly ill and died. Whether he was as ready for death as a good Epicurean should have been was unrecorded, probably unrecordable, not knowable then and certainly not now. Horace was an inconsistent follower of Epicurus at best. His last poems did not suggest the peace of mind required to banish the fear of dying.

His mocking trust in horoscopes, once bantered about between Horace and Maecenas, did, however, turn out to be true: poet and patron did die almost together. Too frail even to write a will, Horace summoned witnesses and declared that he too was leaving all that he owned to Augustus. And he too was buried on the Esquiline Hill, near on the street map to his early haunts after Philippi, in every other way a world away. It was the last week of November. He was in his fifty-seventh year.

CHAPTER NINETEEN

Monumentum

The double loss of Maecenas and his poet reinforced the loss of Agrippa. The world of Augustus became different, smaller, more confined and introverted. It became more concerned with that place where Horace had said no one should look, the future.

That future was concentrated power – and future poets had to see it or leave the stage, to exile if they were lucky. Horace's advice on ignoring what had not yet happened, whether seen as philosophical or frivolous, public or merely private, went as unheeded in the public arena as it had been in his day. Succession gripped the inner state.

Tiberius, sole surviving son of Augustus's wife, was forced to marry the twice-widowed Julia. He continued his northern campaigns, even more successfully when there was no poet to praise him than when there had been. When Augustus asked questions about what and who would follow his own death, the answer was sometimes an Emperor Tiberius and often not. There was carefully manufactured uncertainty. Gaius and Lucius, his own young grandsons, were still the closest to being his official heirs if he were suddenly to need one.

To those who worried that the traditional wheels of government were worn out, locked in pointless corruption, Augustus showed that he still cared for the consulship and the lower rungs of the career ladder by which it was reached. He began a campaign against electoral fraud, keeping warm the hopes of those who hoped that an heir might not be needed, that the republican history of Rome was not over and, in future, would have the Caesars as only a forty-year interlude.

Horace, had he lived, might well have approved of that. He had never attacked Brutus or repudiated his colleagues at Philippi. He had praised Augustus as a man who had brought the peace necessary for recovery, prosperity, and his own work as a poet. He had not praised the principle of permanent succession. He had often shown fellow feeling for losers. Brutus, the man who had first brought him into public life, was there at the last.

The only true concerns for Horace had been his life in the present — sex, wine, and writing — and the future of his work. Politics was linked but secondary to both. He had boasted of leaving a monument more lasting than bronze, higher than the pyramids, an achievement that would survive as long as priests climbed the Capitoline. Such a monument, however, was of words alone. It did not require the politician whose peace made possible his words to hand down power exclusively to his own family.

Horace died at a point when, in the future story of Roman politics and its place in the world, any direction might still have been taken. There did not have to be a dynasty of Caesars. In 6 BCE Tiberius left Rome for Rhodes, a peaceful holiday island that had long since recovered from the depredations of the assassins' army on its road to Philippi. He declared himself to be in retirement. No one knew exactly what that meant. He left Julia behind after five un-happily married years and her five children by Agrippa. Horace's late-life friend Iullus was one of several men to whom Julia turned for protection for her family, beginning a saga of sexual intrigue and battling heirs beyond any story that Horace had ever seen or told.

In 2 and 4 CE, Lucius and Gaius, the official heirs among Julia and Agrippa's children, also died. It was not till 14, at Augustus's death, that Tiberius became finally the answer to the question that so many had preferred not to ask. Rome had an empire long before it had an emperor, but two decades after Horace's death, an emperor was a necessity. Tiberius became that emperor, followed by three others, Caligula, Claudius, and Nero, whose claim to rule came from their place in the family of Julius Caesar and his adopted son.

If Horace had lived he would have seen a tightening in the demands on poets to flatter the regime. Praise of Augustus that had seemed from Horace a little too obsequious would soon be seen as the minimum required. Flattery became the oil of a new admin-istrative machine. That was bad for poetry but not necessarily for government.

The friends that Horace had met in Athens and at Philippi faded away from history even if they stayed alive. Marcus Lollius made the biggest impact on the future through his granddaughter Lollia Paulina, who became empress of Rome as the third wife of Augus-tus's great-grandson Caligula. The complexities of flattery had by that time reached a peak beyond anything that Horace could have conceived.

If he could have seen the future (the least and last thing he had ever wanted to do), he would also have noted a shift in opportuni-ties, which, in one way at least, were much more open to a new boy from nowhere, the kind of person he had once been. Horace had been happy to satirize the fancy-dressed freedmen parvenus of Augustus's early years, writing almost as though he were a disdainful aristocrat himself. But the gradual concentration of decision making within a single household gave new power to the emperor's slaves and former slaves.

Fewer men and women who, like Horace, were libertino patre natum felt the weakness and shame of that status. When Horace's farm entered the imperial estate it became a way station for a massive court of the formerly enslaved moving from one country palace to another. A place of one man's freedom became a part of bureaucracy's birthplace. This new means to administer an empire became as much a monument for the future of politics over the centuries as were Horace's poems for poetry. The legacy of Philippi and Actium lasted alongside that of Pyrrha and Leuconoe, linked and intertwined in the history of Europe and beyond.

CHAPTER TWENTY

Words as Weapons

There were enough uncontroversial poems left in Horace's name to make him immediately suitable for the classroom, exactly as he had feared. His odes, in particular, were short, intricate, well suited for teachers, and, as long as the salacious was edited away, suitable for students for centuries to come. Marcus Fabius Quintilianus, head of Rome's top teaching academy after the death of Nero, decided that Horace's rambling letter to the Pisos was a formal treatise on classical practice, and he promoted its new title, *Ars Poetica*, "The Art of Poetry." With less emphasis on Mount Etna's mad poet and more on *medias res*, less anger and more meter, it quickly reached the schools of Roman Egypt and beyond, further fulfilling its author's hopes and horrors of immortality.

Forty years after the fall of the first dynasty of Caesars, Horace remained famous enough for inclusion among the biographical subjects for the courtier and author Gaius Suetonius Tranquillus, who was writing not only lives of the emperors (for which he became famous) but the lives of Rome's greatest orators, grammarians, and poets. Suetonius was a secretary to Emperor Trajan and had access to the letters of Augustus in the Palatine records, and probably other letters too. He had a good eye for telling detail: he recorded not only the physical frailties of Tiberius but Horace's chamber of mirrors for observing a body from every angle. A chronicler of physical defects and political theory, the techniques of courtesans and teachers, rivers' names and fashions for clothes, Suetonius was a pioneer biographer and a lasting framer of his subjects' lives.

Two or maybe three texts of Horace's work survived the fall of the Roman Empire, when so much else was lost, and emerged in copies during the Middle Ages. Luck and the number of student readers played their part — just as they had for Vergil. Augustus's story of his own achievements, his *Res Gestae,* had been carved on stone many times over, but Agrippa's autobiography disappeared along with all the epics of Varius that might have praised him had Horace had his way. Agrippa's treatises on geography also failed the test of eternity, although his name survived on the Pantheon thanks to the generosity of Hadrian who rebuilt it. M·AGRIPPA· L·F·COS·TERTIVM·FECIT, "Marcus Agrippa, son of Lucius, made this when he was consul for the third time," ran the inscription in front of a massive concrete dome — and it still runs there.

Horace's hopeful boast at the end of his third book of *Odes* was that his fame would last *Dum Capitolium scandet cum tacita virgine pontifex,* "as long as the priest, with the silent virgin, climbs the Capitoline Hill." When the priests were Christian and the virgin was a nun, the boast still stayed true. The Pantheon survived because in the early seventh century it was rededicated to Saint Mary and the Martyrs. A Christian poem in the tenth century, *Ekbasis cuiusdam captivi,* "The Escape of a Certain Captive," told an Easter story of lions, foxes, and magic blankets by means of the mass looting of lines from Horace's *Epistles* and *Satires.*

Not till Petrarch in the fourteenth century did any major writer take inspiration from Horace's odes, the works whose unique durability had been the subject of such confidence in 23 BCE. Petrarch was the new pioneer, putting himself in his own poems as Horace had done, adapting the meters that Horace had adapted from the Greeks. Petrarch's friend Boccaccio did the same. This was a renaissance of a renaissance. Forty-four separate Italian editions were published in the last three decades of the fifteenth century.

In England, Shakespeare found a sinister role for the first words of Horace's ode beginning *Integer vitae scelerisque purus,* "He who is wholesome in life and free from crime." The line must have been famous enough around 1590 for the audience of *Titus Andronicus,* probably Shakespeare's first tragedy, to note its resonance for a play in which no characters are free of crime, their criminal options ranging from rape to tongue-removal, the severing of limbs to burial alive. Horace's words are on a page wrapped around murder weapons — "some mad message" from a "mad grandfather." The recipient notes "O, 'tis a verse in Horace, I know it well, I read it in the grammar long ago." The villain does not understand the message even though he can read it. That was Shakespeare's dramatic point.

It was Shakespeare too who revived the life and death of Brutus in his play *Julius Caesar* ten years later, based on stories from Plutarch, Suetonius's Greek contemporary in the art of writing ancient lives. Plutarch, unlike Suetonius, had not himself written the lives of poets, but his vivid accounts of Caesar, Augustus, Antony, and Brutus brought back the battle that had defined Horace's life: as Caesar's ghost warns Brutus in act 4, scene 3, "Thou shalt see me at Philippi."

Within a wide choice of popular Latin texts in the seventeenth century anybody could have a personal Horace — either as readers or as translators into English. The very difficulty of the translating task attracted some to make their own versions, as though the odes were a fiendish puzzle. Great poets competed with lesser and did not always triumph. John Milton still wins the prize from some for the worst rendition of the querulous ode to Pyrrha, "Quis multa gracilis," "What slender Youth bedew'd with liquid odours / Courts thee on roses in some pleasant cave?" Pyrrha's much-favored blond hair, *simplex munditiis,* became "plain in thy neatness."

Augustus himself, in the spirit of his Centenary Games if not his own sexual life, might have approved the puritan tone. In 1673 Milton described it as "Rendred almost word for word without Rhyme according to the Latin Measure as near as the Language will permit." In the spirit of variety that has always characterized responses to Horace, Milton's Pyrrha has had distinguished admirers too. His contemporary John Oldham, short lived and not well known, freely adapted Horace's bore from the Forum into a bore who "names every Wench that passes through the park" and every one of them who has a sexually transmitted disease.

In the eighteenth century Alexander Pope, even more than Petrarch, absorbed Horace into his writing life. In 1737, in the reign of George II, he gave a vigorous account of Horace's first ode in his fourth book: "Intermissa Venus diu," "Again? new Tumults in my Breast? / Ah, spare me, Venus let me, let me rest! / I am not now, alas!, the man / As in the gentle reign of My Queen Anne."

Lord Chesterfield, one of the king's favorite diplomats, explained to his son in 1747 that serious students kept a cheap copy of Horace's works to hand which they could read in "the necessary house." As required, the pages could be torn out as a sacrifice to Cloacina, goddess of the sewers. Lavatorial uses were not restricted to devotion. Scholars began to think that they knew better than the first manuscript writers what Horace had written — or even what he should have written. Richard Bentley, at Trinity College, Cambridge, pioneer of the modern university examination, was variously judged both a genius in "emendation" and a major exceeder of his brief for his 1711 edition; one critic asked that Bentley's Horace be buried "under his Arse" so that Cloacina could continue to be properly served.

Phrases from Horace were everywhere borrowed and transmitted without too much concern for their original context. Fragments fell into other works like glass into jewelry and mosaics. Critics hailed "in medias res" (beginning in the midst of the action; good advice for storytellers), "ut pictura poesis" (the call for poetry to paint a picture), "silvas academi" (the groves where words are studied, ideally not to death), the "disiecti membra poetae" (the dead poet's dismembered limbs), and perhaps the most popular, in so many places, "carpe diem" (seize the moment, never lose the magical power of now).

"Sapere aude" (Dare to know) was promoted by Immanuel Kant in his 1784 essay "What Is Enlightenment?" Taken from advice to Lollius about his leisure reading, it became a call for a European intellectual revolution and came to mean "Dare to use your reason" and "Dare to be wise." "Incipe!" (Begin!), from the beginning of that poem's next line, became the motto for many schools professing to teach rationality and moderation, including my own in the London suburbs in the 1960s, without, in my case at least, the slightest indication from our teachers of where this thought was from or what precisely we pupils were supposed to begin.

The early works were often judged lesser than the first three books of *Odes*, sometimes not just lesser but the lowest juvenilia. While Vergil had advanced from the delightful shepherds of his *Bucolica* to the full, mature seriousness of the *Aeneid*, Horace's youthful descriptions of the torture of children and his abuse of old women in bed suited no one and in many "complete editions" did not appear at all.

The "Incipe!" school motto was particularly suitable for my own first text of Horace because to begin the second satire was all that we could do with it. After Horace's mysterious opening "ambubaiarum collegia, pharmacopolae" (colleges of flute girls and quacks), followed only twenty-four lines before the poem came to an even more mysterious close. Horace's comments on sex with married women and the particular tastes of Cupiennius, "Mirator cunni Cupiennius albi," had to be found and investigated elsewhere.

Further elucidation of *Satires* 1.2 was elusive. In the 1960s we lacked the advantage of Emily Gowers's scholarly notes in her 2012 edition of the *Satires* on "rape (oral or anal)," the "flounce" by which married women added extra covering to their ankles, and the poetic punning of *tegat*, "cover," with *tetigisse*, "touch," "the natural but perverse wish to touch what is covered." Pope dealt with the translation of *cunni albi* in an anonymous imitation of himself, complete with notes, also by himself, which he attributed to Richard Bentley. The fake Bentley criticized the fake Pope for his translation of *albi* as the white toga of a senatorial wife: "*cunnus albus* by no means signifying a white or grey garment, but a thing under a white or grey garment, which thing may be either black, brown, red, or particoloured." Thus did the Horatians of the eighteenth century amuse and confuse. As the radical British scholar Charles Martindale commented in 1993, "Bentley is mocked for his pedantry and humourlessness, but nonetheless his interpretation of Horace is a persuasive one. Horace's obscenities are frequently glossed over."

In 1747 Horace's late ode "Diffugere nives" reached as far as readers of Cumberland dialect in the English Lake District, where there was perhaps a deeper relief at a new spring than in Bentley's Cambridge. "The snow has left the fells and fled, / Their tops i'green the trees hev' cled," wrote the young schoolteacher Josiah Relph, who died of tuberculosis at the age of thirty-one, translating the advice to Torquatus that every hour steals the daylight that remains: "The year, 'at slips sae fast away, / Whispers we must not think to stay."

In 1819 John Keats absorbed one of Horace's calmer early poems, "Mollis inertia cur tantam diffuderit imis," into the opening of his "Ode to a Nightingale": "My heart aches and a drowsy numbness pains my sense." Horace was replying to Maecenas's question why he hadn't finished his book; the answer was his passion for a freedwoman not content with him alone. Keats was describing his lethargy in terms of wine and drugs — and recognizing that Horace's numbness in the years after Philippi shared something with his own.

Keats did not mention Horace by name, but Wordsworth did, admiring the sense of nature in the description of "the Sabine farm he loved so well." One of Byron's best-known lines, on the joy of leaving school, was "Then farewell, Horace; whom I hated so, / Not for thy faults, but mine." But Byron quoted Horace more than any other classical author. In later years he, and Coleridge too, became predatory students of Horace's letters on literature.

Critics debated whether Horace's intricacy stifled or concentrated emotion. In 1862 the teenage Friedrich Nietzsche requested fine editions of both Horace and Byron for his birthday. In *Twilight of the Idols* in 1888 Nietzsche summarized his view of Rome's literary superiority to Greece. He sought to be *aere perennius* himself, and in what would be the last year of his sanity praised the unique nature of Horace's oeuvre: "this mosaic of words where every piece, as sound, as place, as concept radiates its power right and left and through the whole."

Gentlemen politicians did not always appreciate the mosaic art, but they did like the tone. In 1848, John Quincy Adams, the self-consciously classical sixth U.S. president, translated Horace's now famous poem on divine protection for the pure in heart, a translation that caught its mild self-mockery better than its dignity. "Integer vitae": "A man in righteousness array'd, / A pure and blameless liver, / Needs not the keen Toledo blade, / Nor venom-freighted quiver."

The British prime minister William Gladstone published a translation of all the *Odes* after leaving office in 1894, many of them the product of long train journeys on election campaigns. Comparing himself to Milton and editing away any suggestion of lust for boys, he gave a lordly politician's vigor to "Odi profanum volgus et arceo": "Begone, vile mob, I bar my door!" Rudyard Kipling, in his popular *Stalky & Co.* stories, described the teaching of Horace to schoolboys who became officers in the Indian army. In 1920 he contributed in Latin to a fifth book that Horace had somehow failed to write for his admirers throughout the British Empire. When Britain aimed to rule the world, as Rome had once done, Horace was at the heart of the project.

There was continuing debate over whether Horace's relationship with Augustus was political engagement (potentially a good thing) or political enslavement (not good). When the argument raged over "Divis orte bonis," the fifth ode of the fourth book, on the one side stood the great German refugee from fascism Eduard Fraenkel, who called it "one of his most perfect poems," and on the other Don Fowler, the Oxford literary theorist, who dismissed it as "perhaps of all Horace's odes the easiest to read as straightforwardly fascist."

Horace remained high in the minds of twentieth-century critics of imperial war. Bertholt Brecht was punished at school for questioning whether it was dulce et decorum pro patria mori; he went on in old age to cherish Horace for celebrating poetry's resistance to obliteration. Ezra Pound, who had his own knowledge of war and madness, followed a similar path. Horace has often aged well among his resistant readers.

In 1917 Wilfred Owen wrote one his most remembered lines in calling the claim of "Dulce et decorum" to be "the old lie." His subject was a gas attack on the trenches: "Bent double, like old beggars under sacks, / Knock-kneed, coughing like hags, we cursed through sludge." Both Horace and Owen were participants in the biggest war that their worlds had known. Both saw horrors they had never seen before, on a scale that none had seen before. Both wrote poetry. Each responded in his own way.

In the year before the outbreak of the Second World War, Robert Frost wrote a poem called "Carpe Diem" which stressed the difficulties of seizing the day. The present was too often too hard, too much to bear, too present to make sense. Gathering rosebuds was a burden as well as a delight.

High among the war poetry of the Second World War, always less celebrated than that of the First, stood "Naming of Parts" by Henry Reed, which took for its epigraph the first words of Horace's poem about abandoning love but changing *vixi puellis* to *vixi duellis*: "I have lived enough with war." In 1967, at the height of the Vietnam War, Robert Lowell looked back to Horace and Brutus at Philippi, the heroes who didn't return, the friend who, after so much war, did come back alive.

Over the next fifty years Horace suffered from the rising fashion for the present to disapprove of the past. His art from an age of mass slavery and sexual exploitation was damned with the horrors of its time. Neither his ideas of frankness nor those of freedom fitted the frankness and freedom that men and women required for themselves in our modern age.

His life, whose outlines readers once understood from his work, and even thought that they knew, became clouded by theory as well as distaste. It became fashionable (and in some areas, almost essential) to deny that readers can find any life in a body of ancient work. Such a body, it was said, is all we have, and there is no more a life of Horace in it than there is a life of Empedocles in his philosophical fragments or a life of Homer in the *Iliad*.

These are serious arguments, but if the text must be everything and the life thus nothing, that is a high price to pay. Horace has survived in Western minds for two thousand years. Lovers of Horace's poetry over so long a stretch of time have agreed that the poet lives somewhere behind his lines. Their reasonings and their results may have varied but the capacity to make so many readers sense a human life, its beginning, its progress, and its ending, is itself a monument.

Three Poems

BACK FROM THE WARS

Odes 2.7

O saepe mecum tempus in ultimum
deducte Bruto militiae duce,
quis te redonavit Quiritem
dis patriis Italoque caelo,

Pompei, meorum prime sodalium,
cum quo morantem saepe diem mero
fregi, coronatus nitentes
malobathro Syrio capillos?

tecum Philippos et celerem fugam
sensi relicta non bene parmula,
cum fracta virtus, et minaces
turpe solum tetigere mento.

sed me per hostis Mercurius celer
denso paventem sustulit aere;
te rursus in bellum resorbens
unda fretis tulit aestuosis.

ergo obligatam redde Iovi dapem
longaque fessum militia latus

Three Poems

depone sub lauru mea nec
parce cadis tibi destinatis.

oblivioso levia Massico
ciboria exple; funde capacibus
unguenta de conchis. quis udo
deproperare apio coronas

curatve myrto? quem Venus arbitrum
dicet bibendi? non ego sanius
bacchabor Edonis: recepto
dulce mihi furere est amico.

Who has finally brought you home, old comrade,
oldest of all of my friends from that time
when Brutus led us out and down?
Welcome back to Italy and our fathers' gods!

How many days there were, how many,
dear Pompeius, when we drank and drank,
crowns of leaves in our perfumed hair!
How we drank those days away.

And then we were together through so much more,
the rout at Philippi, the abandoning of my shield
(not my finest hour), the shattering of ancient virtue,
our once menacing soldiers menacing only the dust.

All till our paths parted. Mercury, god of rogues and poets,
wrapped me in a haze and whisked me through the lines,

while a wave of war sucked you away into seething seas,
back to the war which did not end.

So it's time now to give the gods that feast you promised,
to rest your battle-weary body under my laurel tree,
to give no more quarter to the wine jars set aside for you here
than we did when we were together on the road.

Fill full the cups with the red wine of oblivion.
Pour perfume from the shells.
Who is hurrying along the garlands
from the celery and the myrtle?

Who will Venus make the drinking master?
I'm going to party like those old mad Thracians.
It's the sweetest madness to have a friend
back from the wars.

MOTHERS' DAY

Odes 3.8

Martis caelebs quid agam Kalendis,
quid velint flores et acerra turis
plena miraris positusque carbo in
caespite vivo,

docte sermones utriusque linguae.
voveram dulcis epulas et album
Libero caprum prope funeratus
arboris ictu.

hic dies anno redeunte festus
corticem adstrictum pice dimovebit
amphorae fumum bibere institutae
consule Tullo.

sume, Maecenas, cyathos amici
sospitis centum et vigilis lucernas
perfer in lucem: procul omnis esto
clamor et ira.

mitte civilis super urbe curas:
occidit Daci Cotisonis agmen,
Medus infestus sibi luctuosis
dissidet armis,

servit Hispanae vetus hostis orae
Cantaber sera domitus catena,
iam Scythae laxo meditantur arcu
cedere campis.

neglegens ne qua populus laboret,
parce privatus nimium cavere et
dona praesentis cape laetus horae ac
linque severa.

Why is a bachelor like me marking the start of March,
Mothers' Day, you may well be asking.
Why the flowers, the incense in its box,
the hot coals on the grassy altar?

Three Poems

Don't you know, you scholar in the dialogues of Latin and Greek?
This is the anniversary of the day of that fallen tree,
and I've vowed to the wine god a feast of white goat
annually ever since.

On this sacred day, as every year comes round,
a wine jar sealed by pitch on the date of that near disaster,
a living thing itself, will open up and
drink in the smoke.

So now, Maecenas, raise a hundred cups
to the escape of your friend.
Keep the lights lit till dawn. No shouting here.
No anger please.

Forget for a while your cares for the city.
The army of Cotiso the Dacian is done for,
The Medes are doing for themselves by
their usual civil wars.

The Cantabrians, our old enemy in Spain,
are finally defeated and in chains, while the Scythians
begin to move back northward,
their bows unstrung.

So relax, stop worrying whether our people are content.
You are a private man, give yourself a break.
Take the gifts of the present hour and leave
grave cares behind.

Three Poems

SORACTE

Odes 1.9

Vides ut alta stet nive candidum
Soracte nec iam sustineant onus
silvae laborantes geluque
flumina constiterint acuto?

dissolve frigus ligna super foco
large reponens atque benignius
deprome quadrimum Sabina,
o Thaliarche, merum diota.

permitte divis cetera, qui simul
strauere ventos aequore fervido
deproeliantes, nec cupressi
nec veteres agitantur orni.

quid sit futurum cras fuge quaerere, et
quem Fors dierum cumque dabit lucro
appone nec dulces amores
sperne, puer, neque tu choreas,

donec virenti canities abest
morosa. nunc et Campus et areae
lenesque sub noctem susurri
composita repetantur hora,

nunc et latentis proditor intimo
gratus puellae risus ab angulo
pignusque dereptum lacertis
aut digito male pertinaci.

Three Poems

Do you see how Soracte stands white with snow,
how the struggling woods let go of their loads,
how the rivers are stiff
with sharp ice?

Loosen the chill, Party Master,
pile logs on the fire, and be generous too with the wine,
four years old from Sabine jars,
unmixed with water.

Leave all else to the gods for the time when
they've calmed those winds that war with each other
over the furious sea, when the old oaks and ash have
ceased to tremble.

Avoid asking what will come tomorrow
and see as gain each day that Fortune gives.
While you are young neither set aside sweet love
nor say no to parties.

With miserable old age still far away
frequent the sports field and the public squares
at night when lovers' whispers grow louder
in the dark,

where the laugh of a hiding girl betrays her place
in a shadowy corner, just as some token
is snatched from a finger or a wrist,
hardly resisting.

Chronology

All dates BCE.

Chronology

Source Notes

The notes that follow, longer than a reader of a Life might expect, show both historical sources and the range of choices that past writers have made in constructing Horace's life from his poetry. They are necessarily an eclectic, personal selection nonetheless. So many have brought something to the story, and I owe debts to those mentioned here and others who have stood behind them over the centuries. Complete Latin texts are available online at the Latin Library website (https://www.thelatinlibrary .com/hor.html). Currently available English translations of the cited ancient works are in the bibliography. I have included my own basic translations throughout the book solely as a guide to following the original.

INTRODUCTION

For the story of Empedocles, the poet on a volcano in the fifth century BCE, see *Lives of Philosophers* by Diogenes Laertius from the third century CE (viii.51): Diogenes wrote that the fall into Mount Etna was a deliberate decision to die without leaving a dead body, its purpose to persuade his followers that Empedocles had ascended to the heavens. Horace's reference in support of a poet's perfectionism and right to destroy himself was his own. For the most reliable biographical details see Inwood, *The Poem of Empedocles*, 6–8. Mount Etna is on the same volcanic fault line as Mount Vesuvius, and it was much the more active of the two in antiquity as it is today; it was mythologized as the forge of the gods.

On the character of Brutus, the starting point is Plutarch, the prolific Greek moralist and biographer writing in the second century CE, who in his Life of Brutus showed Caesar's assassin as a man of virtue whose character deteriorated into cruelty under the stress of war. That decay was what Horace witnessed, understood, and never directly criticized. For an excellent modern life of Brutus see Tempest, *Brutus*. Plutarch's Lives of Caesar, Crassus, Mark Antony, and Augustus form the background for my *Horace: Poet on a Volcano*. For the best recent political and cultural history of the last years of the republic, see Beard, *SPQR*. For narrative accounts of the Three-Headed Monster alliance see Holland, *Rubicon*, and Stothard, *Crassus*.

Horace's proud boast that he brought ancient Greek song into Italian meters is at *Odes* 3.30.13. For Nietzsche's acute analysis of Horace's writing see the chapter "What I Owe the Ancients" in *Twilight of the Idols*.

In 1939 the critic Cyril Connolly acidly defended Horace "the perfectionist": "Perfection, as the imperfect are proud of telling us, is dead." See "Imitations of Horace," a review of the first volume of the Twickenham edition of Alexander Pope, republished in *The Condemned Playground*, 36. Connolly, most famous for his anthology of disappointment *The Unquiet Grave* (1944), began as an outsider in the British society of his time, was ever conscious of his literary failure, thrived on aristocratic company, and felt a powerful sympathy with Horace. After his death in 1974 his third wife, Deirdre Craven, married the biographer of Horace Peter Levi.

For Augustine's debts to Horace see J. Pucci, "Augustine, Confessions 4.6 and Horace *Odes* 1.3," *Arethusa* 24, no. 2 (1991): 258–281.

The English late-Romantic poet Alfred Noyes, author of an epic on Sir Francis Drake and morale-boosting novels for wartime, wrote an affectionate biography of Horace in 1947. Peter Levi, another neglected poet, who wrote his highly personal *Horace: A Life* in 1997, was an admirer of Noyes. A wide selection from five hundred years of translations of Horace into English is given in Carne-Ross and Haynes, *Horace in English*.

CHAPTER 1. SON OF A SOMETIME SLAVE

All modern writers on Horace must recognize a debt to the German scholar Eduard Fraenkel, whose critical study *Horace* (1957) became a humane and learned introduction for generations of subsequent students. Fraenkel was in many instances open to the poems as biographical sources, too much so for his fellow Oxford scholar Hugh Lloyd-Jones and others. Fraenkel's severity, wrote Lloyd-Jones, citing the Italian Marxist classicist Sebastiano Timpanaro, ensured that "he did not relish anything that savoured of decadence." Fraenkel surprised readers who knew of his narrow escape from fascism by his "evident assumption that Augustus and his regime were in all ways admirable." Lloyd-Jones's barbed but appreciative tribute to a man who "left a gap that no one can fill" is in *Blood for the Ghosts*.

Horace's first biographer, Suetonius, was a slightly older contemporary of Plutarch. Probably from a Numidian town in modern Algeria, he was a secretary to the emperor Hadrian, a senior version of the role that Horace had himself turned down. Suetonius had access to imperial papers, and his account of Horace's life, from his work *De viris illustribus* (On Famous Men), includes excerpts from letters between Horace and Augustus. Suetonius records Horace's birthday and birthplace, his father's status as a former slave, and his short stature, wide waistline, and mirrored room. There are gaps in the account, not because of Suetonius's admiration for Horace's abbreviated narrative technique but because medieval scribes made their own abbreviations. See Fraenkel, *Horace*, 1–23.

There is no record of how Horace's father became enslaved or how long his freedom was lost. It was easy for a man or woman to become enslaved on or near the losing side in Rome's wars with its Italian neighbors. There was then no racial basis to slavery;

the only basis was being a winner or a loser. Outside Italy new slaves would usually be from other races, but in the war between Sulla, Rome's first dictator, and Venusia and its surrounding towns, many Italians became enslaved as well as landless. Plutarch describes Julius Caesar's narrow avoidance of being himself enslaved by pirates at his *Life of Caesar* 2.3–4. Cicero, in his speech *In Defense of Aulus Cluentius Habitus*, describes the long enslavement of a Roman, Marcus Aurius, after Rome's victory over former Italian allies at Asculum in 89 BCE. A good starting point for the difficult discussion of how slavery underpinned the Roman world is Bradley and Cartledge, *The Cambridge World History of Slavery*, volume 1. For slavery in the minds of Roman poets, see Fitzgerald, *Slavery and the Roman Imagination*.

For the varied use of languages in Italy see Adams, *Bilingualism and the Latin Language*. For Spartacus's rebellion and the career of Crassus see Stothard, *On the Spartacus Road* and *Crassus*. Clodia's ironic nickname "Nola" came from the Latin verb *nolle*, "to be unwilling." For Cicero's opportunist abuse of Clodia in his speech *On Behalf of Caelius* see Wiseman, *Catullus and His World*.

Fulvia, who was married to Clodius in around 62 BCE, went on to be an unusually political wife to two other major figures in the life of Julius Caesar, Gaius Scribonius Curio and, most notoriously, Mark Antony. The son of that third marriage, Iullus Antonius, was an equally strong survivor, a poet who was the dedicatee of the second poem in Horace's fourth book of *Odes*.

Lucilius, Horace's predecessor in Latin satire in the second century BCE was a poet with powerful friends. Fraenkel's reluctance to see Horace basing immoral behavior on his own life led him to see more of Lucilius's literary influence and less of Horace's own experience (see *Horace*, 79 ff.). Fraenkel and Williams (*Tradition and Originality in Roman Poetry*, 448 ff.) agree that Horace's view of Lucilius as a stylist became more positive throughout his life as a poet. As a model for a poet laying out his life frankly to trusted friends Lucilius was there from the start. For the text of the limited fragments of Lucilius that survive, see *Remains of Old Latin*. Orbilius, like many teachers in the modern age, complained about the excessive demands of parents, as recorded in Suetonius in the section on *scholars and orators* in *Lives of Illustrious Men*.

CHAPTER 2. POETS AND ASSASSINS

Much of the work in the libraries of Athens would have been as obscure to a student from Rome – both in language and in meaning – as it is for us. Many texts were already in fragments, either from editing or more natural forms of decay.

To Archilochus was attributed the line that a fox knows many things but a hedgehog knows one big thing, a tool for dividing people into different groups that was made famous in the modern age by the philosopher and critic Isaiah Berlin. Under the categories Berlin laid out in *The Hedgehog and the Fox* (1953), Horace and Brutus would have been foxes, knowing many things, and Octavian a hedgehog whose mind was on a single aim. It can only be guessed whether Archilochus was actually the author of the line or, if he was, what he might have meant.

In the first century CE an erotic description by Archilochus of a sexual conquest, probably ending in oral sex, was common enough to end up in the wrappings of an Egyptian mummy on the banks of the lower Nile. See Christopher C. Eckerman, "Teasing and Pleasing in Archilochus's 'First Cologne Epode,'" *Zeitschrift für Papyrologie und Epigraphik* 179 (2011): 11–19. All quotes from Archilochus are collected in Diehl, *Anthologia Lyrica Graeca;* M. L. West's *Greek Lyric Poetry* is the best source for Archilochus in English.

For Callimachus's much-quoted line that a big book was the same as a big evil see fragment 465 in the Loeb Classical Library edition of Callimachus.

Hesiod's advice to farmers, his *Works and Days,* stood behind Vergil's *Georgics* just as Homer's epics stood behind the *Aeneid.* We find an occasional echo of Hesiod in Horace, too, when, for example, Augustus is praised for leading a Rome in which mothers bear children who look like their fathers (*Odes* 4.5.23; cf. *Works and Days* 235). Hesiod, however, was not campaigning against adultery. He merely provided words which Horace, not very sincerely, could use for his master's political purpose.

For Homer's use of fallen leaves to represent generations of the dead fallen in battle see *Iliad* 6.145–149. Greek lyric poets transferred the image to a call to enjoy life while leaves were green. See Mark Griffith, "Man and the Leaves: A Study of Mimnermus fr. 2," *California Studies in Classical Antiquity* 8 (1975): 73–88. In Horace's student days the libraries of Athens held much more evidence of this poetic shift from "kings and wars" to "boys and cups" (Rohland, *Carpe Diem,* 12) than survive today.

Mixing Greek with Latin in the same work was sometimes seen as a mark of culture and precision, at other times an affectation. Horace took issue with it in Lucilius's work (*Satires* 1.10.20 ff.). Cicero criticized it in others (*Tusculan Disputations* 1.15) but used it extensively himself. Later satirists, such as Juvenal (*Satires* 6.184 ff.) and Martial (*Epigrams* 10.68), saw it as a bad habit of pretentious women, particularly in the bedroom. See Adams, *Bilingualism and the Latin Language.*

Cicero's notorious poetic boast that Rome was fortunate to have been born during his consulate, "O fortunatam natam me consule Romam," would later be echoed by Horace in his epistle (*Epistles* 2.1) praising Augustus's intimidation of the Parthians: "Et formidatam parthis te principe Romam." Since Augustus was very proud of his Parthian policy, either Horace was being particularly bold or Cicero's line may not have been as much mocked in Horace's lifetime as it later became. Cicero the poet is cited by Quintilian in *The Orator's Education* 11.1.24 and by Juvenal at *Satires* 10.114–126. Horace's imitation is at *Epistles* 2.1.256; see note on Chapter 15. For a discussion see Emma Gee, "Cicero's Poetry," in *The Cambridge Companion to Cicero,* ed. Catherine Steel (Cambridge: Cambridge University Press, 2013), 88–106. See also A. J. Sillett, "Cicero and Poetry" (1987), What Would Cicero Do? https://whatwouldcicerodo.wordpress.com/2013/10/03/cicero-and-poetry/.

Source Notes

For the unusual description of a Roman maddened by the stresses and losses of war see M. J. G. Gray-Fow, "The Mental Breakdown of a Roman Senator, M. Calpurnius Bibulus," *Greece & Rome* 37 (1990): 179–190.

Brutus and his fellow assassins of Caesar justified their decision from a wide range of philosophical positions. See David Sedley, "The Ethics of Brutus and Cassius," *Journal of Roman Studies* 87 (1997): 41–53. Horace joked about himself as a fat porker from Epicurus's herd in *Epistles* 1.4.16. He was summoning up the popular idea (then as now) of an Epicurean being a pure pleasure seeker. But here as in so many places, Horace was only flirting with Epicureanism. A true disciple would not preach the horrors of death and dark afterlife as Horace so often did; death was to Epicurus a nothingness, the dissolution of the self, the end of the only entity that would have any afterlife if it existed—which it absolutely did not. There was no horror ahead for the dead.

For the "role of philosophy as a tool for reviving republicanism" see Tempest, *Brutus*, 146.

CHAPTER 3. BEHIND THE LINES

The assassins' vicious war against the Asian cities and islands is described by Plutarch (Life of Brutus 30.6–31.7) and by the Greek historian Appian, writing at the height of the empire Octavian founded (*Civil Wars* 4.76–80); see also the vivid, slightly later account by Dio Cassius (*Roman History* 47.34.1.3). If Brutus had won his war for old Roman virtues at Philippi, readers would now know far fewer of these unflattering stories of freedom fighters.

The only source for the story of the Roman buyer Publius Rupilius Rex and the local seller Persius is Horace's satire (*Satires* 1.7). The account of this poem by the Cambridge scholar Emily Gowers, in "Blind Eyes and Cut Throats: Amnesia and Silence in Horace Satires 1.7," *Classical Philology* 97 (2002): 145–161, is sensitive and acute. As to whether the particular incident in the poem is likely to be more fact than fiction, Gow, in his edition *Q. Horatii Flacci Saturarum*, and Bentley, in his *Q. Horatius Flaccus*, saw fact; Fraenkel, for unusually unconvincing reasons, saw fiction. Gowers, *Horace, Satires Book 1*, tended cautiously toward Horace's imagination. I have followed Bentley and Gow. For the drunken "smudge of vowel combinations" in the final line's "operum hoc mihi crede tuorum est" see Morgan, *Horace*.

Two articles by Gowers stand high among the criticism of Horace in our times: the above-referenced "Blind Eyes and Cut Throats" and "Horace Satires 1.5: An Inconsequential Journey," *Proceedings of the Cambridge Philological Society* 39 (1994): 48–66. I have drawn appreciatively on her insight of the use of the letters in Philippi as a code.

The hero from whom Brutus claimed ancestry was Lucius Junius Brutus, the man famed for expelling the last king of Rome, Tarquin the Proud, in 510 BCE. Throughout the early part of his career this connection gave Brutus the grand past that all aristocratic Romans liked to claim. When Caesar was feared by some to be reinstating Roman kingship, it placed added pressure upon him to be a man worthy of his great ancestor.

The course of the two battles of Philippi is discernible from a range of historical sources. The vast scale of the fighting is described by Appian in *Civil Wars* 4.108.454 and Brutus's uncertain maneuverings by Plutarch in Life of Brutus 41.3. Horace's own role is seen only through the poetry of Horace himself, and has to be reconstructed within all the usual evaluations of his memory (the reasoned and the damaged) and his purpose (personal, literary and political). The main references are from *Satires* 1.6, *Odes* 3.4, 3.14, and 2.7, and *Epistles* 2.2. The Italian scholar Mario Citroni in "The Memory of Philippi in Horace and the Interpretation of Epistle 1.20.23," *Classical Journal* 96, no. 1 (2000): 27–56, set out Horace's pride in his military promotion, his mock pride, and his report on the *versa acies*, the turning of his line and his throwing away his shield. This controversial shield has been seen as a solely literary reference to Archilochus and Alcaeus or as a literary hook on which to hang (or hide) real memories. In his ode to Pompeius (*Odes* 2.7) Horace recalls his frightened escape from the battlefield in a cloud conveniently provided by the god Mercury. Horace did not see himself as a Homeric hero in the power of Homeric gods; this was mist in his own mind; and like any powerful image it dispersed only slowly. As Fraenkel rightly wrote: "a poet may invest with a second, though different, life beliefs which in the actual history of mankind have perished long ago" (*Horace*, 165).

CHAPTER 4. WAR POET

Horace's first published poems were written soon after his return to Rome; his last, more sparingly, in the faltering decade before he died. In modern editions, there are four main groups, *Epodes*, *Satires*, *Odes*, and *Epistles*. None of these names is an attraction to readers today. *Epodes* is incomprehensible. *Satires* retains now only the spikier parts of the word's original meaning. *Epistles* are grandiosely named letters, either biblical or too long.

Odes are associated with the old-fashioned and florid despite (and also because of) the towering examples of Wordsworth's "Ode to Immortality" (1804), Shelley's "Ode to the West Wind" (1819), and Keats's "Ode to a Nightingale" (1819); Laurence Binyon's popularly titled "Ode to the Fallen" (1914) and W. H. Auden's "Ode" (1944) continued the tradition of reflections on war. But their history has not made the name attached to Horace's major works a reason to read them or left a meaning as varied and as lively as his.

None of these groups of poems was as unified as publishers have made them look. Horace's work was like that of a modern singer-songwriter whose each individual piece might be defined as a narrative ballad, a love song, or a political statement; each as a song for solo guitar, electric band, or gospel choir; each able to be collected under different descriptive headings, by subject, form, or musical style. Horace differentiated his works by their poetic antecedents as well as their form, by their Greek and Italian predecessors whose subject matter, meter, and sometimes both were his starting point. The writing dates of the *Satires* and *Epodes* (and possibly some of the *Odes*) were overlapping and not in neat order.

Epodes: These were variously influenced by the poems of Archilochus in the seventh century BCE, whose style and spirit which continued for five hundred years into the Hellenistic age. Their first purpose was outrage and assault. They are poems of youth. The basic building block of any metrical line was called a foot, and the iambic foot was considered to carry a kick. Their meter was built in iambic couplets (long short, long short, with certain permitted variations) in which the first line was always longer than the second. The name "epode" was originally designated for the second line of a couplet, then for the whole couplet, and eventually for a poem of such couplets. Horace's final seven epodes used a mixture of dactylic hexameter (long short short, long short short) and iambic lines. Epodes were characteristically public poems: a strong theme was the duty of the poet to harangue his fellow citizens, individually or collectively, almost always very loudly.

Satires: These were conversational descriptions of people and places, usually with some sort of moral point. Horace sometimes called them *sermones,* "conversations." The pioneer of the genre (and contributor to Horace of its hexameter meter) came from closer to home than the Archaic Greeks of the Aegean islands; he was Gaius Lucilius, from southern Italy, a describer of daily life — its journeys, its justice, its moneymakers and money-spenders, its vices and scandals. Lucilius was the closest that Rome had yet had to a literary hero, seen to embody in his style the core virtue of liberty. Horace was keen to be a smoother, more sophisticated chronicler than his predecessor and was bold enough to say so — though he gradually warmed to him as he moved through his own career.

Odes: Horace called these *carmina*, literally "songs." Their inspiration came from the works of the lyric poets of ancient Greece, principally Alcaeus and Sappho. The molding of Latin on to these models was, in Horace's own view of himself, his finest act, the great achievement of his middle age. He selected ancient poems to map on to his own experience, making an introspective self-portrait that was different from the more outward looking *Epodes* and *Satires.* The extent to which Horace chose past writers to mark and intensify specific incidents in his own life remains a matter of scholarly controversy. A modern biographer looks for facts from a poem even if eventually deciding that none are there; a modern academic critic often assumes maximum skepticism from the start. There is a middle way, as Horace sought himself. He did create an imagined persona for himself; he also told the truth. To tell Horace's life is to walk a reasoned line between believing everything and believing nothing.

The *Epistles* were in the form of an older man's letters to patrons and friends, twenty-two in all, written toward the end of his life and divided into two books. They are philosophical but not in as demanding a way as those of Empedocles or Lucretius, whose detailed explanation of Epicurus, *On the Nature of the World* (*De rerum natura*), was published not long before Julius Caesar's assassination. Horace's epistles had some of the conversational style of the *Satires*, his *sermones*, and include elements of his previous work—his reflections on a life of war, work, and leisure, on which parts of himself were appreciated by others, which were not, and how much it all mattered. Sex is absent from the *Epistles*.

A collected edition of Horace has two poems that are usually arranged separately. The first, the *Carmen Saeculare*, "Song of the Century," written in the Sapphic meter like many of the grandest odes, was the kind of poem that a modern Poet Laureate might write. It was a small part of a massive attempt by Augustus to reset Romans' moral sense of themselves. Its commission was both a reward to Horace and a burden.

The second, the *Ars Poetica*, "Art of Poetry," began in the form of a verse letter to some privileged young men before becoming a schoolbook for the creative-writing classes of the late first century CE and gaining its grander title. Quintilian, a fashionable teacher of rhetoric from Roman Spain, pretended to his students that a discursive letter to three members of the Piso family, whom Horace knew in Herculaneum, was the systematic primer that Quintilian would have preferred it to be.

Thasos: The large north Aegean island, where Archilochus fought and Brutus kept his treasury, appears in few popular histories. An exception is Robin Lane Fox's *The Invention of Medicine*, which shows how early Greek doctors followed the early concentration of money.

Epodes 8 ("Rogare longo putidam . . .") and 12 ("Quid tibi vis, mulier . . .") are "repulsive," said Fraenkel (*Horace*), before citing "revolting physical peculiarities" in a possibly related fragment by Hipponax, a cruder and slightly later follower of Archilochus, and then speculating on other Greek poets who might have written in a similar manner. Fraenkel allowed no possibility that Horace's choice of inspiration here was connected to the sensibility of a young poet, newly experienced in the horrors of battle and newly impoverished by the victors. "Astonishing and repellent," said Levi (*Horace: A Life*) of the eighth epode. "The whole disgusting piece is just twenty lines long, and the lady, let alone her characteristics, may be imaginary (let us hope)."

Watson noted the realistic "Roman colouring" of the scenes, the images of ancestors, the pearls and books on Stoicism but denied that epode 12 "has to do with impotence"; it showed merely "revulsion at his aged partner's body" (*Commentary*). "It is of course possible," he added, "to interpret the lurid account of the woman's physical shortcomings as the poet's rationalisation of his own sexual inadequacies," but he preferred to weigh the influence of Archilochus. In Paul Shorey and Gordon Laing's popular American edition of Horace these epodes were excluded altogether—without comment. They have no translation in the Penguin collection by Carne-Ross and Haynes. William's interest in *Tradition and Originality* did not extend this far. For earlier censorship see Stephen Harrison, "Expurgating Horace, 1660–1900," in *Expurgating the Classics: Editing Out in Greek and Latin,* ed. Harrison and Christopher A. Stray (London: Bristol Classical Press, 2012), 115–126.

CHAPTER 5. CONNOISSEUR OF THE CONCEALED

Epodes 5 ("O deorum quidquid!"): Williams in *Tradition and Originality* contrasted the dramatic "agonised monologue by a boy who faces a horrible death" (half-buried alive in sight of food beyond his reach so that his body provides the best remedies for sexual failure) with the narrative style of description that follows.

Epodes 2 ("Beatus ille"): The "hypocritical sham" by which city dwellers claim to love the country was one of Horace's targets which has long outlived him, as Watson noted (*Commentary*).

Epodes 13 ("Horrida tempestas"): This elegant early call for wine and poets' words to promote pleasure became unsurprisingly popular. Levi noted the "serenity" in this poem which is a "relief" from those around it (*Horace: A Life*). R. S. Kilpatrick, in "An Interpretation of Horace Epode 13," *Classical Quarterly, n.s. 20 (1970)*: 135–141, argued that the setting is the tent of Cassius on the eve of the first battle at Philippi, and the foul weather that which dogged the assassins on their march. Watson cited the many admirers for the poem but found "little to be said" for this suggestion, noting that he was not claiming it to be unconnected to the mood in Rome after Philippi: Archilochus and Alcaeus both used storms as "an allegory of political turmoil."

Cassius Parmensis: For the life of a minor poet and minor assassin of Julius Caesar, whose distinction was to survive long enough into Octavian's autocracy to see the consequences of his action, see Stothard, *The Last Assassin*.

Epodes 16 ("Altera iam teritur") and 7 ("Quo quo scelesti"; see Chapter 6) are poems composed by Horace when he was at his most depressed at the state of Rome. The question of exactly when they were written remains. The third-century commentator known as Pseudo-Acro dated epode 7, in which Horace evoked the murder of Remus by Romulus at Rome's foundation, to the time of Philippi: this would require Horace to have been already hostile to a war in which he was himself fighting. In the history of war poets this is not as implausible, Watson and others have suggested (it only takes a bad day to change a mind), but a date in Rome soon after Philippi is more likely. An angry Horace, defeated and poorer than before he joined Brutus's forces, still the son of a former slave, was following the form of Archilochus (fragment 109) and fantasizing a call for a mass exodus from Rome – a mad thought from a maddened man. "Poets do not choose their personae at random," as R. G. M. Nisbet put it in his essay "Horace's *Epodes* and History" (*Collected Papers on Latin Literature*, ed. S. J. Harrison [Oxford: Oxford University Press, 1995]). The "Arva beata," happy fields, were imagined from sailors' tales among what are now the Canary Islands.

Satires 1.2 ("Ambubaiarum collegia"): It is easy to mock the prudery of the past but not so easy to find the right expression of Horace's obscenity for the modern age.

Adams posed the problem in the introduction to his pioneering *Latin Sexual Vocabulary*: "As a rule basic obscenities have no other primary sense to soften their impact. They are unusable in polite conversation, most genres of literature, and even in some genres which might be thought obscene in subject matter." Translating *cunnus* and *muto* is, however, essential to conveying the force of Horace's extraordinary second satire.

In line 121 Horace openly cites Philodemus, a master equally of erotica and metrical theory (see Janko, *Philodemus*, 6). In line 92 he subtly parodies Philodemus's lines on the appeal of his big-footed, long-nosed Oscan girlfriend (*Palatine Anthology* 5.132). Horace may well have joined Vergil's group at Herculaneum in time to meet him as well as read his works. Levi (*Horace: A Life*) blamed "nasty poems by Philodemus" for epode 8. Even a selective reading list of his works would have been vast.

Fraenkel deplored "a rather unpleasant and, in itself, not very interesting theme," the dangers of sex with married women (*Horace*). In Gow's edition, the text of this poem ended at line 24. The commentary explained that "the last 110 lines of this Satire are not read." For a range of perceptive comments, freed from older prejudice and obfuscation, see Gowers, *Horace, Satires Book 1*.

The heroic three-word line about a massive spear, used by Horace in mock grandiosity, is at *Iliad* 15.678. The limbs of the dismembered poet are at Horace, *Satires* 1.4.62. Horace's attack on garlic is the third epode, on the cowardly dog the sixth.

Epodes 10 ("Mala soluta navis"): The unfortunate Maevius had already suffered the distinction (somewhat rarer than abuse by Horace) of abuse by Vergil (*Eclogues* 3.90–91): Fraenkel, *Horace,* accepted this link to the reality of its time but denied that it was of any importance. A younger contemporary poet, Domitius Marsus, also backed by Maecenas, added the detail of the wife who broke the bond between Maevius and his brother by refusing to be passed between them for sex. The fifth-century CE commentary on Vergil by Philargyrius tells this story and includes one of very few surviving fragments of Marsus's work, albeit in a state that has allowed varying textual interpretation. See Hollis, *Fragments of Roman Poetry,* and Watson's commentary. Marsus wrote epitaphs for Tibullus (see Llewelyn Morgan, "Metre Matters: Some Higher-Level Metrical Play in Latin Poetry," *Proceedings of the Cambridge Philological Society,* 2nd series, 46 [2001]: 99–120) and for Augustus's mother, as well as lines that confirmed the enthusiasm of Horace's teacher Orbilius for the rod and strap.

Epodes 14 ("Mollis inertia"): No commentator has liked to dismiss the reality of this poem—a classic call, from patron or publisher, that a writer should get on and finish his book. Maecenas was harassing Vergil at the same time for a final text of the *Georgics* (see Vergil, *Georgics* 3.40–41). Keats so much liked the nature of Horace's reply that he borrowed it for his "Ode to a Nightingale": "My heart aches and a drowsy numbness pains my sense, as though of hemlock I had drunk." See Ellen Oliensis, "Keats's 'Ode to a Nightingale' and Horace's *Epodes*," *Keats-Shelley Journal* 62 (2013): 32–36.

Phryne, a toad in Greek though a friendlier word than *toad* in English, was the name of a famous Athenian courtesan of the fourth century BCE.

CHAPTER 6. OUT OF HERE!

Gaius Asinius Pollio, historian, diplomat, and soldier, was one of the grandees of old Rome who was trying to balance his position against the demands of the new order. His personal sympathies were more with Antony than Octavian. He hoped there might be peace between them, and he was closely involved with the diplomatic missions to that end, one of which Horace himself joined and described in the fifth satire of his first book. Like Maecenas, but with less political purpose, Pollio was a patron of poets. Pollio's history of the civil wars of his time began in 60 BCE, when Horace was five, the date when Caesar, Pompey, and Crassus formed their Three-Headed Monster to rule Rome. Horace would later address to him the first poem in his second book of *Odes,* beginning with the recent history that was like a still active volcano, ever liable to burst out in fire, or, as Fraenkel described it, "a gigantic thunderstorm spreading across the whole *orbis terrarum*" (*Horace*), the nearest that anyone had known to a world war.

Agrippa was as much the new man in Rome after Philippi as Pollio was the old. For a summary of his career see Powell, *Marcus Agrippa.* Sextus Pompeius was the one man from the old world who was still fighting the victors of Philippi. He was a formidable commander. Pollio had suffered a humiliating defeat by him in Spain, only escaping from the battlefield in disguise. See Welch, *Magnus Pius* and *Sextus Pompeius.* Horace's attack on Sextus in the fourth epode for running a pirate force of former slaves was his first foray into what would be later criticized as hypocrisy and propaganda.

Epodes 4 ("Lupis et agnis"): The wolves and the lambs are as much at odds with one another as are Horace and the unnamed rich freedman, whip stripes still on his back, who is an officer for Octavian. Horace took this common theme of attacking the upstart before boldly plowing into problems of his own credibility. This derided man held the same status as Horace, the freedman's son, had held in the army of Brutus. Sextus's appeal spread far beyond slaves, and every army used slaves to fight. Horace himself had friends from Philippi who were now with Sextus. Watson argued that Horace was "deliberately sailing close to the wind" and "intend[ed] us to be amused by his audacity" (*Commentary*). Fraenkel praised "a spontaneous outburst" (*Horace*). To Levi it was "a piece of pure fury, a white-hot blaze" (*Horace: A Life*).

CHAPTER 7. HANGERS ON

Satires 1.1 ("Qui fit, Maecenas"): Fraenkel (*Horace*) saw in this a sophisticated note of thanks to Maecenas in a two-pronged attack on human envy and greed. For Levi (*Horace: A Life*) this was "the most innocent exercise in moral philosophy." Innocence does not make an exercise unimportant.

Satires 1.6 ("Non quia, Maecenas"): According to W. Y. Sellar, a nineteenth-century Scottish classicist who prized knowing Horace over analyzing him into dust, "there is scarcely any individual portrait in all ancient literature which leaves on the mind so real an impression of worth, affection and good sense" (*Roman Poets of the Augustan Age*). Fraenkel cited this approvingly while noting the poem's equally powerful creation of a self-portrait: the son of a former slave who survived the biggest battle of his time to join the architects of peace. Williams noted what a "strikingly ugly phrase" "libertino patre natum" was and suggested that it was part of the real language Horace knew from his first school and the march to Philippi (*Tradition and Originality in Roman Poetry*).

Satires 1.9 ("Ibam forte"): Often titled "The Bore," this satire on the disadvantages of friendship with Maecenas has attracted fine translators in every age, who recognize its reality. The gossiping hanger-on who wants access to power "Names every Wench that passes through the Park, / how much she is allowed and who the Spark / that keeps her," in the version by John Oldham (1681), a satirist much admired by Dryden. "How stand you, Sir, in the good graces of our minister?" asks the bore in Francis Howes's 1845 version. "His favourites are but few, and those select," Horace replies in vain. Fraenkel noted the poem's story as "something that happened to Horace on a very ordinary day" – as well as the "not improbable" existence of a poem by Lucilius that began the same way.

Satires 1.8 ("Olim truncus"): Octavian's plans to clean up Rome – both physically and morally, he hoped – included new gardens, which Maecenas was laying out over the public cemeteries where witches once plied their trade. Horace sets a scene in which a Priapus, a wooden scarecrow with a large erection, scares away two notorious hags with an explosion from his arse. As Gowers explained in her edition of the *Satires*, there was some ambiguity about the scene, the association of farting with fear, "anal or oral rape" as a threat, or a satisfying of "reciprocal anal or oral insatiability." The poet modestly plays the role of a useful piece of wood while, as Fraenkel put it, paying "a handsome compliment" to his patron, the city developer. If this was a compliment, Maecenas was, indeed, a man of broad mind.

Satires 2.1 ("Sunt quibus in satura"): Critics have noted both the firmness and the good humor in Horace's rejection of a lawyer's advice to be a war poet of the epic kind. But this poem shows that it was an anxious time for those wanting to say no, very different from fifteen years previously, when Trebatius was getting his own firm but good-humored advice from Cicero about how to deal with Julius Caesar in Gaul: don't miss chances to make money, avoid Britain, and, if poor Trebatius did have to go to Britain, bring back a chariot. Those were then the main points from the old man to the young, along with tips on dieting, keeping warm abroad, and buying suburban property at home. In the years after Philippi, Trebatius is now himself the wise old man, offering counsel to Horace about how to deal with a new Caesar at a much more difficult and authoritarian time. Like Horace, Trebatius had not been much of a soldier. The lawyer had learned not to push his luck – and this was an important lesson that he wanted to pass on. When Horace in turn passed on the lawyer's opinion he was unlikely to have risked his poem's straying far from the truth, choosing this opportunity to remind his readers that from his very start he had been a follower of Lucilius in fully setting out his life in art (see ll. 30–34 and Shackleton Bailey, *Profile of Horace*, 10).

Cicero's letters to Trebatius – "perhaps the most enchanting pieces that we possess from the pen of that unsurpassed letter-writer," in Fraenkel's view – are in *Letters to Friends* 7.6–22.

CHAPTER 8. UNDER VESUVIUS

If a poet wanted to hurl himself into a pit of fire he might reasonably choose Mount Etna in Sicily as the most reliable spot. The myth of Empedocles – whether of a mad or a calculating man – was set on Etna because its volcano was likely to be active, and, even when only modestly so, it was a permanent reminder of the proximity to the earth of the powers beneath. But the black fields of eastern Sicily were not the only fields of fire. Above Naples in the years after Philippi, Vesuvius was merely a mountain, but the signs of fires were everywhere: sulfurous steam bubbled from lakes, shards of glass glittered in the fertile soil – it offered every reason for Vergil to set the entrance to the underworld there. At the time when Horace and Vergil were visiting Hercula-neum it was a rich town for men with leisure time to read, write, and think about their lives. Not for another century or so did the superheated gas, ash, and mud descend.

For the eruption of Vesuvius in 79 CE see the letters of Pliny the Younger (6.16 and 6.20) and Gibson, *Man of High Empire*. For connections between the countryside around Vesuvius and the study of Epicurus see Stothard, *On the Spartacus Road*, 119 ff. For a modern survey of the arguments about the people and books in what is now called the Villa dei Papyri see Armstrong et al., *Vergil, Philodemus and the Augustans*; also Rohland, *Carpe Diem*, and Janko, *Philodemus*. Philodemus's hometown of Gadara was also the home of Meleager, an early collector of some of the works Horace had discovered in Athens and a major contributor to what became the *Greek Anthology*.

Odes 1.24 ("Quis desiderio sit pudor . . . ?"): On Horace's citing of Vergil in a poem to the muse, Melpomene, warning his friend against excessive grief, see P. Thibodeau, "Can Virgil Cry? Epicureanism in Horace *Odes* 1.24," *Classical Journal* 98, no. 3 (2003): 243–256. The Victorian lawyer C. S. Calverley wrote one of several popular versions in 1861: "Unshamed, unchecked, for one so dear / we sorrow. Lead the mournful choir / Melopomene." Horace's original argument was probably not so different. Both the date and the identity of the dead man in the poem are disputed.

Odes 1.18 ("Nullam, Vare, sacra"): The line "When in their enthusiasm for sex men see too fine a line between right and wrong" ("Cum fas atque nefas exiguo fine libidinum / discernunt avidi") contains strong religious associations, the words *fas* and *nefas* marking days when various actions were permitted or not.

There has been much discussion of the question, not applicable only to Horace, of how much wine the poet drank and how much he merely wrote about drinking. So too on the question of sex, the numeracy, gender, and identity of his partners are sources for speculation. Readers have always had many opportunities to make up their own minds, some Victorian editors even veering toward the claim that no pleasure at all was taken in the making of these poems. See G. Davis, "Wine and the Symposium," in Harrison, *The Cambridge Companion to Horace;* and A. P. McKinlay, "The Wine Element in Horace," *Classical Journal* 42 (1947): 161–168, 229–236. For Roland Mayer, writing in the first decade of the new millennium to the daily drum of public health warnings, "the poem's implicit message might well be endorsed by a society appalled by the binge-drinking of its young" (*Horace: Odes*). For Levi the love of Horace's poetry, "natural no doubt or inbred," was itself "like a taste for alcohol" (*Horace: A Life*).

Even more contentious is the question of whether Horace rehearsed poems before a friendly audience – or even played and sang his odes to them. Proponents of Horace the musician cite Ovid's autobiographical recollection: "Et tenuit nostras numerosus Horatius aures / dum ferit Ausonia carmina culta lyra / Vergilium vidi tantum (*Tristia* 4.10.49–51). Did "Horace master of meter / striking his cultivated songs on the Ausonian lyre" refer to a memory of a concert, or was it merely a metaphor? Did "Vergil I only saw" mean that Ovid did not hear Vergil or simply that he did not ever meet him? See notes for Chapter 15 on Horace the conductor.

Odes 3.26 ("Vixi puellis nuper Idoneus"): Nisbet and Hubbard, pupils of Fraenkel, considered whether the teasing renunciation of sex was intended to refer to love poetry too (*Commentaries*). The Scottish scholar David West, one of the most sensitive interpreters of Horace in the twentieth century, had an acute ear for the cracking G's in this poem. He thought that Horace was planning future sex with Chloe more than *semel* "just once": "One cut of that whip and the most mettlesome of us are brought under lasting discipline" (*Horace Odes III*). For Phryne see epode 14; for Glycera, odes 1.19 and 3.19; and for Pyrrha, ode 1.5.

Augustus's description of Horace as *purissimum penem* (purest penis) and the line from Maecenas about being a skinny nobody if he did not love his poet comes from Suetonius's Life of Horace.

Satires 2.3, line 185 ("In cicere atque faba"): Agrippa became aedile in 33 BCE, a remarkably senior appointment to what was a junior office; he was charged by Octavian with the newly vital role of improving public morale. H. R. Fairclough, translator of the Loeb edition of the *Satires* in 1926, called this "the best constructed" of all the satires. Fraenkel rated it "the worst of all" in a book which generally failed to live up to Horace's first (*Horace*). It is certainly the longest, and it is devoted to madness of various kinds – greed, ambition, superstition, and the failure of the afflicted to recognize the manias of themselves. The madness of war is predominant but is safely diverted to the Trojan War. As Fairclough saw, the tone is light, but the attack is sharp – including upon Horace himself for writing poetry, being bad-tempered, living beyond his means, and forever falling in love.

Source Notes

Satires 2.6 ("Hoc erat in votis"): The god Mercury, whose power was credited with Horace's miraculous escape from Philippi, is here thanked for the farm, the gift of Horace's greatest wish and prayers. Because of the mention of the Dacians, wavering between Octavian and Antony in what is now Romania, this poem is securely dated to the time around the campaign at Actium. The Dacians were punished for their equivocation in the year after Actium, 30 BCE.

The story of the town mouse and country mouse, adapted from a fable attributed to Aesop, made this one the most popular and most translated poems from all Roman literature. It advanced the fashion for seeing Horace as an honorary Englishman himself. Fraenkel stated that there was therefore "no need to praise it again" (*Horace*). In a joint translation by Jonathan Swift and Alexander Pope (1727–1738), Swift took the first 132 lines, leaving the parable of the plausible town mouse to Pope: "But come, for God's sake, live with Men: / Consider, Mice, like Men, must die, / Both small and great, both you and I."

Epodes 1 ("Ibis Liburnis") and 9 ("Quando repostum"): The question of whether Horace and Maecenas were spectators at the Battle of Actium or waiting for news back home is a good example of the choice that any biographer has to make. The first epode begins with the statement to Maecenas, *Ibis Liburnis,* "You will go in a Liburnian," one of the fast, light ships that Agrippa had assembled for the battle. The ninth epode, in which the poet wonders when he and Maecenas will celebrate with the best wine, seems possibly to be set on board a ship and refer to *fluentem nauseam,* "seasickness." An anonymous elegist to Maecenas from the first century BCE says that Maecenas was at the battle. The influential German critic of the late nineteenth century Franz Bücheler concluded firmly that Maecenas and Horace were there on the big day. Lindsey Watson, in his commentary on the *Epodes* in 2003, sided with Bücheler, noting the tradition of taking poets on campaigns to chronicle great victories and arguing that the *Epodes* could hardly have been published with an unfulfilled promise in their first line.

In the meantime, Fraenkel had squashed Bücheler in his characteristic commanding way. He cited Dio Cassius, Appian, and other historians as saying that Maecenas was running Rome for Augustus during the Actium campaign—arguing that these were far superior sources to an unknown elegist struggling to make a point. The fluentem nauseam was not seasickness but referred to overindulgence at a banquet on land where anxious supporters were awaiting battle reports. It was not Horace's way, he wrote, to save such a key fact for the end of a poem—and release it in such a careless way. I have sided with Fraenkel, despite the attraction to a biographer of having Horace back in battle. Horace did not witness war directly after he came home from Philippi. For all his mastery of editing stories and taking sideways views, he would have said more about it if he had.

According to Suetonius's Life of Horace, "It is said that he had no moderation in sexual matters and that in a mirror-lined room he had available women arranged so that whichever way he looked there was an image of himself having sex." This was not a unique feature of contemporary bedroom furniture. A wealthy sybarite from around the same time, Hostius Quadra, is described by Seneca (*Natural Questions* 1.6) as having mirrors that reflected images at abnormal size, causing, for example, a finger to exceed the size of an arm in length and thickness, arranging them so that he could see all his partner's movements and gloat over the imagined proportions of his own body. Fraenkel (*Horace*) argued that the "filthy detail" was the kind of common rumor about great men that Suetonius thought a biographer should pass on regardless of its truth. He had his own image of Horace, and sexual narcissism was not part of it. Hallam (*Horace at Tibur*), though undertaking an imaginative and exhaustive reconstruction from his pilgrimage to the villa site in the 1920s, did not speculate about where the *cubiculum speculatum* might have been.

For the snake in the grass see Vergil, *Eclogues* 3.93. *Eclogues*, from the Greek for a "selection," was the name by which the *Bucolica* came later to be known.

The man who saved Lollius at Philippi and had his favor returned at Actium was Quintus Aemilius Lepidus.

Odes 2.13 ("Ille et nefasto die"): The escape from the falling tree is generally agreed, even by the most skeptical, to have been a real event in Horace's life, comparable to Philippi itself (see *Odes* 3.4.26 ff.). The poem has many literary antecedents in Greek curses, epitaphs, and tours of the underworld, but Nisbet and Hubbard (*Commentaries*) make biographical points that are applicable both here and more widely. "Though Horace's misadventure was a real one, his account of it is written within a literary tradition." Reality and tradition are not mutually exclusive. As in the epodes that attack older women, which some have preferred to see as wholly literary, Horace has chosen past words to sit with present menace: "On the one hand Horace is a Sabine countryman quick to show anger at the brute object that has so nearly extinguished him, but he is also the conscious heir and imitator of Alcaeus's themes and styles." Nisbet and Hubbard are wary of accusations of "mere romantic subjectivism" in sensing an unspoken thought, but they rightly suggest that if Horace sees a past poet escaping "the meaningless accident of fortune, perhaps he himself may have the same capacity to enthral, to console, and to survive." The accident happened in spring, on March 1 (*Odes* 3.8.1). The year is more contested.

Nisbet and Hubbard became major influences on students of Horace through their commentaries on the first and second books of the *Odes*. They were more critical of Augustus the authoritarian than Fraenkel had been, and their partnership inspired the Oxford doggerel of the 1970s: "We now have the Horace of Hubbard and Nisbet but which bits are her bits and which bits are his bits?"

Odes 3.13 ("O fons Bandusiae"): David West noted the vitality "from the truth and vividness of the observations" (*Horace Odes III*). Shorey and Laing called this a "general favourite," and "deservedly" (*Horace, Odes and Epodes*). Fraenkel agreed, praising its "deep colours" and "note of exaltation in the last stanza that lifts up to a higher plane": Horace has the touch to make "light and oblique" what "can easily cloy."

Carne-Ross and Haynes called Wordsworth's version, "To M.H." (1815), "not a notable performance," but cited its clear influence on later poems, concluding that Wordsworth's "small bed of water in the woods," where cattle can drink sheltered from the sun, "comes from Horace and also from life" (*Horace in English*).

Llewellyn Morgan ("The One and Only *Fons Bandusiae*," *Classical Quarterly* 59, no. 1 [2009]: 132–141) showed that the eighteenth-century location of the spring as being near Horace's birthplace, based on a Papal Bull of 1103, was correct and that the recent consensus, formed by Fraenkel and others, that it was on Horace's farm was wrong. West declared it only a "fair guess" that the place of sacrifice of the goat was on the farm and that the poem about Maecenas's gift was "praise of the donor." Nisbet and Niall Rudd, Nisbet's new partner for the third book of *Odes*, accepted that the original fons Bandusiae was on the Appian Way but suggested that Horace had reused the name for his new home (*Commentary*). To Morgan the "fair guess" is not fair; and "the kindest description of the compromise is that it is inelegant."

Odes 1.37 ("Nunc est bibendum"): The opening phrase came direct from Alcaeus (GL 1.332), but the first word, "Now!," rings out three times like a peal of bells to Romans who were not and were never going to be readers of ancient Greek. The defeat of Antony, dressed for political purposes as the defeat of Cleopatra, marked the end of the uncertainty for Horace that began at Philippi. Rather than see the poem as too political, Mayer preferred to see Horace as "the victim rather than the echo of propaganda," a man in no position to shape the conflicting stories of Actium and after (*Horace: Odes*). Either way, the poem suited Octavian well. There has long been admiration for Horace's deft, deep respect for an enemy in defeat. For Fraenkel it was rare in being "so jubilant and so profoundly humane." This was the vital message from classical civilization, however often ignored in practice, that "you ought not to humiliate your defeated enemy and that by trying to degrade him you will, in fact, degrade yourself."

Odes 1.1 ("Atavis edite regibus"): Maecenas's mother's family were said to be the Cilnii, and fifty years ago students were told that Horace was flattering Maecenas in tracing his ancestry to Etruscan kings (per Nisbet and Hubbard). The subsequent publication of a sixteenth-century transcription of an Etruscan inscription showed that a Cilnius was, indeed a *lucumo*, an Etruscan king, and that Horace was not quite such a flatterer after all. See Adriano Maggiani, "*Cilnium genus*: La documentazione epigrafica Etrusca," *Studi Etruschi* 54 (1986): 171–196.

Odes 1.9 ("Vides ut alta stet nive candidum"): See my full translation of the poem in this volume. Scholars have long appreciated the technical skill in this ode, its eerie beauty – and they have argued about whether winter is here a symbol of old age, and whether the boy in charge of the party is Horace's lover, a possibility judged by Mayer as "a harmless enough reading" without much enthusiasm that it be true. Known usually as "the Soracte ode" it had a sentimental afterlife as the shared schoolboy memory of the writer Patrick Leigh Fermor and a German general he had captured on Crete in 1944, a lens through which civilized values were deemed to shine in dark times. See Patrick Leigh Fermor, *A Time of Gifts* (London: John Murray, 1977). Mary Beard, with her characteristic skepticism for the staler pieties, called the joint recitation "an upmarket equivalent of singing 'Silent Night' across the trenches" and queried how civilizing were the consequences of the kidnapping for the Cretan civilian population (*London Review of Books*, August 16, 2005).

CHAPTER 11. TREACHEROUS GROUND

Odes 2.1 ("Motum ex Metello"): Page cited the "peculiarly difficult and delicate task" identified by the nineteenth-century historian of England Lord Macaulay in writing about James II in Ireland. "To borrow the fine image used on a similar occasion by a Roman poet," every step is a peril, "on the thin crust of ashes beneath which the lava is still glowing" (*Odes of Horace*). Nisbet and Hubbard noted that Augustus might have found the image less fine than "unnecessarily tactless" (*Commentaries*).

Odes 3.8 ("Martiis caelebs quid agam Kalendis"). See my full translation in this volume. David West noted the new intimacy between Horace and Maecenas that this poem showed (*Horace Odes III*). They were going to get drunk together on a hundred ladles of wine from the year when Maecenas first gave him the farm where the poem was set. The wine jar, West sees, is almost a character in the dialogue, like a jar in *Alice in Wonderland,* a drinker itself, learning to drink the smoke from the sacrificial fire, Horace's "taste for the surreal" at its best.

Maecenas knew Greek and the art of intellectual dialogues like those of Plato, but his learning did not help him understand what this bachelor party on the Matronalia was all about—until he found that it was all about him. A likely date, based on the "military communiqué" at the poem's end, is 28 BCE.

The stories of Horace enjoying sex with a high number of partners (even by the standards of milieu and time) may originate in *Satires* 2.3.325, where the character Damasippus refers to the poet's "affairs with thousands of girls and boys" ("mille puellarum puerorum mille furores"). Or it may have other sources. Numbers in ancient texts, like most boasts about the quantity of sexual partners, are generally more indicative than accurate.

Odes 1.22 ("Integer vitae scelerisque purus"): In Fraenkel's comments on "one of the best-known Horatian odes," he recalled that German schoolboys at funerals used to sing the first stanza about the man of blameless life who feared not the weapons of wild enemies (*Horace*). Their tutors could presumably be sure that without direction their boys would not reach the final stanza, where the fearless poet, terror of the local wolves, is the crazed lover of the sweetly laughing, sweetly talking Lalage. Horace feared the impact of schoolteachers on his work as soon as he saw that he had any literary success. The early Christian polemicist Lactantius (fourth century CE) began the process of turning the "integer vitae scelerisque purus" into a model man (*Divinae Institutiones* 5.17.18), and his spirit lived on ironically in Shakespeare (*Titus Andronicus*, 4.2) and John Quincy Adams (see Carne-Ross and Haynes, *Horace in English*, 215). It is possible, though not certain, that the thunderous opening was taken by Horace, equally out of context, from Alcaeus (see Mayer, *Horace Odes*, 166). In support of the reality of wolves on Horace's farm Fraenkel listed various relevant sightings and a report of a postman attacked and eaten nearby in 1956.

Odes 1.25 ("Parcius iunctas"): "A coarsely expressed ode. It has no merit and may be omitted with advantage": that was the verdict of the first editor of the Loeb classical library, T. E. Page (*Odes of Horace*). "The crudest and nastiest poem in Horace's lyrics," according to the authority on language N. E. Collinge (*The Structure of Horace's Odes*). Few have liked to share Horace's bitter memory of the woman who spurned him once and is now a lustful mare whom on a windy night no one wants. Why would a woman like Lydia even need to be outside on such a night? asked Bentley in 1788 (*Q. Horatius Flaccus*). For a more sympathetic modern account see L. W. Catlow, "Horace Odes I, 25 and IV, 13: A Reinterpretation," *Latomus* 35, no. 4 (1976): 813–821.

Odes 1.2 ("Iam satis terris"):. "Improvisatory" became a common way to describe this poem, which was early but, when the time came to collect the *Odes* for publication, still seen as the best candidate for the important second place after the dedication to Maecenas. See Mayer, *Horace Odes*, 73.

CHAPTER 12. ODES AND EELS

For Aulus Murena's role or lack of it in plots against Augustus, see Suetonius, Life of Augustus 56.4, 66.3, Seneca, *De clementia* 1.9.6, and Dio Cassius, *Roman History* 54.3. For a modern account see Bowman et al., *The Cambridge Ancient History*, 87–98. For difficulties in dating see R. A. Bauman, "Tiberius and Murena," *Historia* (November 1966): 420–432. The references to Licinius Murena in Horace are at *Satires* 1.5.38 and *Odes* 3.19, a promise of a heavy night celebrating one of his electoral successes. There is much uncertainty at every point.

Odes 1.6 ("Scriberis Vario"): For Agrippa criticizing Vergil for being a puppet of Maecenas and the inventor of a new kind of affected style, see L. P. Wilkinson, "The Language of Virgil and Horace," *Classical Quarterly* 9 (1959): 181–192.

Odes 2.7 ("O saepe mecum"): See my full translation in this volume. Nisbet and Hubbard felt uncomfortable with so subtle and gentle a response to a battle in which more than 50,000 died, 24,000 on the first day alone (*Commentaries*). Their best verdict was "a masterpiece of tact," a triumph for Horace in simultaneously respecting Pompeius's choices, avoiding the rejection of his own, and thanking Octavian for his

Source Notes

friend's freedom to return without any of the obsequiousness often thought appropriate for pardons. Both men had seen too many dead soldiers; both would now leave behind empty wine jars instead, a view which some might today find offensive but one that was essential to Horace both as storyteller and a man. The linguistic subtleties with which Horace moved between wine and war, the suggestions that he and Pompeius had been both led and misled by Brutus were set out in detail by John L. Moles, in "Politics, Philosophy, and Friendship in Horace *Odes* 2.7," *Quaderni Urbinati di Cultura Classica* 25 (1987): 59–72. For dead soldiers at parties in Cambodia see the chilling poem "Dead Soldiers" by James Fenton in his *The Memory of War* (1982).

Odes 1.5 ("Quis multa gracilis"): "Dazzling mastery" was Mayer's verdict on the lines predicting Pyrrha's inevitable betrayal of the slender young boy (*Horace Odes*). The placing of the words is central to the description of the scene, the girl pressed down by the boy, them both by roses, the perfect example of what Nietzsche noted in Horace: "the mosaic of words where every piece, as sound, as place, as concept, radiates its power right and left and through the whole" (*The Twilight of the Idols*).

Odes 1.4 ("Solvitur acris hiems"): "The placing of this ode so prominently in the collection makes it 'political' in a way that its content would never suggest," wrote Mayer in his commentary. Lucius Sestius, revealed as the dedicatee in only the fourteenth line of a twenty-line poem, was a few years older than Horace but as a child had been more fiercely entwined with Rome's struggles for power. In 56 BCE, while Cicero was defending his father on political charges from his populist enemies, the young boy was brought into court to arouse the sympathy of the jury, and heard what would become Cicero's classic account of how the senatorial and business classes should unite in hostility to absolutism and mass democracy (*On Behalf of Sestius* 136–137). Cicero found the elder Sestius a steady friend albeit often morose, but although they won the case, the policy of the middle way was doomed by Clodius's gang violence and the rise of Caesar. The younger Sestius was pardoned after Philippi but stuck to his hopes of a balanced constitution and prospered as a useful proof of Augustus's clemency and tolerance. He became consul in the year Horace's *Odes* were published. A conventional poem about winter turning to spring became a warning that Sestius's success in adapting to the new age – and his great wealth from wine exports, elegantly indicated in the poem – was no defense against *pallida mors*, "pale-faced death." "Lovely" was the verdict of Fraenkel (*Horace*).

Odes 2.10 ("Rectius vives, Licini"): Every cliché was fresh once. The Golden Mean, the successful middle way between extremes, was a vivid metaphor in this poem, the *auream*, "shining gold," set beside the *mediocritatem*, the "mean" that meant also the mediocre. Among the competing philosophies which Horace and Brutus heard in Athens the *mediocritas* of Aristotle and his followers, the so-called Peripatetics, was still popular despite the fashion for Epicurus and newer rivals. Aulus Murena was at one point close to the Peripatetic Athenaeus (see Strabo, *Geography* 14.5.4).

The argument for a middle way through life's daily dilemmas became a yet more useful comfort among later courtiers in autocratic regimes. Richard Tottel's pioneering *Miscellany* of poetry, published in 1557 just as Elizabeth I was about to ascend the throne of England, contained two anonymous versions of this ode for dangerous years — set alongside the first published poems of Thomas Wyatt and the Earl of Surrey. In Surrey's words, he "who so gladly halseth the Golden Meane, / voyde of dangers advisdly hath his home" ("Ode II.10"). Through Horace's intervention in the most murky episode of Maecenas's career, he came to be present at the birth of English lyric poetry.

CHAPTER 13. HOROSCOPES

Odes 2.17 ("Cur me querelis exanimas"): "If interpreted with discretion," conceded Nisbet and Hubbard, this poem gives a biographer useful insights into the character of the most important man in Horace's life after the death of his father (*Commentaries*). Maecenas was highly conscious of his health, prone to hypochondria as well as to the *perpetua febris,* the "permanent fevers" that swirled around Rome (Pliny, *Natural History* 7.172). He was an insomniac who needed music and the sound of waterfalls to help him sleep (Seneca, *Dialogues* 1.3.10). He liked to contemplate his own death but prayed to stay alive whatever his physical handicaps. Horace humored him "with deft sensitivity."

Odes 1.11 ("Tu ne quaesieris"): The advice to seize the moment, *carpe diem,* made this short piece one of the most quoted of all Horace's poems. Horoscopes were becoming a fashionable eastern import in Rome. Horace's advice that the future was invented only to ruin the present stemmed both from the ideas of Epicurus and his own idea that Leuconoe's present time should be spent in bed with him. See Rohland, *Carpe Diem,* for a fine modern account of the two words in a multiplicity of contexts — from drinking cups to jewelry.

Odes 1.7 ("Laudabunt alii"): Many later readers have found this poem difficult. It "largely resists analysis," according to Collinge (*Structure of Horace's Odes*). Its historical place belonged with the ode to Sestius (see discussion of *Odes* 1.4 in notes to Chapter 12, above) since Plancus too was a prominent opponent of Octavian whose rehabilitation Horace had observed. Its emotional power is very much its own, with its beautiful ending in which the brother of a war-maddened hero sails the seas to find some kind of peace. Analysis has not always been the best approach to Horace, whose quiet defiance of his critics is a defining characteristic of his work.

Odes 2.3 ("Aequam memento"): Horace was not always recommending "carpe diem" to the reluctant or the "auream mediocritatem" to extremists. In this poem he was urging "hedonism to a hedonist," as Nisbet and Hubbard put it. Quintus Dellius had as checkered a career as Plancus but attracted no reputation for self-doubt. The vision of the underworld to which every puritan or pleasure seeker must pass was as "brilliant" as any of Horace's other imaginings on the same theme.

Marcus Egnatius Rufus, the founder of a fire brigade, seemed to have been a threat in the manner not of Brutus but of Clodius, the populist rabble-rouser in Horace's youth.

Odes 3.1–6 ("Odi profanum volgus"): Horace never called the first six odes of his third book the Roman Odes but that is how they came to be termed. Because all were in the same Alcaic meter and all showed Horace at his most public and preacherly, this was not unreasonable, despite the recognition by careful readers of significant differences among them. The theme of social, moral, religious, and political revival attracted admirers and translators, including Byron and Swift, as well as more conventional authors. The attack on excess ambition attracted rulers, like Augustus himself, who distrusted ambition in other people.

The line "Dulce et decorum est pro patria mori" challenged those who loved Horace for throwing away his shield at Philippi and then making light of it. David West searched in vain for an earlier Greek poem that might soften their discomfort. "For two millennia Horace's line has been valued by mourners and young men in all ages have acted upon it in the heat of battle," he concluded, noting that "many a mother and daughter have stood on city walls from Spain to Mesopotamia and looked down on their menfolk waiting to receive the Roman legions" (*Horace Odes III*). Horace knew directly the reason and unreason of battle; the fields of Philippi had defined his life more even than those of his farm. "Because a thing happens in literature, that does not mean that it does not happen in real life": this was a wise verdict from West that should be extended throughout Horace, well beyond these words of war.

Odes 3.14 ("Herculis ritu"): This poem too, beginning with a public welcome for Augustus as a Herculean hero and ending with Horace's party plans, has long puzzled readers. Llewellyn Morgan ("A Yoke Connecting Baskets: *Odes* 3.14, Hercules, and Italian Unity," *Classical Quarterly* 55, no. 1 [2005]: 190–203) argued persuasively that the role of Hercules as a mythical unifier of Italy flows through both parts. David West noted both the personal warmth in Horace's praise for Rome's first family and the public politics in a party where the wine is seventy years old and the host is a so much calmer man than he was "consule Planco," in the year of Philippi. Unity might not be essential in a poem, but for those who prize it, there is more unity than appears at first sight.

CHAPTER 14. DEATH OF VERGIL

Odes 1.3 ("Sic te diva"): "Modern interpreters" too easily dismissed as a failure this anxious appeal to Vergil's ship, according to Mayer, because "we do not share Horace's misgivings about man's ambitious nature" (*Horace Odes*). He suggested that "the present state of the planet's ecology might induce some rethinking." Mayer then went on to complain that the argument of the poem "crumbles on analysis" since, after the perils of the sea, Horace's choices to illustrate our reckless daring were Prometheus, who was a god; Daedalus, whose only failure was the folly of Icarus, his son; and Hercules, who was not so much daring as forced to perform his labors. For Williams, "the personal element is obviously real and emotional," but this third ode of Horace's first book was an early display of "the basic dilemma of the ancient poet" (*Tradition and Originality in Roman Poetry*). On the one hand stand the "traditional themes and formulas" and on the other "the poet's immediate feelings and perceptions." An important criterion for judging ancient poetry, in Williams's view, is to inquire "how successfully—if at all—this fusion of elements has been managed." The phrase "animae dimidium meae" was used by Augustine as he confronted his guilty feelings for a dead friend in *Confessions* 4.6.

Odes 1.24 ("Quis desiderio sit pudor aut modus?"): Mayer commented that the question implies "more bleakly than any statement" that there can be no way to put any restraint (*pudor*) or limit (*modus*) upon the sense of loss (*desiderium*). The consoling translation by the Victorian wit, and unfortunate skating accident victim, C. S. Calverley (1861) comes without the opening question.

Odes 3.30 ("Exegi monumentum"): Great men with a nervous sense of their own legacy have often translated Horace's moving claim on immortality. In the hands of such as Gladstone ("Now I have reared a monument more durable than brass") and Ezra Pound ("This monument will outlast metal") it has not always been so moving.

Vergil's picture of the three stags is at *Aeneid* 1.180–194, and of Mount Etna erupting at 3.578: "sed horrificis iuxta tonat Aetna ruinis" (but Etna's throat, its roar of ruinous terror, thunders near).

Epistles 1.1 ("Prima dicta mihi"): No poet had a greater love for Horace than Alexander Pope, or a more instinctive sense of his sensitivities to criticism. Pope gave a witty account of Horace's pick-and-mix approach to philosophy in his version of this epistle to Maecenas: "But ask not to what Doctors I apply?/ Sworn to no master of no Sect am I:/ As drives the storm at any door I knock,/ and House with Montagne now, or now with Locke" ("Epistle 1.1, An Imitation" [1738]).

Epistles 1.11 ("Quid tibi visa Chios, Bullati"): This poem was chosen by Williams to note, though not quite to deplore, the habit of extracting maxims from Horace's work that ignore their context. "Caelum non animum mutant qui trans mare currunt" is a favorite. Milton used it to show that a good Protestant could visit Catholic Italy. The writer David Lodge used it to introduce his campus novel *Changing Places* (1975), about an American and British academic who exchange jobs and wives.

Epistles 1.12 ("Fructibus Agrippae Siculis, quos colligis: Icci"): Profits from Sicily were very high. It was hardly more than a prison island for the slaves who worked its wide cornfields. By controlling Sicily—and freeing slaves to fight for him—Sextus Pompeius had threatened starvation for Rome as well as invoking fears of a new Spartacus. Agrippa's victories for Octavian had made the island a brutal food factory again, restoring the slaves to their fetters, if they survived, and rewarding the successful commander with vast estates run by managers like Iccius. Horace would have been disappointed if he had visited the cliffs from which Sappho jumped to her death or the woods mythologized by the poets of Alexandria. In the age of Augustus only Empedocles' volcano was as it had been when Sicily inspired poets rather than financiers. Fairclough noted the "somewhat ironical vein" in which Horace suggested that Iccius could spend his time in the shadow of Mount Etna studying physics rather than trying to become as rich as possible (*Horace, Satires, Epistles and Ars Poetica*).

Epistles 1.2 ("Troiani belli scriptorem"): Lollius Maximus was a relative, possibly the son, of the Lollius from Philippi and Actium who became consul in 21 BCE. Horace certainly seemed to take a strong personal interest in him. He was the addressee of both this and another epistle, 1.18, offering similar courtly advice; and in receiving the advice "sapere aude" about his literary homework, his name became attached to a defining motto of the modern age after its use by Kant in answering the question from a Prussian government official: "*What Is Enlightenment?*" (1784).

Epistles 1.20 ("Vertumnum Ianumque, liber"): In the last line of his poem pimping out his own latest papyrus rolls Horace confirmed his age. If anyone, in the manner of a modern journalist, were to ask, he had completed his forty-fourth December in the year when Lollius, his fellow fighter at Philippi, had become consul, 21 BCE.

Epistles 2.2 ("Floro bono claroque"): In 20 BCE Julius Florus was in the entourage of Augustus's stepson Tiberius on a diplomatic mission to appoint the next king of Armenia. This was his second letter from Horace. The first, 1.3, was a more routine request for news and the offer of worldly advice. The madman in the empty theater may have been something of a shock.

CHAPTER 15. GAME SHOW

Carmen Saeculare ("Phoebe silvarumque potens Diana"): "Not often translated and not much admired," as Carne-Ross and Haynes explained in his introduction to English translations of Horace, before giving a sympathetic account of C. H. Sisson's version of 1963 (*Horace in English*). Sisson was a Christian, monarchist, and patriot, writing pleadingly against the spirit of his time: "There was, at one time, even Modesty. Nothing is so dead it does not come back." Five years later Williams gave an equally sympathetic scholar's explanation of why Horace had to focus on public morality: "The most poetically acceptable justification of the Augustan regime – viz. that it had put a final end to civil war in Rome – could scarcely be mentioned on this day of celebration" (*Tradition and Originality in Roman Poetry*).

The account of the twenty-seven girls in Livius Andronicus's choir in 207 BCE comes from Livy, *History of Rome* 27.37. Livy says that his namesake's hymn to Juno would seem coarse and unstructured if it were performed in his own sophisticated times.

Many critics, keen to reject every possible biographical reality in Horace's poems, have denied that the poet used the beat of his thumb as conductor of his own choir.

Source Notes

For a rebuttal, and a wider attack on academic consensus, see Peter Wiseman's vigorous letter to the *Times Literary Supplement* of February 9, 2024: "And so it goes on, with scholars just citing each other (or themselves)." The argument went on for several weeks with neither side, each well argued, admitting defeat.

Fraenkel gave a vivid account of the discovery in 1890 of "a huge block of white marble" inscribed with the official account of the games and the one line "containing the momentous words *carmen composuit Q. Horatius Flaccus*" (*Horace*).

Epistles 2.1 ("Cum tot sustineas et tanta negotia solus"): Suetonius's Life of Horace contains an exchange between Augustus and Horace in which Augustus, "after reading various conversational poems complained that he made no appearance in them himself: 'You must know that I am displeased with you, that in your many works of this sort you do not talk with me, only with others. Are you anxious that your future reputation would suffer because it appeared that you were my friend?'" In this way, writes Suetonius, Augustus forced from Horace the poem which begins with these words: "Since you alone are bearing so much weight of work and expectation, protecting Italy with arms, providing it with morals, improving it by laws, I should err against the public good, Caesar, if I wasted your time with a long discourse." This poem, which was not short, would become the first in Horace's second book of epistles. The poems from which Augustus may have felt excluded were the letters to Maecenas and Horace's young friends in the first book.

Epistles 2.3 ("Humano capiti"): "Puzzling" was Williams's verdict on the epistle to the Piso boys which, within a century of Horace's death, had been renamed *Ars Poetica,* "The Art of Poetry," and elevated into a thesis (*Tradition and Originality in Roman Poetry*). The problem for Williams, and probably for the young Pisos too, was that Horace was not a man for a thesis. While some of the subject matter — the right number of characters in a play, the proper role of music, and so on — seemed to be imitating Aristotle and other systematic critics, the poem itself resisted any "such a structure." The Pisos might possibly have noted a connection to Neoptolemus, a third-century philosopher from Parium on the Asian side of the Hellespont, whose arguments found no favor, but some attention, from their house intellectual Philodemus. Or at least so said Porphyrio in the third century CE, one of the first commentators on Horace. Or equally the Pisos might not have connected these men to it at all. Horace's general preference was for the modest *aut ego fallor,* "if I am not mistaken," and for the lightest possible links to anything fixed unless politics demanded otherwise. If that later left critics "puzzled" — and struggling to get beyond his quotable phrases — this was probably part of his poetic purpose. Pope, who had as profound an understanding of Horace as anyone, wrote thus of the *Ars Poetica:* "Horace still charms with graceful negligence, / And without method talks us into sense" ("An Essay on Criticism," 1711). The most potent parts of the poem are its opening and bitter ending, the horse-headed human fish bird and the mad poet on the volcano, the two like lurid bookends with a shelf of quotation dictionaries in between.

Odes 4.1 ("Intermissa, Venus, diu"): "Cinara is different from the many girls who pass through his songs; she seems to be more real than any of them" (Fraenkel, *Horace*). Fraenkel argued that here Horace was genuinely recalling "the bygone days of his youth."

Odes 4.10 ("O crudelis adhuc et Veneris muneribus potens"): The warning to a reluctant boy that his charms will soon fade and no one will want him was a popular theme in the poetry of Alexandria. Thomas cited "the whole run of Palatine Anthology 12, 24–41" with variations including the epigram that "it was time to move back to women now that Theron and Apollodorus have become hairy-arsed" (*Horace Odes Book IV and Carmen Saeculare*). In A. T. Bradshaw's view ("Horace, Odes 4.1," *Classical Quarterly* 20, no. 1 [May 1970]: 142–153), Ligurinus "has no closer contact with reality than fair-haired Ganymede in the talons of an eagle." However confidently expressed by Bradshaw, this does not mean that Horace did not direct the sentiment toward a real boy with a real name. Page, ever keen to protect his schoolboy readers, presented the poem with minimum explanation.

Odes 4.6 ("Dive quem proles"): Fraenkel found "perhaps no better example" to show how Horace used a traditional form of lyric poetry, "even when its essence sprang from a very personal experience."

Odes 4.2 ("Pindarum quisquis studet aemulari"): Carne-Ross and Haynes noted the typical "gracious sidestep" with which Horace sketched out the necessary praise of Augustus while protesting that a fitter writer would be Iullus, Mark Antony's pardoned son (*Horace in English*). "'Tis thine with deeper Hand to strike the Lyre, / For Caesar's Glory shall his Bard inspire," in the translation by the notoriously "extravagant and largely unsuccessful" Irish cleric Philip Francis (1746).

Odes 4.7 ("Diffugere nives"): Thomas noted that "scholars take a particular delight" in letting us know whether this or the fourth poem in book 1 of the *Odes* is their "favourite" treatment of their shared theme. For the poet and scholar A. E. Housman, *Odes* 4.7 was "the most beautiful poem in ancient literature" (Richard Gaskin, *Horace and Housman* [London: Palgrave Macmillan, 2013], 12). Whether such feelings for poetry (or the arguments about them) help the biographer and textual critic was the subject of a vigorous exchange in 2000 between the playwright Tom Stoppard, whose play *The Invention of Love* centered on the poem, and the New York classicist Daniel Mendelsohn. See Tom Stoppard, Reply by Daniel Mendelsohn, "On 'The Invention of Love': Another Exchange," *New York Review of Books,* October 19, 2000.

Odes 4.9 ("Ne forte credas"): Lollius was not an easy man to praise. He had neither been a victorious general nor died in honorable defeat. As Thomas set it out, Horace's view of Lollius's integrity, however cautiously expressed here, was not generally shared. A "somewhat laboured" eulogy, claimed Fraenkel, but "not the poet's fault."

CHAPTER 17. CAPTOR AND CAPTIVE

Odes 4.4 ("Qualem ministrum fulminis alitem"): Williams used this poem to attack modern readers who found nothing where "the appeal is not primarily to the emotions" (*Tradition and Originality in Roman Poetry*). As a very learned critic himself, he saw a special virtue in a poem which "makes severe demands of a critic," considering it "one of the greatest of Horace's odes on public themes." The statesman and historian T. B. Macaulay, in a letter of February 8, 1835, judged the lines about the weapons of Drusus's opponents to be "the harshest, queerest, and most preposterous digression in the world" (*Life and Letters of Lord Macaulay*, ed. Sir George Otto Trevelyan [1876]).

Odes 4.5 ("Divis orte bonis"): Those who saw Horace as the authentic devotee of Augustus much prized this poem. For others it tipped too far into fascist idolatry. See Don Fowler, "Postscript: Images of Horace in Twentieth-Century Scholarship," in Martindale and Hopkins, *Horace Made New*, 273.

Epistles 2.1 ("Graecia capta ferum victorem cepit et artis / intulit agresti Latio," ll. 156–157). An often quoted line but "demonstrable nonsense," declared Wiseman in *Unwritten Rome*, deploring the too common tendency of classicists "to believe what a classic author tells them." "Tortuously careful" was Lyne's verdict on the struggle behind epistle 2.1: "walking tightropes is not pleasant to the unaccustomed funambulist and can induce anxiety in the spectator" (*Horace*). Fraenkel noted the need for those criticizing "their own incomparable nation" to tread with care: even when the recipient is not an authoritarian emperor, "there is always the possibility of a sudden change of front" (*Horace*). Horace's view that there were too many, too prolific writers, suffering from too much *insania*, well stood the test of time.

CHAPTER 18. ON THE ESQUILINE

Dio Cassius (*Roman History* 55.2.1) described Tiberius's arrival just in time to see Drusus before he died. Alternative dates for this event are set out in Bowman et al., *The Cambridge Ancient History*, 98.

Suetonius (Life of Tiberius 30.3, Life of Claudius 1.4) suggested that Drusus might have been in favor of a return to politics without an emperor. There may have been a crisis in 9 BCE prefiguring later murderous scenes within the family of the Caesars, but if so, Horace gave no sense of it. He liked neither squabbling heirs nor unknowable futures — and died before he needed to address them.

The final paragraph of Suetonius's Life of Horace gives the date of Horace's death as November 27, 8 BCE, fifty-nine days after the death of Maecenas: "he was in his fifty-seventh year."

Source Notes

CHAPTER 19. MONUMENTUM

For a survey of Horace's relationship with Brutus see Mario Citroni, "The Memory of Philippi in Horace and the Interpretation of Epistle 1.20.23," *Classical Journal* 96, no. 1 (2000): 27–56. For the future changes in political power at Rome see Andrew Wallace-Hadrill, "The Imperial Court," in Bowman et al., *The Cambridge Ancient History*. See also Stothard, *Palatine*.

CHAPTER 20. WORDS AS WEAPONS

Shakespeare quoted directly from Horace in act 4, scene 2, of *Titus Andronicus* when Titus wrapped weapons in the line "integer vitae scelerisque purus" in order to threaten the rapists of his daughter. The taunt of the just man not needing javelins was "Quite literally a barbed allusion" (Heather James, *Shakespeare's Troy*, cited in Jonathan Bate's Arden Shakespeare edition of the play). The "grammar" into which Horace's line fell in the sixteenth century was William Lily's *Brevissima Institutio*, the standard Latin textbook for schools, in which, Bate noted, "the quotation occurs twice." Even though the recipient of the weapons is able to recognize the lines he is too stupid to recognize what the gift means: "Shakespeare knew very well that reading something in a grammar long ago does not necessarily mean that one understands it," commented Colin Burrow (*Shakespeare and Classical Antiquity* [Oxford: Oxford University Press, 2013]) in analyzing how Shakespeare's own knowledge of complete poems by Horace was backed up by many quotes passed on through other authors.

In the same early play, Shakespeare, in Bate's view, also "perhaps adapts" the line in Horace's gardening advice to plant vines – and his warning about the moral risks of drinking like a centaur or a Thracian (*Odes* 1.18). "Sit fas aut nefas," be it right or wrong (*Titus Andronicus*, 1.1.618).

Milton's "To Pyrrha" is "generally regarded as the worst rendition in English," according to the American classicist Glenn W. Most in his detailed survey of Horace's posthumous influence in Grafton et al., *The Classical Tradition*. Carne-Ross and Haynes, more sympathetic than many, considered it a uniquely successful example of a translator who "more or less abandons the genius of his own language and seeks to create something new, an amalgam of the foreign or alien and the native" (*Horace in English*). Cyril Connolly called Milton's "To Pyrrha" "one of the most exquisite lyrics in English" (*The Condemned Playground*). Martindale and Hopkins reminded readers how "weirdly experimental" the original *Odes* would have seemed to most Roman readers – and how difficult it was to convey this strangeness in English (*Horace Made New*).

Lord Chesterfield's comments come from a letter dated December 11, 1747, in *The Letters of the Earl of Chesterfield to his Son,* ed. Charles Strachey and Annette Calthorp (London: Methuen, 1901). *The Gentleman's Magazine* of 1733, reporting on the funeral of John Underwood of Cambridgeshire, noted, "The coffin was painted Green, and he laid in it with all his Cloaths on . . . in his Left Hand a little edition of Horace . . . and Bentley's Horace under his Arse."

Connolly defined the modernism of Horace as the characteristic product of a metropolitan clique, "fascinated by the mechanism of clique life, by conversation without brawls, disinterested friendship, criticism without duels, unpunished sex." In the growing city of Rome, as in the London of Charles II, there was "a newly developed city sense and an interest in the more mundane ethics, in friendship, or the use of riches, in the value of moderation or the follies and rewards of youth and age."

Pope's "Sober Advice From Horace, to the Young Gentlemen About Town. As Deliver'd in his Second Sermon. Imitated in the Manner of Mr. Pope. Together with the original text, as restored by the Rev'd. R Bentley, . . . And Some Remarks on the Version" (1734) is discussed in Martindale's introduction to Martindale and Hopkins, *Horace Made New.*

Josiah Relph's version of *Odes* 4.7 appeared in his collection *A Miscellany of Poems, Consisting of Original Poems, Translations, Pastorals in the Cumberland Dialect, Familiar Epistles, Fables, Songs, and Epigrams by the Late Reverend Josiah Relph of Sebergham, Cumberland* (1747). Among almost eight hundred subscribers was the man who would be Wordsworth's maternal grandfather, William Cookson. Wordsworth's own thoughts on Horace are in his 1824 poem "Liberty."

Byron's lines upon learning Horace at school came at *Childe Harold's Pilgrimage,* Canto 4, stanza 77:

> Then farewell, Horace; whom I hated so,
> Not for thy faults, but mine; it is a curse
> To understand, not feel thy lyric flow,
> To comprehend, but never love thy verse,
> Although no deeper Moralist rehearse
> Our little life, nor Bard prescribe his art,
> Nor livelier Satirist the conscience pierce,
> Awakening without wounding the touch'd heart,
> Yet fare thee well – upon Soracte's ridge we part.

For *Satires* 1.2 reduced to twenty-four lines see Gow, *Horatii Flacci Saturarum Liber 1,* the text still used in schools, including mine, sixty years later.

The year of *Twilight of the Idols,* 1888, was the last before Nietzsche's madness took over his mind. For his admiration of Horace and the image of the mosaic see R. Bett, "Nietzsche and the Romans," *Journal of Nietzsche Studies* 42, no. 1 (2011). For a comparison of Nietzsche's approach to discussing literary style with that of Horace and others see Allan L. Carter, "Nietzsche on the Art of Writing," *Modern Language Notes* 39, no. 2 (1924).

In his diary entry for January 1, 1786, John Quincy Adams gave a cynical politician's verdict on finishing the third book of Horace's *Odes*. "Many of them are very fine, and the last one shows he was himself, sufficiently Sensible of it. When a Poet promises immortality to himself, he is always on the safe side of the Question, for if his works die with him, or soon after him, nobody ever can accuse him of vanity or arrogance: but if his predictions are verified, he is considered not only as a Poet, but as a Prophet."

Gladstone claimed, in his preface to his own translations of the odes, the neglected "necessity of compression" as his reason for becoming a translator of Horace, citing Milton as one of the few who before him matched this necessity. He also argued for the importance of avoiding ugly English genitives – even when "these are supported by the authority of Shakespeare in 'Come, Cassius's sword, and find Titinius's heart'" (*Julius Caesar,* 5.3). Modesty was never Gladstone's greatest virtue, but Horace did not encourage it.

Fraenkel's praise of "Divis orte bonis" is in *Horace;* Fowler's contrary opinion is in the postscript to Martindale and Hopkins, *Horace Made New.*

References in English poetry to "Dulce et decorum est" begin Kenneth Baker's wide-ranging anthology *The Faber Book of War Poetry (1996)* – Jonathan Swift (1716) and Wilfred Owen (1920) among them.

For Robert Frost's "Carpe Diem" see Frost, *A Witness Tree* (1942).

Henry Reed's "Naming of Parts," with its sardonic emendation of the opening to *Odes* 3.26, was published in in *New Statesman and Nation* in August 1942 as the first of his *Lessons of the War.* Robert Lowell's "Two Odes from Horace" were published in the *New York Review of Books* (January 28, 1965).

For the "error" of deriving life from work, among other aspects of "biographical fallacy," see Roland Barthes, "The Death of the Author" (1967), and Michel Foucault, "What Is an Author?" (1969), and too many followers to mention.

Bibliography

Adams, J. N. *Bilingualism and the Latin Language.* Cambridge: Cambridge University Press, 2003.

———. *The Latin Sexual Vocabulary.* London: Duckworth, 1982.

Appian. *Civil Wars.* Vol. 5: *Books 3–4.* Ed. and trans. Brian McGing. Loeb Classical Library 543. Cambridge: Harvard University Press, 2020.

Armstrong, David, et al., eds. *Vergil, Philodemus and the Augustans.* Austin: University of Texas Press, 2004.

Baker, Kenneth, ed. *The Faber Book of War Poetry.* London: Faber and Faber, 1996.

Balsdon, J. P. V. D. *Romans and Aliens.* London: Duckworth, 1979.

Bate, Jonathan, ed. *Titus Andronicus.* London: Bloomsbury, 1995.

Beard, Mary. *The Roman Triumph.* Cambridge: Harvard University Press, 2007.

———. *SPQR.* London: Profile, 2015.

———. *Twelve Caesars.* Princeton: Princeton University Press, 2021.

Bentley, Richard, ed. *Q. Horatius Flaccus.* Amsterdam, 1728.

Bowman, A. K., et al. *The Cambridge Ancient History.* Vol. 10: *The Augustan Empire, 43 B.C.–A.D. 69.* 2nd ed. Cambridge: Cambridge University Press, 1996.

Bradley, Keith, and Paul Cartledge, eds. *The Cambridge World History of Slavery.* Vol. 1: *The Ancient Mediterranean World.* Cambridge: Cambridge University Press, 2011.

Brink, C. O. *Horace on Poetry.* Vol 2: *The "Ars Poetica."* Cambridge: Cambridge University Press, 1971.

Callimachus. *Miscellaneous Epics and Elegies. Other Fragments. Testimonia.* Trans. and ed. Dee L. Clayman. Loeb Classical Library 550. Cambridge: Harvard University Press, 2022.

Carne-Ross, D. S., and Kenneth Haynes, eds. *Horace in English.* London: Penguin, 1996.

Cicero. *Letters to Friends.* Trans. D. R. Shackleton Bailey. 3 vols. Loeb Classical Library 205, 216, 230. Cambridge: Harvard University Press, 2001.

Coarelli, Filippo. *Rome and Environs.* Los Angeles: University of California Press, 2007.

Bibliography

Collinge, N. E. *The Structure of Horace's Odes*. Oxford: Oxford University Press, 1961.

Connolly, Cyril. *The Condemned Playground*. London: Routledge, 1945.

Diehl, Ernst. *Anthologia Lyrica Graeca*, 3rd ed. (Leipzig: Teubner, 1952).

Dio Cassius. *Roman History*. Vol. 5: *Books 46–50*. Trans. Earnest Cary, Herbert B. Foster. Loeb Classical Library 82. Cambridge: Harvard University Press, 1917.

——. Dio Cassius. *Roman History*. Vol. 6: *Books 51–55*. Trans. Earnest Cary, Herbert B. Foster. Loeb Classical Library 83. Cambridge: Harvard University Press, 1917.

Fitzgerald, William. *Slavery and the Roman Imagination*. Cambridge: Cambridge University Press, 2000.

Fraenkel, Eduard. *Horace*. Oxford: Oxford University Press, 1957.

Gerber, Douglas E., ed. and trans. *Greek Iambic Poetry: From the Seventh to the Fifth Centuries B.C. (Archilochus, Semonides, Hipponax.)* Loeb Classical Library 259. Cambridge: Harvard University Press, 1999.

Gibson, Roy. *Man of High Empire*. Oxford: Oxford University Press, 2020.

Gladstone, W. E., trans. *The Odes of Horace*. London: John Murray, 1894.

Gow, James, ed. *Q. Horatii Flacci Saturarum Liber 1*. Cambridge: Cambridge University Press, 1901.

Gowers, Emily. *Rome's Patron: The Lives and Afterlives of Maecenas*. Princeton: Princeton University Press, 2024.

Gowers, Emily, ed. *Horace, Satires Book 1*. Cambridge: Cambridge University Press, 2012.

Grafton, Anthony, Glenn W. Most, and Salvatore Settis, eds. *The Classical Tradition*. Cambridge: Harvard University Press, 2010.

Hallam, G. H. *Horace at Tibur and the Sabine Farm*. Rome: Vecchie Letture, 1927.

Harrison, Stephen. *The Cambridge Companion to Horace*. Cambridge: Cambridge University Press, 2007.

Holland, Tom. *Rubicon: The Triumph and Tragedy of the Roman Republic*. London: Little, Brown, 2003.

Hollis, Adrian. *Fragments of Roman Poetry*. Oxford: Oxford University Press, 2007.

Horace. *Satires, Epistles, The Art of Poetry*. Trans. H. R. Fairclough. Loeb Classical Library 194. Cambridge: Harvard University Press, 1926.

Inwood, Brad, ed. *The Poem of Empedocles*. Toronto: University of Toronto Press, 1992.

James, Heather. *Shakespeare's Troy*. Cambridge: Cambridge University Press, 1997.

Bibliography

Janko, Richard, ed. *Philodemus, On Poems*. Oxford: Oxford University Press, 2000.

Jay, P., ed. *The Greek Anthology*. London: Penguin, 1981.

Lane Fox, Robin. *The Invention of Medicine*. London: Allen Lane, 2020.

Levi, Peter. *Horace: A Life*. London: Duckworth, 1997.

Lloyd-Jones, Hugh. *Blood for the Ghosts*. London: Duckworth, 1982.

Lowrie, Michele, ed. *Horace: Odes* and *Epodes*. Oxford: Oxford University Press, 2009.

Lyne, R. O. A. M. *Horace*. New Haven: Yale University Press, 1995.

Martindale, Charles, and David Hopkins, eds. *Horace Made New: Horatian Influences on British Writing from the Renaissance to the Twentieth Century*. Cambridge: Cambridge University Press, 1992.

Mayer, Roland, ed. *Horace: Odes, Book 1*. Cambridge: Cambridge University Press, 2012.

Millar, Fergus. *The Emperor in the Roman World*. London: Duckworth, 1997

———. *A Study of Cassius Dio*. Oxford: Oxford University Press, 1964.

Morgan, Llewelyn. *Horace: A Very Short Introduction*. Oxford: Oxford University Press, 2023.

Mouritsen, Henrik. *The Freedman in the Roman World*. Cambridge: Cambridge University Press, 2011.

Nietzsche, Friedrich. *The Twilight of the Idols*. Trans R. J. Hollingdale. Harmondsworth, UK: Penguin, 1968.

Nisbet, R. G. M., and Margaret Hubbard. *Commentaries on Horace Odes I and II*. Oxford: Oxford University Press, 1970, 1978.

Nisbet, R. G. M., and Niall Rudd. *Commentary on Odes III*. Oxford: Oxford University Press, 2004.

Noyes, Alfred. *Horace: A Portrait*. New York: Sheed and Ward, 1947.

Obbink, Dirk, ed. *Philodemus in Italy*. Ann Arbor: University of Michigan Press, 1995.

Page, T. E., ed. *Odes of Horace*. New York: Macmillan, 1883.

Plutarch. *Lives: Demosthenes and Cicero. Alexander and Caesar*. Trans. Bernadotte Perrin. Loeb Classical Library 99. Cambridge: Harvard University Press, 1919.

———. *Lives: Dion and Brutus, Timoleon and Aemelius Paulus*. Trans. Bernadotte Perrin. Loeb Classical Library 98. Cambridge: Harvard University Press, 1918.

Powell, Anton, and Kathryn Welch, eds. *Sextus Pompeius*. London: Duckworth, 2002.

Bibliography

Powell, Lindsay. *Marcus Agrippa*. Barnsley: Pen and Sword, 2015.

Remains of Old Latin: Lucilius. The Twelve Tables. Trans. E. H. Warmington. Loeb Classical Library 329. Cambridge: Harvard University Press, 1938.

Rohland, Robert A. *Carpe Diem*. Cambridge: Cambridge University Press, 2023.

Sellar, W. Y. *Roman Poets of the Augustan Age: Horace and the Elegiac Poets*. Oxford: Oxford University Press, 1892.

Shackleton Bailey, D. R. *Profile of Horace*. London: Duckworth, 1982.

Shorey, Paul, and Gordon Laing, eds. *Horace, Odes and Epodes*. Pittsburgh: University of Pittsburgh Press, 1910.

Stothard, Peter. *Crassus*. New Haven: Yale University Press, 2022.

———. *The Last Assassin*. Oxford: Oxford University Press, 2020.

———. *On the Spartacus Road*. New York: HarperPress, 2010.

———. *Palatine*. Oxford: Oxford University Press, 2023.

Suetonius. Life of Augustus. In *Lives of the Caesars*. Vol. 1: *Julius. Augustus. Tiberius. Gaius Caligula*. Trans. J. C. Rolfe. Loeb Classical Library 31. Cambridge: Harvard University Press, 1914.

———. Life of Horace. In *Lives of the Caesars*. Vol. 2: *Claudius. Nero. Galba, Otho, and Vitellius. Vespasian. Titus, Domitian. Lives of Illustrious Men: Grammarians and Rhetoricians. Poets (Terence. Virgil. Horace. Tibullus. Persius. Lucan). Lives of Pliny the Elder and Passienus Crispus*. Trans. J. C. Rolfe. Loeb Classical Library 38. Cambridge: Harvard University Press, 1914.

Syme, Ronald. *The Roman Revolution*. Oxford: Oxford University Press, 1939.

Talbert, Richard J. A., ed. *Barrington Atlas of the Greek and Roman World*. Princeton: Princeton University Press, 2000.

Tempest, Kathryn. *Brutus*. New Haven: Yale University Press, 2017.

Thomas, Richard, ed. *Horace, Odes Book IV and Carmen Saeculare*. Cambridge: Cambridge University Press, 2011.

Warmington, E. H., ed. *Remains of Old Latin III*. Cambridge: Harvard University Press, 1938.

Watson, Lindsay C. *Commentary on Horace's Epodes*. Oxford: Oxford University Press, 2003.

Welch, Kathryn. *Magnus Pius: Sextus Pompeius and the Transformation of the Roman Republic*. Swansea: Classical Press of Wales, 2012.

Welch Kathryn, ed. *Sextus Pompeius*. London: Duckworth, 2002.

Bibliography

West, David, ed. and trans. *Horace Odes III: Dulce Periculum*. Oxford: Oxford University Press, 2002.

West, M. L., trans. *Greek Lyric Poetry*. Oxford: Oxford University Press, 2008.

Williams, Gordon. *Tradition and Originality in Roman Poetry*. Oxford: Oxford University Press, 1968.

Wiseman, T. P. *Catullus and His World*. Cambridge: Cambridge University Press, 1985.

——. *The House of Augustus*. Princeton: Princeton University Press, 2019.

——. *Unwritten Rome*. Exeter: University of Exeter Press, 2008.

Acknowledgments

To Mary Beard, Heather Glen, Emily Gowers, Susan Laity, Caroline Michel, Llewelyn Morgan, Ruth Scurr, Andrew Sillett, Paul Webb. *Optimi lectores,* the very best of readers.

Index

Index

Index

Byron, Lord (George Gordon), 5, 249, 284; *Childe Harold's Pilgrimage,* 291

Caesar, Gaius Julius: army of, 227; assassination of, 1, 27, 29–30, 41, 114, 115, 143, 205; basilica of, 212; as chief priest, 205; and Cleopatra, 88; as dictator, 19, 184; divinity of, 90; family of, 15, 241; former soldiers of, 28–29; and Fulvia, 265; in Gaul, 19, 28, 62, 80, 97, 108, 109, 274; home of, 212; as leader, 43; and Mamurra, 85; and Octavian, 2, 3; opposition to, 155, 226; Plutarch's biography of, 265; as poet, 72; vs. Pompey, 21, 44, 46, 62, 134; Shakespeare's play, 245, 292; sister of, 2, 28–29; son of, 140; in the Subura, 65, 75; Suetonius's account of, 245; supporters of, 71; and the "Three-Headed Monster" (Triumvirate), 13, 17, 18, 19, 27, 29, 138, 151, 183, 263, 273; wife of, 10, 114. *See also* Caesar's assassins

Caesarion, 140

Caesar's assassins: army of, 2, 37, 41, 43, 44, 49, 199, 240, 271; after the assassination, 31, 182, 213; Cimber, 41, 50; Cinna, 28; deaths of, 48, 50, 92, 182; destroyers of, 122; ideals of, 35, 46, 186–187, 267; pardon for, 50, 80, 180; Parmensis, 69; at Philippi, 2, 48, 88, 92, 143, 267; proscription of associates, 31, 32, 93; supporters of, 29, 32, 50, 61, 120, 123, 180, 181; Turullius, 69. *See also* Brutus, Marcus; Cassius, Gaius

Caligula, 241

Callimachus of Alexandria, 25, 60, 163, 175, 266

Calliope, 189

Calpurnia, 114, 115

Calverley, C. S., 275, 285

Cape Palinurus, 57

Capito, Caius Fonteius, 84–85, 88, 120, 161

Capito, Gaius Ateius, 206

Capua, 15

Carmen Saeculare (*Song of the Century*), 207–213, 223–224, 225, 270, 286

carmina. See Odes

Carrhae, 61, 183

Carthage, 17, 117, 137, 205, 209, 230

Cassius, Gaius: army of, 33, 37–38, 42, 44, 46–47; assassination of Caesar, 27, 30, 115; and Crassus, 18–19; as criminal, 31; death of, 48; as Epicurean, 86; followers of, 40, 59, 104, 182; and Messalla, 133; at Philippi, 48; planned assassination of, 94

Catullus, Gaius Valerius, 13, 16, 85, 155

Centaurs, 21, 22, 70, 117, 290

Centenary Games. See *Ludi Saeculares*

Cerberus, 138

Chesterfield, Lord, 246, 290

Chiron, 70

Choerilus, 233

Cicero, Marcus Tullius: Antony and, 30–31; and Cratippus, 32; friends of, 107; and the Greek language, 266; *Letters to Friends,* 275; Philip of Macedon, 35; Philippics, 34; in Plato's Academy, 21; as poet, 26, 72; proscription and death of, 34–35, 71, 93, 120; response to the assassination of Caesar, 28, 31, 33, 34, 180; rhetoric of, 162; ships of, 142; writing about Clodia, 13–14

Cicero, Marcus Tullius (son): and the Battle of Actium, 136; with Brutus,

Index

Index

Index

Index

tus), 189–190; pedagogical use of, 243, 244, 250; phrases quoted from, 247; for Plancus, 180–183, 227; praising Drusus, 229–231; about Rome, 185–190; about Rupilius Rex, 53–56; on the Subura, 65–66; translated into English, 5, 245–252; for Vergil, 192; about women and sex, 59–60, 62–64, 75–76, 100, 110–111, 118–119, 156, 188–189, 248, 280. See also *Epistles; Epodes; Odes;* poetic meter; *Satires*

Horatius, 9

horoscopes, 177–178, 179, 237, 283

Housman, A. E., 288

Hubbard, Margaret, 276, 278, 279, 280, 281, 283

iambi, 6, 59, 76, 91, 95–96, 100, 110, 127, 128, 129, 137, 144, 199. See also *Epodes*

Icarus, 225, 285

Iccius, 200, 286

idylls, 67

Iliad (Homer), 23, 70, 117, 202, 227, 252

Juba, 154

Julia (daughter of Augustus), 171, 216, 234, 239, 241; children of, 216, 230, 241

Juno, hymn to, 208, 286

Jupiter, 90, 212

Juvenal, 266

Kant, Immanuel, 247, 286

Keats, John, 249, 268, 272

Kipling, Rudyard, 5, 250

Lactantius, 281

Laenas, 35

Lebedos, 37, 199–200

Legion of the Lark, 227

Lepidus, Marcus, 151

Lepidus, Quintus Aemilius, 184, 278

Lesbia, 16, 129, 137

Lesbos, 25, 32, 145, 155, 199

Leuconoe, 177–178, 242, 283

Levi, Peter, 264

Libitina, 194

Libya, 104

Licinius, 173

Lily, William, 290

Livia (wife of Augustus), 163, 169, 216; sons of, 229, 230

Livy, 286

Lloyd-Jones, Hugh, 264

Lodge, David, 285

Lollius, Marcus, 40, 46, 50, 57, 136, 149–150, 184, 241, 247, 278, 288; on the Rhine, 217, 227, 231

Lollius Maximus, 201–202, 206, 286

Lowell, Robert, 251, 292

Lucilius, Gaius, 15, 17–18, 56, 69, 72, 73, 83, 84, 109, 110, 111, 265, 266, 269

Lucius Antonius, 71

Lucius Caesar, 216, 230, 239–240, 241

Lucretius, 115, 270

Ludi Saeculares (Centenary Games), 16, 205–213, 224, 227, 231–232, 246

Lupercalia, 212–213

Lycymnia, 217

Lydians, 99, 143

Macaulay, T. B., 289

Maecenas, Gaius Cilnius: in Actium, 128; and Agrippa, 149; death of, 236, 239; and the Esquiline cemeteries, 103, 105; gift of property to Horace, 123, 125, 132, 235; health concerns, 177, 283; Horace as friend/companion, 100, 106, 120, 140, 152, 159, 168, 175, 177, 179, 180,

Index

Maecenas, Gaius Cilnius (*continued*)
192, 194, 199, 274, 280; Horace's
letter to, 199; in Horace's poetry,
95–96, 97, 98–100, 101, 103, 127;
journey to Brundisium, 82–85,
86, 89, 161, 187, 200; as patron of
Horace, 77, 82, 91, 92, 96, 98, 99,
107, 116, 117, 119–120, 141–142, 144,
150, 151, 153, 155, 158, 175, 177, 182,
192, 194, 211, 236–237, 249; as
patron of poets, 73, 92, 106–107,
114, 116, 117, 119–120, 121, 141, 150,
151–152, 158, 162, 168, 215; political
position of, 81, 89, 90, 92, 122, 132,
135, 142, 143, 144, 158, 188, 211; in
Rome, 72–73, 129, 132; wife of, 85,
161, 162, 174, 217
Maleventum, 15
Mamurra, 85
Marcellus (nephew of Octavian), 169,
171, 175, 193
Marsus, Domitius, 272
Martial, 266
Martindale, Charles, 248
Matronalia, 152
Mayer, Roland, 276, 279, 280, 282, 284,
285
Medea, 16
Media, 104
Meleager, 275
Melpomene, 275
Mendelsohn, Daniel, 288
Mercury, 114, 157, 254, 268, 277
Messalla Corvinus, Marcus Valerius:
and Agrippa, 133; in Athens, 33, 34;
brother of, 33, 43, 93, 136; Horace's
praise for, 218; as patron of poets,
206; at Philippi, 40, 46, 47–48, 49,
50; political position of, 61, 93, 95,
136, 158, 183; with Sextus, 144;
surrender to Antony, 57

Messapians, 191
Metellus, Quintus Caecilius, 13–14, 16,
151, 156
Milton, John, 246, 250; "To Pyrrha,"
290
Mimnermus, 23
mirrors, 131–132, 156, 166, 176–177, 223,
244
Morgan, Llewellyn, 284
Most, Glenn W., 290
Mount Etna, 4, 69, 87, 189, 197, 219,
243, 263, 275, 285–286
Mount Garganus, 10, 41
Mount Soracte, 145, 146
Mount Vesuvius, 113, 219, 263, 275
Mount Voltur, 10, 15
Murena, Aulus Terentius Varro,
161–162, 163, 174, 177, 281, 282
Murena, Lucius Licinius, 85, 161–162,
281
Muses, 24, 139, 154; Calliope, 189;
Melpomene, 275; Sappho as tenth,
155, 207

Naevius, Gnaeus, 17
"Naming of Parts" (Reed), 251
Naples, 57, 93, 113, 115, 119, 142, 186, 198
Naulochus, Battle of, 93, 167–169, 200
Neptune, 90, 92, 167, 168, 186
Nero, 241, 243
Nerva, Lucius Cocceius, 84–85, 86, 206
Nerva, Marcus Cocceius, 94, 206
Nietzsche, Friedrich, 5–6, 249, 291
Nisbet, R. G. M., 271, 276, 278, 279,
280, 281, 283
Noyes, Alfred, 264

Octavia, 89, 105, 122; daughter of, 224
Octavian (Augustus): alliance with
Antony, 3, 32, 35, 93; vs. Antony,
58, 61, 103, 104, 105–107, 125, 127,

· 308 ·

Index

133–134, 140, 164, 167; army of, 40, 42–43, 48, 69, 70–71, 135, 202; in Athens, 196; as Caesar's heir, 2, 28–29, 167; campaign to Parthia, 183–184, 187–188; and the Centenary Games, 205–207, 210–211, 213, 246; and Cicero (son), 93; commission to Varius, 142; as consul, 171; daughters of, 234; depiction of, 141; as dictator, 184; divinity of, 90; feasts and entertainment ordered by, 120; vs. Fulvia, 89; in Gaul, 229, 231, 235; heirs of, 216, 239–240, 241; and Horace, 106–107, 110, 122, 250; Horace's letters to, 231–234, 264; in Horace's poetry, 91, 96, 109; ill health of, 29, 45, 150–151, 171–172, 179; as Imperator, 142; letters of, 244; military plans, 150; moral legislation passed by, 206, 208; mother of, 28–29; as object of flattery, 119; at Philippi, 45, 48, 49, 88; and Plancus, 180; poetic praise for, 225, 229–231, 241; political position of, 158; power of, 120, 122; public bath campaign, 105; *Res Gestae* (What I Did), 244; response to Horace's poem, 175–176; in Rome, 31, 57, 79–80, 93, 141–144, 169, 188, 196, 217; as Romulus, 143; seeking public support, 229–230; vs. Sextus, 129, 168; in Spain, 163; Suetonius's account of, 245; supporters of, 182–183; and Terentia, 162; and Tigellius, 75

Odes (*carmina*), 6, 169–172, 243, 247, 268–269; 1.1 (*Atavis edite regibus*), 143, 279; 1.2 (*Iam satis terris*), 156, 175–176, 281; 1.3 (*Sic te diva*), 192, 284–285; 1.4 (*Solvitur acris hiems*), 172–174, 226, 282, 283; 1.5 (*Quis multa gracilis*), 170–171, 246, 276, 282, 290; 1.6 (*Scriberis Vario*), 163–164, 281; 1.7 (*Laudabunt alii*), 180–181, 283; 1.9 (*Vides ut alta*), 145–147, 258–259, 279–280; 1.11 (*Tu ne quaesieris* [*carpe diem*]), 177–179, 218, 251, 283; 1.18 (*Nullam, Vare, sacra vite*), 117, 275–276. 290; 1.19 (*Mater saeva cupidinum*), 276; 1.22 (*Integer vitae scelerisque purus*), 153–154, 245, 249–250, 280–281; 1.24 (*Quis desiderio sit pudor . . . ?*), 193, 275, 285; 1.25 (*Parcius iunctas quatiunt fenestras*), 156, 281; 1.37 (*Nunc est bibendum*), 140–141, 279; 2.1 (*Motum ex Metello*), 151, 280; 2.3 (*Aequam memento*), 182–183, 283; 2.7 (*O saepe mecum*), 165, 253–255, 268, 281–282; 2.10 (*Rectius vives, Licini*), 173–174, 282–283; 2.13 (*Ille et nefasto die*), 137, 278; 2.17 (*Cur me querelis exanimas tuis?*), 177, 283; 3.1 (*Odi profanum volgus*), 185–186, 188, 250, 284; 3.1–6 ("Roman Odes"), 185, 284; 3.2 (*Angustam amice pauperiem pati*), 186–187, 250, 251, 284, 292; 3.3 (*Iustum et tenacem propositi virum*), 188, 189; 3.4 (*Descende caelo*), 189, 268, 278; 3.5 (*Caelo tonantem*), 188; 3.6 (*Delicta maiorum*), 188; 3.8 (*Martiis caelebs quid agam Kalendis*), 151–152, 255–257, 278, 280; 3.13 (*O fons Bandusiae*), 138–140, 278–279; 3.14 (*Herculis ritu*), 268, 284; 3.19 (*Quantum distet ab Inacho*), 276, 281; 3.26 (*Vixi puellis nuper idoneus*), 118–119, 251, 276, 292; 3.30 (*Exegi monumentum*), 194–196, 263, 285; 4.1 (*Intermissa, Venus, diu*), 223, 246,

Index

Index

.